D0448040

COW PEOPLE

COW PEOPLE

J. Frank Dobie

UNIVERSITY OF TEXAS PRESS
Austin

International Standard Book Number 0-292-71060-7

Library of Congress Catalog Card Number 80-53427
Copyright © 1964 by J. Frank Dobie
All rights reserved
Printed in the United States of America

Sixth University of Texas Press Printing, 1997
Reprinted by arrangement with Little, Brown and Company,
Inc.

Requests for permission to reproduce material from this work
should be sent to Permissions, University of Texas Press, Box
7819, Austin, Texas 78713-7819.

∞ The paper used in this publication meets the minimum requirements of American National Standard for Information Sci-
ences—Permanence of Paper for Printed Library Materials,
ANSI Z39.48-1984.

TO

Walker Stone and Ralph Johnston, contributors to my life. Their friendship with each other goes back to youth in Oklahoma.

I knew Stone as a student in my English class at Oklahoma A. and M. College forty years ago. He lives in Washington, D.C., editor-in-chief of the Scripps-Howard newspapers published over the United States. All these years he has kept on actively remembering me. Ralph A. Johnston, of Houston, is another civilized rememberer. For years his Rancho Seco in southwest Texas has been hunting ground for Stone and Stone's friends. There the deer and the wild turkeys are positives of the hunt, but what we most anticipate and cherish in memory is the comradeship and talk around an evening fire that seems to emanate from our genial host.

Contents

Introduction

THE USUAL makes social history. The unusual makes interesting reading. It may be untypical; it is likely to be representative. However singular some characters and narratives in chapters that follow may sound, they are out of reality. No attempt at the "definitive" has been made. My aim is to reveal human beings. Nearly all the characters are dead. They represent vanished ways and a vanished tempo. Yet no life of one time is alien to another time. Herodotus and Chaucer come nearer belonging to the present age than certain troglodytes in the United States Senate.

On a ranch down in the brush country of southwest Texas, I was born and reared to the life herein represented. My father and his brothers were ranchers and drove up the trail to Kansas. My mother was born to ranching. My grandparents on both sides of the house were cow people. I grew up on good books. At college, English poetry entered my life and I wanted to teach it. For three years I served as instructor of English at the University of Texas. All along I was dabbling at writing. Two years of Field Artillery in World War I put fibers in my brain.

Cow People

In 1920 I took charge of my Uncle Jim (J. M.) Dobie's ranch of fifty-six thousand acres attached to two hundred thousand acres of leased land. We kept two crews of Mexicans going: an outfit of vaqueros and one of fence-builders and tankers. Here for the first time I became conscious in a writing way of the people I had all my life belonged to. Cattle prices slid to the bottom and cattlemen, my uncle included, were going bankrupt. I went back to the University of Texas. I belonged to ranch land and ranch people, but wanted something beyond. I fitted into university teaching. It allowed me free time. My purpose was to gather into a book traditional tales of Texas. That meant talking with people who belonged to the land, though many owned not an acre of it. That meant writing. Horizons kept expanding. They keep on expanding. With perspectives afforded by literature and history, by experience and civilized life, I have for about a third of a century been putting into writing the land on both sides of the Rio Grande, expanding north into Canada and south to the pampas, the animals, the people, their stories. Life at Cambridge University during World War II expanded my perspectives.

Early in the 1920's I began setting down on paper narratives by old-time men of the soil and the saddle. As one talked, I might jot down proper names, but seldom took notes. Immediately after hearing what was meat to me, I would go apart and write out, either by hand or on typewriter, the talk while it was still hot and detailed in memory. To write down, not write about, has been a continuing aim. Spinning out opinions is dead easy. Some of the character sketches and incidents that follow have been in my files a long time; some have appeared under my name in magazines and newspapers. To fortify myself, I have read most of the travel books and reminiscences of the Americas touching on cattle and cattle people.

Too much reading — even good reading — and too much listening to canned amusement stifle personal narrators. The best ones associate with themselves. They tell out of experience. Before airborne murder of silence atrophied oral communication, *what he said* and *what she said* were common to it. Honest directness of speech, revealing an easy intimacy with ranch life, never has been common to journalism or to big-selling fiction.

One night, about 1940, on my way to Little Rock, Arkansas, an airplane deposited me in Fort Smith, where I had to wait for a bus the next day. Having plenty of time, I set out after breakfast to explore three bookstores listed in the back of the telephone directory. The first turned out to be a furniture store that sometimes acquired books with used furniture; the few on hand were worthless. The second specialized in stationery, and all the books it had could have been utilized by a business college. As soon as I stepped into the third, my eyes picked out three shelves of books. The first was stocked with Bibles, the second with cookbooks. The third was longer, crowded with Zane Grey novels, many titles in duplicate.

For more than a hundred years, tracing their lineage back to dime novels, the cowboys of popular Westerns, of pulp magazines, of Hollywood pictures, and now of television gun-smokers have come no more from homes of people than the Aphrodite sprung from sea foam came. They have never known humanity, sucking calves, before-daylight freshness, evening shadows. Cow people true to life and occupation as in *The Log of a Cowboy* by Andy Adams, in *Pasó por Aquí* by Eugene Manlove Rhodes, and in autobiographies up to the standard of Agnes Morley Cleaveland's *No Life for a Lady* and Ike Blassingame's *Dakota Cowboy* never pass the requirements of film and TV. I am not counting on *Cow People*'s coming up to those requirements.

All of us live in debt to each other. Human nature is so healthy that few are oppressed by the feeling of debt. On many pages that follow I mention names of individuals who told me this and that. The person to whom I owe most is a critic of style and a thinker named Bertha McKee Dobie. She has overlooked every line and influenced me to exercise the never sufficiently accomplished art of omission.

COW PEOPLE

1

Hunting Cousin Sally

"YES," SAID COLONEL IKE, "I believe in Providence, luck, chance, whatever it is outside a man that directs his destiny."

But nobody could be around Ike Pryor long without perceiving that he cherished also a high opinion of his own interior factors and exterior features.

His title was by courtesy, but it was fixed. He was one of the few old-time cowmen ready in public speaking. His high-pitched voice was anything but oratorical and he was too factual for flights, but good judgment and a well-stored mind always furnished him something definite to say. In my time, at least, he never wore a range hat, but a black one of modest brim matching his black bow tie. He had been president of the two most powerful livestock associations in America, and for a while entertained the idea of running for governor of Texas on the Republican ticket. As a businessman, he had lost his ranginess. While his business was primarily cows and land, a city office was his homing place. On the wall facing his desk, in San Antonio, hung the mounted head and horns of a Longhorn steer. The Longhorn in Colonel Ike had diminished in visibility under coverings of hard financial success, ambition, greed, sophistication, vanity, but it was there.

He was among the few big speculators of open range days who adjusted themselves to change and did not go permanently broke. After his hundred-thousand-acre ranch down in the brush country became worth a million, he loved to tell how he had bought it for $1.40 an acre. He related his experiences well. Every time I heard him tell — always with self-gratulation — of a tract of land he bought for a song, sold at a high price to a buyer who made a good down payment and then went broke, letting the land revert to him, I would wonder why he thought Providence had picked him out for ownership. While the land, by title, was still his, it became a gas field. Providence!

"I've always been a winner," he would confess. He did not often bet on games of chance, but one night in Mexico City he allowed a professional sharp to guide him through the principal gambling houses. Finally they came to the richest in the city. Stacks of gold and silver glittered on broad tables.

"If you are going to bet at all," said the gambler, "here is your last chance."

Colonel Ike placed a silver dollar on a certain number; the roulette wheel revolved; he won eighteen dollars. He kept placing bets and kept winning. After he had won steadily with only minor setbacks for two hours, the gambler advised him to stop.

"No," said Colonel Ike, "I'm going to win three hundred dollars more."

He placed his money; the wheel turned; three hundred

IKE (ISAAC) THOMAS PRYOR. He started trading in cattle almost as soon as he started driving them. He never went broke and never ceased to regard himself with approbation. His big ranch was in the Brush Country below San Antonio, Texas.

pesos in silver were counted out to him. When the two men left they carried two heavy sacks of coins.

The next night there was to be a raffling of a thousand-dollar diamond. Chances for it cost five dollars apiece. Colonel Ike bought one chance. When the time came to draw, he hunted up the gambler guide. "You are my mascot," he said. "I want you to stand behind me with your hand on my shoulder while I draw. I'll draw the lucky number." He drew it, and his wife wore the diamond the rest of her life.

The years wilted him as they wilt all, but until he died, in 1937, at the age of eighty-five, Colonel Ike considered himself a lady-killer. The day after he died Texas newspapers carried a biographical sketch. About noon I met my old friend Horace Shelton on Congress Avenue in Austin. He was a lawyer, but a quarter of a century back he and I had been reporters on the San Antonio *Express*.

"I'll tell you a little story on Ike Pryor," he said. "One winter he got mighty sweet on a lady from the North staying at the St. Anthony Hotel. One evening she informed him she was leaving a few nights later on the eleven-o'clock Katy train, which carried several Pullmans. Ike Pryor said he had to go north also and was figuring on taking the same train. She let him know what Pullman she'd be on and the number of her berth. He told her he would see her. She said, 'All right.' After the lights were out, he opened the curtains to her berth. She said, 'I was waiting for you. Now you fork over five thousand dollars or else get exposed.' He paid over the five thousand dollars."

Knowing how close Ike Pryor was gives the anecdote, probably a folk creation, point. He was seldom guided by sentiment. At every meeting of the old trail drivers in San Antonio he would make a speech — essentially the same one, giving anecdotes of his experiences on the trail. The organization had commissioned Gutzon Borglum to make a monument to the trail drivers. Ike Pryor, richest man in the organization, contributed virtually nothing to the fund and Borglum received enough money to justify his making only a small model — a bronze casting of which is now in front of the Witte Memorial Museum in San Antonio. One of the professional guards on train-loads of cattle from lower Texas named Harry Singer was worn out when I came to know him. He had accompanied thousands of steers shipped by Ike Pryor to the Indian Territory, the Flint Hills of Kansas, Kansas City, Chicago, and elsewhere. When he was old, poor, and ailing, but always self-respecting, he asked Ike Pryor, as he told me, for a little help. He got five dollars. "That's all he gave me," Harry Singer said. Ike Pryor used to predict falling cattle prices just before he got ready to buy yearlings in the spring.

In the end, all of Ike Pryor's beliefs and creations about luck and Providence were based on events that brought him into the cattle business. After spending two days taking notes on his narrative, I wrote it down and submitted it to him for corrections and approval. Here, without quotation marks, is the final form.

I was born in Tampa, Florida, June 22, 1852, the youngest of three boys. When I was two years old my father died. My mother had nursed him constantly for a long time; now she developed tuberculosis, the disease that took him off. This infection, combined with the struggles she had to provide for her three children, brought her down; I was close to five when she died. This was in Alabama, where she had relatives. She had prayed for us constantly and she died praying.

Before she died she called in three sisters and gave a boy to each of them. I went to an aunt who had married a doctor. He was exceedingly strict, and I did not get along well there. I was passed on to a second aunt. Within six months I was in the home of the third aunt. She was a widow with six children when she married a widower with six more children. I made the thirteenth child in that household. There wasn't much room for me, and naturally I was pecked on. But there was Cousin Sally Lightfoot, my aunt's eldest daughter. She was eighteen and an angel.

One day when I was crying because the other children had shut me out of some game, Cousin Sally came to me and said, "Iky, I've got a wonderful gingerbread man baking in the oven. He's for you. Come, let's go get him." From that minute I was Cousin Sally's own child. She could not have loved her own offspring more devotedly. And I loved her with all the passion of a child. She saw to my clothes, took up for me when the older children bullied me, and let me sleep in her own bed.

When I was something past six years old, a rich uncle named Orville McKissack, who lived at Spring Hill, Tennessee, forty miles south of Nashville, came to visit us.

"Why, sister," he said, "you have too many children. You tell me that Iky there is Sister Emma's youngest child. I'll take him with me, give him a good home, and educate him."

My aunt was loath to give me up. Cousin Sally and I were both brokenhearted at the idea, but the transfer was made. As I left, I resolved to run away and come back to Cousin

Sally. This new home had a plenty of everything and I could not in reason complain. Still, I suffered spells of homesickness for Cousin Sally. Time went on, and I heard that Cousin Sally had married and gone to live in Nashville. When I was nine the Civil War broke out. Not long after that my uncle and adopted father gave me a good switching. He was stern, no matter how high-minded.

After he whipped me, I went to my room and there resolved to go to Cousin Sally in Nashville, forty miles away. The idea that I could not find Cousin Sally once I arrived in Nashville did not enter my mind. I was raging mad. In my room was about a bushel of "scaly-barks" — thin-shelled hickory nuts — that I had gathered. Instead of loading myself with clothes, I took these in a sack and slipped out, walking up the road towards Nashville. I don't know why I took the nuts unless for meanness. I did not want my uncle to get them. Once I was on the road, I began throwing them away, right and left. I do not know whether it is true or not, but I have heard that for some distance from Spring Hill the Nashville road is lined on both sides with beautiful scaly-bark hickory trees. If so, perhaps I can claim to be the unwitting Johnny Appleseed who planted them.

I set out in the afternoon. By dark I had gone nine miles and had thrown away all my hickory nuts. The road had a few travelers, but they all seemed to be in too big a hurry to pay any attention to a small boy. I stopped at a tollgate kept by an old woman.

"Lady," I said, "I don't have a penny to pay you, but will you let me stay all night? I'm going to Nashville."

The good old woman led me inside and gave me supper. While I ate she questioned me. "Why, child," she said, "don't you know there is a terrible war on and that soldiers are everywhere about this country? They are fighting right now between here and Nashville. You might be run over by horses or get shot."

All I knew was that I was going to Cousin Sally. I didn't know enough about war to be scared. I slept on a clean cot, ate hot pancakes and eggs about daylight, and went on.

After I had walked two or three miles, I heard shooting; then I saw men running and firing at each other. Instinct told me to get out of the way. I crawled into some bushes and lay hidden. The firing and chasing receded the way I had come. History will tell you that the Federals surprised the Confederates near Franklin and drove them south. I was now within the Federal lines, and the Federals had possession of Nashville. That battle saved me. As I learned later, when my uncle missed me at dark, he ordered two men to set out early next morning and bring me home. He found out somehow that I had gone off towards Nashville. When, next morning, those men on my trail encountered the battle, they turned back.

Finally I reached Nashville. The city was in utter confusion — troops everywhere, business paralyzed, martial law in charge. A city the size of Nashville would have confused a country boy just nine years old at any time.

At last I asked a soldier who seemed to be on guard at one of the street corners if he could tell me the way to Cousin Sally's.

"Cousin Sally?" he repeated kindly. "What's her other name and what street does she live on?"

I couldn't tell. All I knew was that before she married she was Cousin Sally Lightfoot. Her husband's name I had forgotten. The street she lived on I had never heard. In fact, I did not know that streets had names and numbers. I went on inquiring for Cousin Sally. This person and that person knew of a Sally somebody. I went into hundreds of private homes, asking, asking for Cousin Sally. It seemed to me there were forty thousand Sallys, but not one of them my cousin. I slept in alleys and barns, picked food out of garbage heaps, went with no food at all. During normal times a child living as I lived would have been taken in. This was wartime.

For days I wandered around continuing the futile search. One morning I went out to the camp of the 3rd Ohio Cavalry. Here I saw a man selling newspapers to the soldiers. He was the sutler, proprietor of the camp canteen. I got him to let me sell some papers. That night I ate with a squad of soldiers and had a full meal. One of them said I could crawl into bed with him. I slept like a log. After that I belonged to the 3rd Ohio Cavalry. I was its mascot. The sutler had a portable printing press on which he ran off news sheets when there was a battle or some other excitement. I sold these sheets and also some magazines.

Sometimes I slept with one soldier and sometimes with another. My clothes wore out. When a soldier was issued new clothes, he discarded his old uniform. I was free to appropriate these discards. I would take a pair of breeches, cut off the legs, tie up the seat, and manage to hitch the waist around me. For two years I remained with the 3rd Ohio Cavalry. I was with them at Lookout Mountain and Missionary Ridge. A stray horse became mine, and I rode him to Murfreesboro. During the battle he was shot dead under me. I don't believe any boy of my years ever saw more dead men than I had seen by the time I was eleven years old. I don't know how many I saw, but I saw thousands, maybe tens of thousands. I saw men shot down not five feet from where I stood.

The regimental surgeon, Dr. R. Wirth, now began to pay me particular notice. He had me sleep regularly in his tent, and he often spoke of how wrong it was that a boy of my age should be living in such a way. Every time a batch of prisoners came in, he would send me down to the provost guard to see if some relative of mine might be among them.

The excitement and adventure appealed to me, and I was making money. Food, clothing, and shelter cost me nothing. Every nickel I made was clear gain. Finally I had a hundred dollars saved up. It needed a purse to be safe in. I killed a mole, skinned it, and stuffed the skin with bran. Then, when the skin was well cured, I put the hundred dollars in bills inside the moleskin purse and stuffed it into my pocket. I made a mistake. Instead of putting the moleskin head down, I put it tail down. It had a tendency to work up with the grain of hair. It worked out of my pocket. I could not tell exactly where or when I had lost it, but as near as I could figure, it was out in a ten-acre field. For three days I searched that field over and over, trying to find the moleskin purse. It was lost for good. In later years I lost over half a million dollars on cattle in a Colorado blizzard, but that loss did not come as close to me as the loss of my first hundred dollars.

I had now been with the Federal soldiers going on three years. Not long after I lost the purse, Dr. Wirth wrote his wife about me. She wrote back that she wanted to take care of me. A wounded captain going on furlough would take charge of me and deliver me at the doctor's home in Ottawa County, Ohio, on Lake Erie. I agreed to go.

Hunting Cousin Sally

It was a cold country I went to. Every morning I had to get up before daylight, make fires, milk, and then, while Mrs. Wirth cooked breakfast, tend to her two babies. I changed their diapers, fed them, packed them about, nursed them like a nursemaid. I feel grateful now to the Wirth family for their adoption of an orphan, but this life made me terribly homesick for the free life in camp. And I was still homesick for Cousin Sally. I thought of her more here by Lake Erie than I had thought of her on the battlefields. I determined to go to her. I had learned a lot about the world, and I felt sure that I could now find her in Nashville, even if I did not know the name of her husband or what street she lived on.

Lake Erie was frozen over, and the shore near town was lined with ice-locked boats. I walked that shoreline every day on the way to the post office. One of the boats appealed to me in a particular way. I mustered up courage to go aboard it. I found the captain in his warm cabin and told him I wanted to be his cabin boy. He agreed that when the ice broke he would stow me away and then after we were out would hire me. I had to tell him that I was running away. That was all right with him.

But I was never to make the voyage. Here I'll have to tell something that at the time I was unaware of. It confirms my belief in Providence and in the effectiveness of my mother's prayers.

While I was on Lake Erie nursing babies and waiting for the ice to break so that I could run away and try once more to find Cousin Sally, the Union forces around Vicksburg used up all available forage within the vicinity and called for more. The 3rd Ohio Cavalry was at Vicksburg. A captain of this regiment went to Nashville with an order on General

Rosecrans for wagons, teams, and men to gather forage for shipment to Vicksburg. The captain was to commandeer hay, oats, corn, and other provender, giving each owner a receipt and an order on the government for pay.

Starting out of Nashville with his wagons, the captain went ten miles before he halted. The halt was at a prosperous-looking farmhouse with promising-looking barns. The barns fulfilled their promise. The captain loaded several wagons from them. Then he went into the house, where he met a woman. He told her the government would pay for what he was hauling off. He called for pen and ink.

While he was writing out a warrant, the woman said to him, "Captain, there is one question I ask every Union soldier I meet. About three years ago while the Federal troops were taking Nashville, an orphan boy named Ike Pryor ran away from his uncle at Spring Hill, in this state, with the intention of finding me. He never reached me. I love him as a mother; he loves me as a son. We have heard that he fell in with some Federal troops. Have you ever seen this orphan boy?"

While the woman was talking, the captain quit writing. "Madam," he said, "is your name Sally?"

"Yes," she replied, "but why do you ask? I have given you my husband's name."

"Why, madam," the captain went on, "I know this boy well. He has stayed in my tent many a night. A hundred times I have heard him tell how he looked and looked for his Cousin Sally in Nashville. He had forgotten the name of the man you married. The 3rd Ohio Cavalry with which he took up is at Vicksburg in Mississippi. I have just come from there. I am the only man in Tennessee now who knows about Iky Pryor. I rode ten miles this morning without halting, and the first house I stop at I meet Cousin Sally. It looks like the hand of God."

Then the captain told Cousin Sally how Dr. Wirth had befriended me and sent me to his home. He gave her the doctor's address in Ohio.

One morning when I asked for Mrs. Wirth's mail, having dawdled a little while, as usual, on the road to look at the boat I was going to escape in, the postmaster called me inside. He took me to a corner where nobody could overhear our talk. "I understand that your name is Ike Pryor and that you are living with Mrs. Wirth and her children," he said.

"Yes, sir."

"I have a letter concerning you," he went on.

"Who wrote it?"

"A relative of yours named Mrs. John O. Ewing, near Nashville, Tennessee."

Like a flash, the name Ewing came back. I was so eager to hear more that I was in a tremble. Then the postmaster read me the letter from Cousin Sally. She had learned of my whereabouts through a captain of the Union Army rustling forage. She had written to Mrs. Wirth but had no answer. She wrote again and again heard nothing. Now she was calling on the postmaster for help. She wanted to know if I was really at the Wirth home. She wanted to know how I was — and she wanted me.

The postmaster was a sympathetic man. I saw that I could trust him. I told him my whole story and how I was even then planning to leave on a boat as soon as the spring thaw came

— in order to find Cousin Sally. He sat down right there and wrote Cousin Sally. He read the letter aloud to me, and I saw him post it.

Cousin Sally sent that letter, together with one of her own, to Washington. Very likely Abraham Lincoln knew nothing of it, but some humane official took notice. General Rosecrans sent for me. Shortly after I arrived at his headquarters Cousin Sally came and got me.

I was now twelve years old. For seven of those twelve years I had been batted from pillar to post, but I was born headstrong and willful. For the past three years I had been trying to get back to Cousin Sally. At last I had found her and found a home. The ten thousand prayers sent up by my mother were answered.

Cousin Sally sent me to school. After I had gone three years her husband went broke. I took a job to help her and worked for three years. Meantime we had moved back to Alabama.

Here, when I was eighteen years old — in 1870 — one of my brothers showed up. He was fresh from Texas and was full of talk about opportunities in that new country. Many people were going to Texas. I told Cousin Sally I wanted to go. She said she no longer needed me and to go on. She gave me some money and a Bible and kissed me goodbye.

I came down the Mississippi River to New Orleans, took boat for Galveston, and made my way overland to Austin. There I hired to a man named Neil Cain. He had a farm out about ten miles from town and put me to plowing at fifteen dollars a month. His field had a fence around it to keep cattle out. The only fences in Texas in those days were to keep stock out of fields; nothing fenced them in. There were not many fields. The Chisholm Trail from south Texas to Kan-

sas passed right by our field. I could watch the herds of Longhorns trailing by, see cowboys riding, smell the dust of movement. I wasn't a bit satisfied with keeping my eyes on a pair
of mule ears and walking up one row and down another between a pair of plow handles. Moreover, I had learned that
cowboys were getting thirty dollars a month, while here I was
getting just fifteen dollars. I took the cow fever.

About this time a phrenologist named O. S. Fowler* came
to Austin analyzing people's heads and telling them what
they were suited for. I borrowed a horse from Mr. Cain and
rode in to find out what I was good for. Mr. Fowler sat me
down beside a table, pulled out a blank chart, told a young
woman assistant to write as he dictated, and began feeling my
head. He felt this bump and that bump, and the young lady
wrote down everything he said.

"Young man," he concluded, "you will always be under the
spell of some woman. That woman should be your wife."

I asked him what I owed him.

"Ten dollars."

I paid it — two-thirds of a month's salary. Then I rode
back to the farm.

While we were eating breakfast before daylight the next
morning I pulled out the sheet of paper I had paid ten dollars
for and put it on the table. Then I thumped my head and
said, "Mr. Cain, everything in this head is in this paper. It
don't say a damned word about plowing. I'm going to follow
cows instead of mules."

I have often wondered what would have happened to me

---

* His reputation was nationwide. After he had made a fortune from books
and lectures on the contours of the human head, he established the town of
Fowler in Colorado.

if I hadn't consulted that phrenologist. He appears like some gigantic hand thrust out by Providence to jerk me from one trail into another — from the trail of a plow mule into the widest and longest trail ever beat out by cattle.

I got a job with Bill Arnold of Llano County and in the spring of 1871 went up with his herd to Coffeyville, Kansas. We had twenty-five hundred aged steers. After snailing along for six weeks at the rate of about fifteen miles a day, I realized that the cowboy's life was not all glory; still, I liked it. I learned as much about cow psychology as Dr. Fowler knew about phrenology. One steer in our herd bawled and bellered all through the first night on the trail. A few nights later he stampeded the herd, leading one run after another until daylight. When Bill Arnold found he was fifty head short and I told him that this steer was the troublemaker, he shot him dead with his six-shooter.

The next year I was twenty and bossed the drive. Then I went to work for Charles Lemberg of Mason County and was soon manager of his ranch.

The question of honesty among cow people often comes up. Sometimes I say that any cowman of open range days who claimed never to have put his brand on somebody else's animal was either a liar or a poor roper. But that's a joke — in a way.

Not long after I went to work for Charles Lemberg, a man came to the ranch to receive a herd of cattle he had contracted for. He brought the money in a morral (Mexican fiber bag) tied to his saddlehorn. The night before the cattle were to be counted out they stampeded. The buyer jumped on his horse with the rest of us and tore after the running herd. It was dark, but the pounding of hoofs and the cracking of horns could have been followed a mile off. The buyer had his morral of gold and silver still on his saddle. Why he had not hung it up in camp, I don't know, for morrals and sacks of money were frequently left lying around. When the buyer's horse began to run, the morral began to flop. It wasn't even tied down.

The cattle ran for hours. The buyer had made a good purchase and was anxious to stop them. He finally took that morral off his saddle and hung it on a tree. When daylight came, he could not go back to it. Of course he appealed to us. "I don't know where I left it," he said — "on a limb somewhere." Every hand that could be spared from the herd turned out to hunt the money. The buyer had no fear that a finder would hide it or make off with it. There were thousands of trees in the country over which the cattle had chased; the fear was that the right one would not be sighted. On the second day a cowboy brought the morral in. A blanket was spread on the ground and payment for the cattle was counted out right there.

To give another illustration of old-time cowman honesty, in 1884 I put fifteen herds of three thousand cattle each on the trail. They went to Kansas, Wyoming, Colorado, and Nebraska. I did well on them, but trailmen could count on a loss of about three per cent from deaths, escapes in stampedes, animals dropping out in brush, drowning in rivers, etc. Inevitably out of the forty-five thousand head of cattle in my herds perhaps a thousand or so were lost. They were all branded P on the left loin — my road brand. For years after this drive I attended annual meetings of the American National Live Stock Association at Denver, Cheyenne and other places. Several times some cowman would come up to me and say something like this: "Didn't you have a herd passing through such-and-such a range in 1884?"

"Yes."

"Well, what was your road brand?"

"P on the left loin."

"I thought so. Your outfit lost three steers in my country, and I finally sold them. Here's the money."

When I began buying cattle in Llano and Mason counties to take up the trail, the owners asked for checks in hundred-dollar denominations. I did not ask questions but nearly took writer's cramp writing out fifty one-hundred-dollar checks. When I got back from Kansas six months later, I found my money still in the bank, most of the checks uncashed. Those fellows were keeping some in their trunks; the others were passing from hand to hand as currency. A cowman's name on a check was considered as good as a bank note.

My strangest experience on the trail was in 1875. That was the year Dodge City opened as the main market for Texas cattle. I had a herd of three thousand head bound for Colorado. After the trail crossed Red River into the Indian Territory, it ran due north three hundred miles for Dodge City and then one prong turned west up the Arkansas River a hundred and fifty miles into Colorado. I decided to cut straight across in a northwesterly direction, instead of making the elbow, and save maybe a hundred miles. I knew the country was fairly well watered and was willing to take a chance on the Indians. It was my practice to scout in the lead, looking for water and camping grounds. About the third day out, I met two men riding east. I told them I was scouting ahead of a herd of cattle and asked them about the lay of the land.

"My God," they exclaimed, "you'll never in this world get to Colorado!"

"Why?"

"Because there are millions of buffaloes that you can't possibly drive a herd through."

I told them I thought I could and went on. It was a beautiful country, level as a sea and as rich in grass as any hayfield. That night we stopped by fine water and the cattle didn't move till daylight. The next afternoon I was scouting ahead, the cook in his wagon right behind me, when I saw something that made me halt.

"What is that dark cloud away yonder ahead of us?" I asked.

The cook did not know. We could see that it was coming towards us. Our cattle were following a mile or so back. I soon realized that the dark cloud was buffaloes. The front of the herd was so wide that neither edge was in sight. As far as the eye could reach there was no break in the mass of buffaloes as they came on.

I turned back towards our cattle, telling the cook to follow, which he did in a gallop. Then I halted the wagon, and had the remudero bring up the horses. After catching fresh mounts, we roped all the other horses and tied them to a rope that was run around the wagon. I detailed six men to hold the herd. Then with six more I galloped to meet the oncoming buffaloes. We met them half a mile away. I placed three men on either side of me. Shouting, shooting, beating our leggins with quirts, and waving slickers, we managed to split the herd, so that half of them went on one side of our cattle and half on the other. Those buffaloes were passing us all night long. We had a double job: keeping our restless cattle together and keeping the buffaloes spread out. At daylight next morning they were still passing by but the tail end was in sight. I estimated these drags to number about a thousand.

I have no idea how many were in this herd. Certainly there were hundreds of thousands. The famous buffalo hunter Wright Mooar declared that he once rode all day through a herd, he going in one direction, they in another, opening out to afford him in a narrow passage. I believe as many buffaloes passed us that night as Wright Mooar rode through. After we were clear of them I veered northeast to intersect the Dodge City trail. I was afraid that if we kept on the way we were headed we might run into the main herd of buffaloes.

About this time I contracted for a thousand dry cows in Mason County. When I went to receive them in the spring, half of them had calves too young to stand the drive. I told the owner I didn't want them; he didn't either. He said for me to do as I pleased. I put the cows in a pen, a bunch at a time, and had the calves killed — five hundred of them. Wild razorback hogs, thick in the country, devoured the veal. At that time trail drivers customarily killed every morning any calves that had been dropped on the bed grounds. As cattle got higher, trailers of stock cattle took "calf wagons" along to haul the young calves until they were old enough to make their own way. A herd of cows and calves went much slower than one of steers.

In 1876 Charles Lemberg propositioned me to buy him out. He gave terms that I could handle. I bought a twenty-thousand-acre ranch, stocked with fifteen hundred cattle. The cattle boom that was to last for nearly ten years was on. In 1877 I drove to Ogallala, Nebraska, with a herd only partly owned by me. The next year I had my own herd of three thousand head — the most economical size for a trail herd. In 1879 I had two herds on the trail. In 1884, steer yearlings bought in Texas at $12 sold in Montana at $16; two-year-olds bought at $16 brought $20, and big steers bought at $20 were in demand at $24. The cost of driving from Texas to Montana was not over a dollar a head.

My brother and I bought more cattle, and in 1885 put twenty thousand head on free grass in Colorado. They had no more than got located when a syndicate made up of Cleveland, Ohio, capitalists bought a large grant of land we were using. I understood they wanted to get into the cow business. I took a train for Cleveland. They put up $100,000 on contract to receive our cattle the next spring. On paper we made a $700,000 deal. On the way back to Texas I stopped in Chicago and while there received a telegram from my brother in Colorado saying that the worst blizzard in years was raging. Eighteen inches of snow covered the grass all over the plains and then froze deep enough to hold up a steer without breaking through. After six weeks of starvation not many cattle were left. When spring came we delivered $65,000 worth, leaving us $35,000 in debt to the Cleveland men on their contract. I owed a livestock commission company $30,000 besides, but they extended the note and put up $70,000 for me to operate on. The partnership was closed out.

For several years nobody seemed to want cattle. In 1885 I had offered the Cross S outfit in southwest Texas $25 around for their stock, everything but calves counted. In 1893 I contracted for the Cross S cattle at $6.30 a head, calves thrown in and twenty-five hundred head of big steers guaranteed. I shipped the grown stuff to Oklahoma to fatten, and that fall sold fat cows on the Kansas City stockyards at 85 cents a hundred pounds. I held the steers through the winter, feeding them on corn at 15 cents a bushel. In the spring of '94 they brought up to $4 a hundred.

After the Spanish-American War broke out in 1898, I figured that as soon as we won and the blockade was raised, Cuba would be the best market on earth for cattle. I sent an agent to Cuba to keep me advised by cable, in code language. He was with General Shafter's troops at Santiago while negotiations for surrender were going on. When the blockade was raised, two ships I had chartered for freighting cattle to Cuba were in port and I had a virtual corner on all other available ships. In six weeks I loaded out eight thousand cattle that cost $15 around and that brought as high as $80 around in Havana, the freight cost running about $5 a head. Within two weeks after I quit shipping, the market was glutted and many good men went broke on the business.

Pinned down, Colonel Ike would admit that he did not see the hand of God directing profits in this kind of business. Just the same, he attributed his success in life to the way affairs turned out while he was hunting Cousin Sally.

2

Ab Blocker, Trail Boss

AB (ALBERT PICKENS) BLOCKER, generally known as
Mister Ab and by some called Uncle Ab, born of cultured parents near Austin, Texas, in 1856, was the most original-natured trail boss I have known. He claimed to have looked down the backs of more cows and to have drunk water out of more cow tracks than any other man who ever pointed a herd towards the North Star. He was not a boaster. His face was sorrowful, his voice was sorrowful, he loved to celebrate in a quiet way.

I recall one celebration in the Gunter Hotel in San Antonio during a gathering of the Old-Time Trail Drivers of Texas. Prohibition was in force, but John Doak had procured a pint of good bourbon. He invited his compadre Bob Lauderdale, Ab Blocker and me up to his room. It would never have occurred to him to order ice and glasses. He owned a good ranch. Uncorking the bottle while we stood, he handed it to Ab first. Ab looked at it with marked approbation and said, "I want to give a toast." So far as my association with him went, it was the only toast he knew and he never failed on a proper occasion to give it. In his declining years he lacked money to buy whiskey — the time of life when a man needs it most.

Now he held up the brown bottle in his massive, weathered hand and, with added strength to his deep voice, but no light added to his tristful countenance, pronounced the toast slowly, earnestly, as if wishing to impress on both God and men his belief in its philosophy:

> We come into this world all naked and bare;
> We go out of this world we know not where.
> But if we have been good fellows here,
> We need not fear what will be there.

He passed the bottle to Bob Lauderdale, of Scotch descent, soft-spoken, as honest as daylight, very modest. He said nothing. John Doak's turn came last. "Boys," he said, "I'm going to give a toast I heard here in this town in the Iron Front Saloon on Main Plaza in 1885. I was just back from a drive to Kansas. To give the toast right you have to look at the bottle hard while giving it and then when it's ended do what you can to demolish the whiskey." He held the bottle out at arm's length and, gazing at it, recited:

"Here's to the vinegarroon that jumped on the centipede's back. He looked at him with a glow and a glee and he said, 'You poisonous son-of-a-bitch, if I don't git you, you'll git me.' "

The bottle went around a second time, the partakers being careful that at least a few drops would be left for John Doak to finish off.

Ab Blocker could not come to town without getting sore-footed from walking on pavement. For sixty years, he wore the same kind of hat and the same style of boots, most of

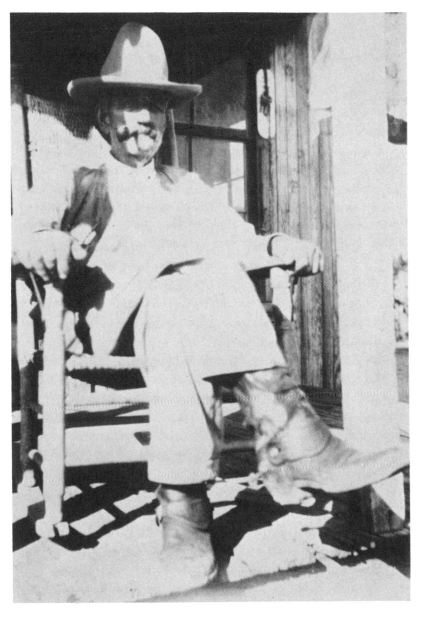

AB (A. P.) BLOCKER, perhaps the most noted of all trail bosses. He claimed to have looked down the backs of more cows and to have drunk more water out of more cow tracks than any other man who ever pointed a herd toward the North Star.

them made by the same bootmaker. As a young man, to help his mother out, he quit trailing cattle to farm, and nearly broke his back picking a bale of cotton, which sold for four cents a pound. After it was ginned, to quote his words, "I got down on my knees and promised God A'mighty that if I ever planted another cotton seed I would boil it first for three days so as to make sure it would never come up." Once while he was having trouble with Mexican customs officials crossing a herd out of Mexico, a friend who knew the ropes offered to take him to the *jefe*. As they got to the door of the little office, this friend advised Mister Ab to take off his hat. Ab said nothing and kept it on. "When you are in Rome, do as the Romans do," the friend urged. "If that's the case, I'll back out of Rome," Mister Ab said. He could be as final as a judge's sentence to hang. He kept his hat on, got the official paper, and crossed the cattle.

One fall on a drive to the Cherokee Strip in the Indian Territory, it went to raining and the cattle stampeded. Every night for six nights they stampeded and drifted, and Ab Blocker was with them all the time. On the seventh afternoon the skies cleared, the winds died down, and the whole world seemed pacific. The bedding more or less dried out, and after an early supper Mister Ab changed his clothes. Garbed in fresh red flannel underwear, he said to the cook, "I'd give the price of a gallon jug of whiskey to sleep this way through the night." He always slept in his underwear, long-handled summer and winter. He probably never had a nightshirt or a pair of pajamas on.

"Why, Ab," the cook said to him that clear night, "go on and sleep. There won't be any trouble tonight."

According to invariable custom, Mister Ab had his horse

Jovero saddled and tied to the right front wheel of the chuck wagon. Nobody else could bring a horse within a stake rope's length of the wagon. He lay down on his pallet near the rear of the wagon and in a minute was dead asleep. About eleven o'clock he felt the earth shaking and heard the roar of the stampede. He jammed on his hat as he arose from bed — for he always dressed from the top down — and took time to pull on his boots but could not spare enough to get into breeches. He untied Jovero, swung into the saddle and coiled up the tie-rope on the run. Heavy clouds had gathered; man and horse had to go by sound rather than sight. By the time he caught up with the herd, it had split. He found himself cut off with about a hundred head of steers.

He checked them down, but they kept drifting, now and then breaking into a trot or run, and before long he had no more idea than the man in the moon where the main herd was — if there was a main herd any more. His bunch kept getting farther and farther away from camp. At daylight he saw that he was on a draw running into the Salt Fork of the Brazos River and knew that camp was fully fifteen miles away. He tried to course his big bunch of steers towards it, but they wanted to graze south. They were plenty tired.

After a while he saw smoke coming up in a timbered bottom. Where there was smoke there must be coffee. He left the steers grazing while he rode to the smoke. About the time he got in sight of a cabin he saw woman clothes and baby clothes hanging on bushes to dry. He kept out of sight until he saw a man and then called to him. The man looked surprised when he got a view of a rider dressed only in red flannel underwear. He urged him to come in and get some breakfast, but Mister Ab would have starved before appearing as he was in front of a woman. The man went to the cabin and brought out a pot of coffee, some greasy bacon and cold biscuits. By the time Ab got back to his steers they were refreshed enough to travel. He reached camp with them early that afternoon. The rest of the men had been out bringing in scattered cattle all day, and two of them were ready to try to trail him down. They were short over a hundred head, and they naturally figured he was hanging with them somewhere — even if he'd left his clothes behind.

He married once but was not accommodated to domestic life. Yet he was gentle to women, especially to those he liked. He belonged only to cattle, grass, trails, cow camps. One day while he was in Cotulla shipping, Mr. Maltsberger, after the train of steers had pulled out, invited him to the house for dinner (lunch). Mrs. Maltsberger asked, "Mister Ab, how's your wife?" This was about a year after he had married. "Oh," he said, "she's just as poorly as she can be. She's had everything from hollerhorn to a baby." Nearly anything wrong with a cow was ascribed to hollowhorn. As a cure Ab had sawed or cut off the horns of many a cow. He did not remain married.

When he died in 1943 at the age of eighty-seven, he had never put his hands on the steering wheel of a car. He ignored all machinery of the machine age. The first airplane he ever saw stampeded a bunch of cattle he was driving through the brush. He always swore that at the time he thought it was a flying pearburner. (This contrivance for singeing thorns off prickly pear so that cattle can eat it throws a flame through a flexible nozzle from kerosene and compressed air and roars a little like an airplane engine.) He actually never learned to be at ease with mechanical contraptions. He might listen to talk about politics, foreign wars and economic complexities; he might say something about the prices of cattle and grass leases, but he had absolutely no conception of this world's affairs beyond the range. The range included whiskey, in which he had an abiding interest. The only vegetable he ate was potatoes, but he had to have meat.

As for owning anything, he was as unworldly as Chaucer's Poor Parson. He never had any cattle of his own. Most of his life he bossed trail herds and ranches for "Brother Johnnie," as he always called John Blocker. Starting in 1871 with five hundred head of trail cattle, John R. Blocker was in 1886 "interested" in eighty-two thousand between southern Texas and northern Montana. When Brother Johnnie prospered, Ab Blocker glowed; when Brother Johnnie lost, he sympathized but remained serene. One year while he was driving a herd to Wyoming for his brothers John and Bill, they rode out from Dodge City to inspect it. The three of them rode over for a look at a herd of twenty-five hundred heifers grazing nearby. Ab said, "Johnnie, if you and Bill had ten thousand like that in the Chupadero country, we'd be sitting purty, wouldn't we?"

"Teddy Blue" (E. C.) Abbott of the Three Deuce Ranch, Gilt Edge, Montana, used to tell a story on John Blocker he heard from a Suggs cowhand called Jack on Powder River in 1884. When he was fifteen, Jack and an old Negro gathered up about a hundred beef steers in his mother's brand and then Jack and his sisters (aged ten and twelve) grazed them under herd by day, penning them every night. Their mother had no money at all, and when she heard that John Blocker was putting up a herd in the region to drive north, she sent for him to come over and buy her steers. He came and said, "They are mighty good. I would buy them but couldn't pay you until I come back. Tell you what I'll do. I'll drive them north with my cattle, sell them for you and deliver the money this fall." "Give me ten dollars a head and take them," she said. "No," John Blocker answered, "they'll bring a lot more in Kansas." He put them in his herd and that fall rode up to her ranch and counted her out $1500. "I'm sure obliged," she said, "but how much do I owe you for all you've done?" "Nothing," John Blocker said. "The boys didn't know they were in the herd so far as work goes. That money is all yours."

Ab Blocker's pride was in being a superb cowman, and he boasted that he always tried to treat all hands fair, whether white, black or brown, but he never learned to talk Mexican. To him every boy, Mexican or Anglo, was "Bolivar." A cowman may own only steers; he may not own anything. The essential quality of a cowman is that he savies the cow — cow psychology, cow anatomy, cow dietetics — cow nature in general and cow nature in particular. He must know how to water a herd, graze it, drive it, hold it up, string it out, manage it at will and yet leave it free to thrive and be contented. One afternoon Ab sent a man from Doan's Store near Red River to see how the water was. "It's up to the last willow back from the bank," the cowboy reported. "We'll split her wide open in the morning," Ab said. He always stayed with 'em and got there.

He loved to tell about certain cows, certain horses, certain range characters. One character was Hell Bitch. In the winter of 1876, this cow dog helped him and three other brush poppers catch hundreds of mavericks out of the Blanco breaks in central Texas. Hell Bitch learned to distinguish between branded and unbranded cattle and would never bulldog anything but a maverick — so Mister Ab said. At least five hundred head of the thirty-seven hundred steers roped out and bought by the Blockers that year had horns spreading five feet or more from tip to tip.

There was a certain cowman accused of having cheated Brother Johnnie on a trade. He did not go broke one year when most other cowmen, including Brother Johnnie, went broke. He grew richer and stingier. "I knowed him," Mister Ab would say, "when he couldn't flag down a gut-wagon." Of someone he had known a long time he would say, "I've knowed him since he sucked. I'd know his ashes in a whirlwind."

There was a strawberry roan cutting horse with a white streak down his face. "He could do everything nearly but talk Mexican." Working in a herd, he'd watch with his ears. He'd keep both ears pointed at a steer being cut out. If he was behind a cow and calf, he'd point one ear down towards the calf and the other towards the cow. If he got tired and hot, he would simply take the bit in his teeth and walk straight out of the herd to rest. Then, if Mister Ab would get down, loosen the cinch, shift the saddle blanket and let him breathe a spell, he would be willing to go back in and cut some more.

Ab Blocker often took the bit in his own teeth. He had a sympathy for independence in others. He did not like cornbread and would not eat it. One year he set out to deliver a herd for Tom Coleman and John Blocker, partners. Cornmeal was considerably cheaper than flour, and Tom Coleman believed in saving expenses. When Ab Blocker loaded up his chuck wagon at Coleman's ranch store, Coleman insisted on putting in four fifty-pound sacks of cornmeal. Three months later Ab was back at headquarters with the wagon. "You'll find them four sacks of cornmeal still in it," he said to Tom Coleman.

He delivered the first herd bought by the Capital Syndicate for stocking their three-million-acre ranch on the Texas–New Mexico line. He found the manager undecided as to what brand to adopt. "I want about three letters in the brand," he said, "something that cow thieves can't burn out. We've got running irons." It was customary for deliverers to help receivers brand out a herd. Ab Blocker was in a hurry to deliver, ride back south and get another herd. With his spurred boot-heel he drew three letters on the ground. "That brand will hold 'em," he said. Thus the famous X I T brand had its origin.

Ludie Dobie, my brother Elrich's wife, knew him at Big Wells, Texas, when she was young and Mister Ab was old. He was staying on at the John Blocker ranch after his brother died and no cattle were left for him to tend to. These are some of Ludie Dobie's recollections.

"Uncle Ab rode every day into Big Wells — for mail that seldom arrived — from the John Blocker ranch about six miles away. He had two horses, Tony and Baldy. His favorite, Baldy, was a bay with a blazed face, from the Blocker and Jennings Piedra Blanca ranch in Mexico.

"The only use he seemed to make of stirrups was in mounting a horse; he didn't brace his feet in the stirrups, just dangled his feet in them. His horses knew the way to our pen, always came there when they had a chance. No matter what the time of day, Uncle Ab upon dismounting would say, 'I God, Ludie, ain't you got a cup o' coffee?' One time he said, 'I God, Ludie, this ain't coffee. I can see the bottom of the cup.'

"One time he came to our house after some hunters had left a bottle of gin. This was during bootleg days. We gave it to Uncle Ab and he said, 'I God, Ludie, gimme something to chase this poison with.' Before long he got confused on which was water and which gin, both being clear. After he had chased the water with the gin a few times, the telephone rang and the operator said, 'If Mr. Blocker's there, tell him to go home quick. His house is on fire.' He could hardly crawl up on old Baldy. I was afraid he'd fall off, but he made it to the ranch in time to see a bucket brigade save everything but the kitchen.

"He never left his quirt on his saddle. The string to it was around his wrist wherever he went. He rode with one end of the rope around his horse's neck and the other end coiled and tied to the left-hand side of his saddlehorn. His boots had low heels, tops up nearly to the knee, not scalloped in front but even — like a stovepipe. Long leather ears hung down from the boot tops. He always had his breeches tucked inside the boots. He wore a white shirt fastened at the neck with an old brass collar button that had once been gold-plated. After the style changed to sewed-on collar buttons, he'd bring any new shirt he bought to me to cut the button off and make a buttonhole. He wore a white handkerchief around his neck — never a bandana, never a necktie. He wore a woolen vest, the pockets always handy, summer and winter, along with long-sleeved undershirts and long-legged drawers — never changing from anything he was used to. In a vest pocket, he carried a big watch with a long gold chain attached by a gold bar through a buttonhole of his vest. His pocket knife, long-bladed and white-handled, was as old as his collar button, watch, and spurs. He kept it very sharp, often whetting it on a boot-leg. His heavy felt, wide-brimmed, high-peaked hat was black. Very likely he'd never had a straw hat on his head.

"Once in a while somebody driving to San Antonio would take him to see his nephew Billy Blocker, son of Mr. John Blocker. Getting back to Big Wells late, he would stay in the hotel. In those country towns you didn't register. You just found an empty room and went to bed. Sometimes the landlady knew you were there and sometimes she didn't. The night the Big Wells hotel burned down nobody knew Uncle Ab was upstairs. People were getting roomers and furniture out when here came Uncle Ab through a window. The boys brought him to my aunt's rooming house, where I lived. He was wearing a pair of shoes. The boys had gotten them for him out of a store. They had given him a drink, too, to calm his nerves. I said, 'Uncle Ab, what happened to your boots?' He said, 'Girlie, I'll tell you. You know when I waked up I smelled smoke. I went to that stairway and fire was coming up the stairs. Ab ran back to his room and threw his clothes out the window and then Blocker jumped out on top of them, but he didn't get his boots. He just threw his clothes out.' Of course, he was dressed in his longies when he woke up.

"He always wore spurs, never unstrapped them — 'unstropped,' as he would say — when he pulled his boots off. The next morning he had the boys searching through the ashes, where they found his spurs. The silver was melted off, but some friend had them resilvered for him. His boots were handmade in San Antonio. This was the first pair of shoes he could remember having worn. When Uncle Ab couldn't ride any more I kind of kept an eye on old Baldy. One winter during a drouth I brought him into town and fed him. He died of old age. After Uncle Ab quit riding he kept on wearing his spurs. He was undressed without them.

"One time while my baby was little, he came to see me. The weather was hot and the baby was crying. This crying irritated Ab, but I was used to hearing it and now I was busy preparing lunch. Finally he said, 'What's wrong with that baby?' I said, 'Oh, really, Uncle Ab, nothing. He's hungry, I suppose.' After awhile he said, 'I God, Ludie, why don't you let that baby suck?'

"When he was taken to a San Antonio hospital in his final illness he would not let the nurses bathe him or put pajamas on him. 'Annie' (Brother Johnnie's wife) or his own daughter brought him freshly laundered underclothes every day. He did not die in the hospital, but at Annie's. He wanted to be buried with his boots on. He was, the spurs strapped to them. The old brass collar button was in his shirt and a fresh white handkerchief was around his neck."

A verse written of another earth-man long, long ago might have been graved on his headstone: "Thou shalt be in league with the stones of the field: and the beasts of the field shall be at peace with thee."

3

Shanghai Pierce and the Flapjacks

O F ALL THE old-time cowmen of open range days Shanghai Pierce, with the possible exception of Charlie Goodnight, has come nearer becoming a legend than any other. They were opposites, Goodnight quiet, public-spirited and modest, Pierce loud, rough and vaunting, though each was "a character unto God."

How Abel Head Pierce got the nickname of Shanghai is speculative, but probably it was from his resemblance in youth to a cocky Shanghai rooster. Old Shang liked it so much that it is a wonder he did not use it instead of his initials in signing checks. He landed in Texas — from Rhode Island by way of Virginia, six foot four, nineteen years old. The published explanation of his leaving Rhode Island is that he simply had to get away from"too many doses of sanctimony." According to one of his lawyers, he said: "When I lay down in Rhode Island I'd find my head on the tits of some woman in Massachusetts and my feet tickling another woman's legs in Connecticut. I was just too fenced in." His one ambition was to get rich. As he gathered land and cattle, he seemed to be increasingly set on having his way.

Shanghai Pierce and the Flapjacks

When he landed at Port Lavaca, he had seventy-five cents. When he died in 1900, at the age of sixty-six, he owned over two hundred thousand acres of land besides other property. After he had acquired two hundred thousand acres he changed certain field notes to add a few more sections of land. He fenced in little men and poor widows and drove off their milch cows in his big herds — unless one of them leveled a double-barreled shotgun on him, and then he was very obliging. He'd as soon bribe a judge as tip a waiter. In fact, he was against tipping any functionary. He asserted that "if six bits won't bribe an Italian it is useless to offer more." After he had contracted a thousand steers to an Indian agency he considered it fair sport to count in 118 that he did not have past the "army greenhorns." He got his start working for $200 a year putting up a picket fence, but didn't really prosper until mavericking got on a boom following the Civil War.

Probably no mavericker of the ranges ever boomed higher than Shanghai Pierce. There were lots of cattle on the coast and lots of them unbranded. Shanghai imported four (some say only two) brothers named Lunn to maverick for him. After a while they went to mavericking for themselves, starting a brand of their own on the side. Pierce had taught them to burn his brand on any big calf — soon to be weaned — following a cow in some other man's brand. When he learned that they were stealing for themselves instead of for him alone, Pierce turned on the Lunn brothers like a tiger. He and some other ranchers surrounded them in a thicket. One vigilante persuaded them to come out and talk. The talk consisted of disarming them, putting a rope around the neck of each man while he sat on his horse under a limb to which the other end of the rope was tied, and then driving the horse away.

Before quirts were applied to a horse so that the rider would be left hanging, the youngest of the Lunn brothers was asked if he had anything to say for himself. "Yes," he replied, "I'd like to have ten minutes to tell that long-legged son-of-a-bitch," pointing to Shanghai Pierce, "what I think of a man who hired us to steal for him and then after we learned his methods wants to hang us." The hangers gave the Lunn boy's horse a lick and he was left kicking in the air. He was about eighteen years old. Joe Pickering, a cowman from way back, of Victoria, Texas, gave me this account in 1935. He said the Lunn tree was still identifiable.

After the hangings for practices that he himself had been prospering on, Shanghai Pierce found the climate too hot in Texas and, as Joseph G. McCoy tells in his honest book *Historic Sketches of the Cattle Trade* (1874), spent a considerable time in Kansas, where he also prospered.

Most of his troubles were with big guns. "I am eternally lawing," he once wrote. Records of his lawsuits enliven Chris Emmett's biography *Shanghai Pierce: A Fair Likeness*. He lawed with George Miller, founder of the 101 Ranch, and with Dan Sullivan, a San Antonio "private" banker noted for foreclosing on cowmen. In Sullivan's declining years, two loyal-Irish, devoted-Catholic bookkeepers got away with a million dollars of his money. Once in a terrible drouth he refused to renew Jim Chittim's note. "Pay up or turn over the mortgaged stuff," he said. "I'll see what I can do," Jim Chittim left saying. Five days later he was back. "I guess you've got the money," Dan Sullivan said, exuding iron and irony, after the two had sat down in his private office. The door was closed. "I've decided to renew the note," Jim Chittim said, reaching and pulling out his private example of the Great Persuader. "Now take your choice. You're not going to get title to *my* land and cattle." Dan Sullivan chose to make out a new note.

Seated in the witness box, Shanghai Pierce shouted, "I think the best commercial record a man can make is to prove in court that he has robbed Little Dannie Sullivan. I'll be very popular for this. The people will descend upon me and pluck my locks for souvenirs and charms." As for the owner of the 101 Ranch, Shanghai Pierce, again on the witness stand, bellowed out, "Miller is known to be the biggest liar on the North American continent, and not only the biggest liar but the biggest thief and a son-of-a-bitch."

His voice, he realized, was "too loud for indoor use," and he delighted in using it. His talk was even more picturesque than loud. Once in New York he noticed a boy among strangers circled around to listen to him. "Son," he boomed, "just what do you want?" "Please, sir," came the reply, "I just want to hear you talk." Shanghai brought the boy to Texas, where he could hear runty cattle called "swamp angels" or "saddle-pocket dogies," and coastal cattle called "sea lions," they were so practiced in swimming.

Shanghai Pierce was the loudest man in the country. He would sit at one end of a day coach and in normal voice hold conversation with some man at the other end of the coach, who of course had to yell, while the train was clanking along. He knew everybody, yelled at everybody he saw. A certain cowman upon arriving in Victoria one day asked a friend if he had seen Shanghai Pierce in town. "No," the friend replied, "I haven't seen him, but I know just the same he's not here.

I haven't heard him." As another old joke goes, he built the bunkhouse at Rancho Grande fully three hundred yards away from the main house — so that the hands could not hear him whispering to his wife. "Being in the most conspicuous part of a Barnum and Bailey circus parade would be no more conspicuous than being in company with Shanghai Pierce," Judge Fred Proctor, himself a very modest man, told me.

Once while Proctor was on a train going through to Houston, Shanghai, at the station outside, saw him. The train was moving out, but Shanghai yelled to the conductor to hold it. He went inside, asked Proctor how much he owed him, grumbled at the amount, and then wrote out a check for it.

Everybody knew where he stood, both physically and mentally, with respect to individuals and things. Once when he went into a hotel at Columbia, Texas, to register, his eye caught the freshly written name of R. L. Stafford. Pointing to the name, he said to the clerk — and to everybody else in the block who had ears to listen: "I know this is a comfortable hotel with ample accommodations for ordinary men, but, by God, sirs, it is entirely too small for Bob Stafford and Shanghai Pierce at the same time." He arrived at a hotel in Hot Springs, Arkansas, without a reservation, and the manager, after listening to his bluster, refused him one. "By God, sir," Shanghai bellowed out, "is this hotel for sale?" "I own a half interest, and I'll sell it for fifteen thousand dollars," the manager-owner replied. "Sold," shouted Old Shang, and he reached for his checkbook — and went up to a room he now owned. A cattle solicitor was after him to stop his herd at Dodge City, Kansas. "No, I'll not ship any more cattle to your town," Shanghai thundered. "Why, I can get a room right here in the heart of your city, with a nice clean bed, plenty of soap, water and towels, and occupy it for twenty-four hours for two bits. And your stockyards, way out past the edge of town, want to charge me twenty cents a head and let my steers stand out in the weather. No, I'll not ship any more cattle to your town."

A lawyer for his opponent in a court suit came to see him at his ranch and made what Shanghai considered a shady proposal. After being referred three or four times to Pierce's own lawyer, the visitor stood up and said, "Colonel Pierce, I don't believe you are going to commit yourself on anything." Colonel Pierce replied, "When a man owns a dog, there is no use for him to do the barking himself."

While his daughter was in school in Virginia he received a special bill for "equestrianism." He put it in his pocket until he could see his banker some weeks later. "Look at that," he said, pointing to the balance due and the word "equestrianism." "My God," he asked, "what has she done now?" It was just a charge for horsemanship, the banker explained. Shanghai Pierce waved his hand and cried out, "Horsemanship! Here I am paying out money to teach her to ride a sidesaddle in Central Park and she was raised riding straddle on a bareback Texas pony."

After a railroad built through his ranch and Pierce's Station was established near headquarters, he decided to "introduce religion in the community" and built a church. Upon seeing it, a visitor asked, "Colonel Pierce, do you belong to that church?" "Hell, no," he retorted, "the church belongs to me." The son of a cowman friend once asked him, "Mr. Pierce, do you really think there is a heaven?" "I doubt it, son," he replied. "I don't see how the good Lord would voluntarily take upon himself the immense job of cutting back so many culls out of the human race."

He was wont to identify himself as "Shanghai Pierce, Webster on cattle." "There is not a man in the United States can beat me on a ranch," he boasted, "and I have some stuff to show for it, sir."

Nobody knew him better than Fred C. Proctor, who in representing the O'Connors, Jim Chittim, Ben Q. Ward and other big cowmen came to understand the breed well. In 1932 I got him to talk about Shanghai Pierce, and immediately wrote the notes that now follow.

Ben Q. Ward had a ranch on Carankawa Bay. He and Shanghai Pierce had been neighbors for many years and at one time were partners. He went to speculating in Houston real estate at the wrong time and became so deeply involved that his whole estate was in jeopardy. About 1900 he applied to Shanghai Pierce for a loan. Shanghai instructed his counsel, Fred C. Proctor, to look into Ward's affairs and see if a loan were warranted.

Proctor looked and told Ward that his collateral would not back a loan for more than $70,000.

"But I need ninety thousand," declared Ward. "Seventy thousand won't save me. It won't do me any good."

"Well," said Proctor, "I have followed Mr. Pierce's instructions. I am his adviser, you will understand. Involved as your property is, seventy thousand is all it seems worth as collateral."

"Do you mind if I see Shanghai myself?" asked Ward. He seemed to have an idea that Proctor was acting as watchdog over Pierce.

Shanghai Pierce and the Flapjacks

"Why, of course not. I have nothing to do with Mr. Pierce's decisions. He makes them himself. I act only under his instructions."

Ward left. Two days later he was back in Proctor's office. "I saw Shanghai himself," he gloated. "He's going to let me have the ninety thousand. Said he would wire you."

The next day the telegram arrived. It read: "Let Uncle Ben have the $90,000. His mother used to give me flapjacks."

Proctor made out the papers and Ben Q. Ward got the $90,000. The next time Proctor saw Shanghai, he said to him, "I understand all right what you meant by saying, 'Let Uncle Ben have the ninety thousand,' but what on earth did you mean by adding, 'His mother used to give me flapjacks'? "

Shanghai laughed loud and hard. Then he told something of the story of his life.

"The first thing I did when I got to Texas was hire out to W. B. Grimes at fifty cents a day. That was in 1853, on Matagorda Bay. Directly I was put to breaking horses. It happened this way. One morning a prize buck nigger was riding a wild horse out in the pen close to the Grimes house. This horse was a terror. He was a-squalling and the nigger was a-hollering and other niggers joining in. Well, Mrs. Grimes came running out, saw what was happening, and pitched into old Bing [W. B. Grimes]. 'Don't you know,' she stormed, 'that that horse is liable to kill that nigger? He's worth a good eighteen hundred dollars. What do you mean by letting him ride pitching horses when you got a Yankee here working for four bits a day that could take the risk just as well?'

"Grimes saw the point, and from then on I took the risks. I was too poor to buy decent clothes, and the Grimes family

[45]

didn't allow me to come into the polite part of the house. I ate in the kitchen and slept out in a shed. The Wards lived over on the Carankawa, where Uncle Ben still has the ranch — mortgaged to me. Once in a while I'd ride over in that country — all unfenced then, of course. Whenever I did, they'd treat me like sure enough white folks. Old Lady Ward knew I could eat more than a whole livery stable. She'd just pile the flapjacks up and keep on piling them until I was full. I can taste them yet. I'll never forget them and the good, kind woman who made them. Now you know why I let Uncle Ben have the ninety thousand against your advice."

Yet Shanghai was a businessman. When he came to write his will he asked Proctor how much he was going to charge. Proctor finally said $2500. Old Shanghai fumed, went outside, kicked a dog, and yelled at a boy. Then he came back. "All right. Agreed, is it?"

"Yes."

"Do you know how much I expected you to charge?"

"No."

"I expected you to charge five thousand."

Then he dictated the peculiar will by which his estate was to be kept intact, to be known as the A. H. Pierce Estate, until his youngest grandchild was thirty-five years old. "Nobody has any sense until he is thirty-five years old," he said, "and damned few after that." He was openly anxious to be remembered, and seemed to think that keeping the estate intact would preserve his memory. And when he later erected a monument to himself and Proctor asked him why, Shanghai answered: "If I didn't have it put up, nobody would."

Once he and Proctor went together to Galveston on business. Upon getting off the train, Proctor got into a cab. Pierce struck out on foot. Proctor called him and asked why he would walk. "Waste of money," he said, "to ride such a little distance. Why are you riding?"

"Because," answered Proctor, "I am rich, rich as hell."

"Yes, and you will charge it to me," roared Pierce.

"Certainly I will. You walk, and when you die not long hence your son-in-law will ride."

"By God, I hadn't thought of the thing that way," Shanghai exploded. "I'll ride with you, and from now on I'm a-going to ride every time I feel like it."

A few years before he died he commissioned a San Antonio tombstone-maker to execute a statue of himself out of gray marble, "higher than any statue of any Confederate general, a fair likeness of myself, big enough to be buried under, so people can look at it and say, 'There stands old Pierce.'"

"Old Pierce" still stands in one of the pastures of the Pierce Estate, not far from Blessing. After the Galveston storm (September, 1900) he wrote, about three months before he died, a check for $80,000 to be used for the relief of Wharton County people who had been "wrecked." He could also be kind. Perhaps he thought more of old Neptune, the Negro who used to ride with him on cow-buying expeditions and carry the gold for cash payment, than of anybody else. It was old Neptune he sent to pass on the statue. "It looks like you, Mr. Shang," Neptune reported — and then Mr. Shang wrote the check.

I know what the book gives as the facts on the end of Shanghai Pierce. I know, too, from long observation that folk anecdotes about certain characters are sometimes more revealing of truth than documented facts. I know two anecdotes breathing truth about the end of old Shang. I'll tell the milder one, from Joe Pickering.

One night while he was staying with Jonathan Pierce, brother to Shanghai, a rider came with a note. After reading it Jonathan growled, "Well, I've got to go to Pierce."

"Nothing wrong, I hope," Pickering said.

"Yes, Shang's dead. I told him all along that if he didn't leave them nigger gals alone they'd sap his log."

My old friend Jim Ballard of Beeville, now dead, knew Shanghai and knew his breed. To my mind he summed him up justly in these words: "He was always bragging — and didn't have a thing to brag about but his money. He talked big but was easy tamed. He was rough even for his time, rough in ways, rough on people he rode over, and rougher in language. The day his daughter married he said, 'That feller's going to stick his pecker into a gold mine tonight.' "

4

A Little Near

HE'D SKIN A FLEA for its hide and tallow, but he ain't as near as he used to be. He's got so that when it rains he'll go out and drink all the water he wants from the creek running into the big tank — plumb extravagant. He used to get up out of bed to turn over so's not to wear out the sheets. He'd have his cook make bread a day ahead so that it would harden and dry beyond human appetite. He would not buy sugar: it cost money and, besides, anything sweet softens a hired man.

A New Mexico ranchman named Ben Blanks had a way of feeding his hands nothing but frijoles and cornbread made of water, salt and meal — no shortening of any kind. This was fare three times a day. One day a man seemed to be shredding his throat in a cough.

"What's the matter with you, Luke?" Mr. Blanks asked.

"Oh, nothing much," Luke replied. "I've just got the cornbread heaves."

After that the cornbread had shortening.

Dan Waggoner of the ꓷꓷꓷ (the Three D's) ranch lived on the edge of Decatur, Texas. He and other cowmen brought saddle horses to the south. This was in the days of open range. Of a winter these horses were likely to drift back home. One early spring Burk Burnett, who ran the 6666 (Four Sixes) brand, sent men south to pick up his horses. They saw several in the Three D brand. Since they were driving north by Decatur, they put them in their herd.

They penned at Waggoner's house and showed him his horses. He thanked them, gave them some picket ropes, and asked them to catch the horses out and stake them. After they had done this, they said they would like to noon at his tank, near the house. That was all right. Shallots growing in a garden near the tank looked fresh to the Burk Burnett men. They had not tasted anything green for a long time. They asked if they might have a few to flavor their dried beef. Mr. Waggoner hesitated a second, then said, "Pull up a few." They helped themselves, ate dinner and were saddling up to leave when Mr. Waggoner came out. "I guess I'll have to charge a nickel for the shallots," he said. They paid it. That was the last time they or any other man to whose ears the story came picked up a stray horse for Dan Waggoner.

Lewis Ikard, in the same part of the country, had contracted for a string of cattle from a cowman named Black and was working with the outfit while they gathered. One morning a cowboy forefooted a fat cow and broke her leg so that she had to be killed. Black said nothing, but at noon while looking about the chuckwagon he discovered on the ground under it a match and half an onion. He went up in the air, began on the wagon boss, then one by one gave his hands a raking over for wastefulness. Finally he paid his respects to Lewis Ikard — the buyer merely along with the outfit. Throwing away half an onion and a match was, to him, outrageous thriftlessness.

By night he had cooled down, and Ikard said to him: "Mr. Black, you are a mystery to me."

"Why?"

"This morning you saw a cowboy forefoot a cow and break her leg. She had to be killed for beef. You said nothing. We've been eating her ribs — damned good. At noon you saw a match and half an onion lying under the chuck wagon, and you raised unmitigated hell with every man in camp, myself included. I don't understand your principle."

"Maybe," Black replied, "that cowboy could not help breaking the cow's leg. But somebody damn sure could have helped throwing away my property, leaving that match and piece of onion to waste."

Saving from a dread of waste or from necessity is not the same thing as greedy stinginess in a propertied man as mean as gar soup. As a boy I was helping my father pull pipe out of a pasture well to repack the pump. The wrench was too worn to catch securely and it kept slipping as the pipe joints were uncoupled. "Why don't you buy a wrench that will hold?" I asked. "They say," Papa replied, "that poor people have poor ways and rich people have mean ways."

Burk Burnett was rich in city as well as ranch properties. He is credited with having won, while a young man, the Four Sixes brand of cattle in a poker game. For him, money bred like thrifty cows. Oil wells on his ranch land increased into oil fields. As the years piled up he, in the manner of all flesh, came to seek health — energy — with more longing than he sought money.

As my friend Raymond Dickson used to relate, he and Hal Mangum, both ranchers, encountered ailing Burk Burnett in the Palmer House at Chicago. They were on a money-raising expedition and were spending freely. Burk Burnett was in Chicago to consult a medical specialist. He had to stay there some time. He was going out of the fine hotel and down side streets to eat in cheap restaurants. One evening Raymond Dickson and Hal Mangum persuaded him to come up to their suite of rooms. He had been forbidden to drink whiskey and barely smelled the glass given him. He did respond to a fine dinner ordered up.

Dickson and Mangum had gone beyond smelling whiskey and were feeling free. "Mr. Burnett," Raymond said, "here you are one of the richest men in Texas. Everybody knows you could throw a hundred thousand dollars into a garbage can and not miss it more than a nickel dropped in a cow pen. You would give a fortune to have the juices of life running in your veins again. The only reason you are in Chicago is to recover a spark of life. Yet at mealtime you go out in a sleety blizzard, down a back street, to save six bits or maybe a dollar on eggs and coffee. Honestly, why do you act that way?"

"I'll tell you honestly," Burk Burnett replied. "I don't need to save money, but I began saving it when I thought I had to save. I wanted to make more money. I got into the habit of saving. The habit stayed with me. It's fixed in me. I know I'm not going to take anything with me to the next world. Just the same, the habit stays in me. I guess it'll hang on till I die."

Burk Burnett died in 1922. It was his wife who gave an undivided one-half of the Four Sixes to Texas Christian University in Fort Worth, which now receives from it between seven and eight hundred thousand dollars a year, mainly in oil royalties.

Jake Holderman was a "Dutchman" and he knew horses from who laid the chunk. As a boy he broke horses at the rate of a dollar a year according to age — one dollar for a yearling, two dollars for a two-year-old, and so on up to five dollars for a five-year-old. In 1878 he set out for California with hundreds of mares and a score or more stallions. Instead of herding them at night he would point them west, turn them loose, and rely on the stallions to cut out a manada each and keep it together. About daylight his hands would locate the bands heading back east and throw them into herd formation to drive on. He owned a horse ranch of three thousand acres of the best land in Live Oak County, Texas, between the converging Frio and Nueces rivers. He acquired a watering in New Mexico and ran horses on free grass out from it also — at least until he "got into trouble" out there.

He was notoriously saving, close, stingy. One time my Uncle Jim Dobie started west with him, going along with a herd of horses, to prospect for a new range. The Jake Holderman wagon was provisioned with cornmeal, baking powder, sowbelly, beans, coffee, and little else. Uncle Jim always believed in eating well. He discovered a jug of molasses in the wagon and asked Jake when he was going to pull the corncob stopper out. "Saving it for hard times," Jake replied. At Devil's River Uncle Jim decided that the times and the range were both hard enough, and turned back.

While my father as county commissioner was going regularly to Oakville, the county seat, for court, he came to know

J. M. DOBIE (1856–1929). This picture was made in the Dan Sullivan Bank in San Antonio about 1900. So far as I ever learned, Uncle Jim Dobie and his brothers Neville Dobie and R. J. Dobie (my father) never cowboyed for anybody but worked and traded for themselves. Their father and his brother were ranching in Harris County, of which Houston is the seat, while Texas was still a republic. They drove horses to Kansas, then changed to cattle. I began managing Uncle Jim's ranch down in the Brush Country in 1920. He owned 56,000 acres and had about 200,000 acres leased. At the end of World War I he was supposed to be worth a million dollars. By 1925 he was bankrupt. His name was a synonym for honesty. Nearly all his hands were Mexicans. In a stampede he wanted only one good man with him to stop the cattle and put them into a mill. The idea of shooting six-shooters ahead of cattle to stop their running was absurd to him and other genuine cowmen. He was saving without being tight. His generosity to me is still in my consciousness.

Jake Holderman fairly well. The population of Oakville was not over two or three hundred, but it had what passed for a hotel. When Jake Holderman came to town, he camped down on Sulphur Creek, ate soda biscuits his wife had tied up in a flour sack, and boiled his coffee in an old tomato can. Instead of broiling slices of salt pork with a green stick over the fire, he fried them in a small iron frying pan that he habitually carried. He did not want to lose the grease. He soaked his biscuits in it hot and then saved what was left to spread on boots, saddle and harness.

I was a mere child when he drove his buggy to our ranch late one evening, ate supper, and then sat out on the front gallery with Papa, neither saying anything much, while Mama cleaned up the kitchen. All I know of the visit came from her years later. Mr. Holderman's buggy harness was patched with rawhide and baling wire. He did not mention business until morning. He wanted to buy mares, and since Papa wanted to get rid of a few, he bought them.

Once when John Rigby was at the Fort Worth Stock Show, he noticed a blanket and a morral back in one of the stalls at the stockyards.

"Don't bother that stuff, please," an attendant said. "It belongs to an old man camping out here."

"I ain't going to bother it," John Rigby told him. "I just want to look on the bottom side of that morral."

He looked, and, as he suspected, it was painted X T, Jake Holderman's brand. "Why," Jake Holderman said later when John Rigby saw him, "they wanted to charge me a dollar and a half for a room at that hotel. I just won't pay out money that way."

Jake died according to lifetime practices. An Irishman

named Pat Saxon was sitting up with him for a dollar a day-and-night. Holderman quit breathing a while before midnight. Saxon straightened out his body, drew a sheet over it, and put a quarter over each of his eyes to keep them closed. Only he and Becky Holderman were on the ranch. She shared her husband's feelings for money, did not mind grinding corn into meal and seldom having flour. Now she said to the helper, "Pat, we've been out a lot on expenses, and I'll have to buy a coffin — though maybe I can get a carpenter in Oakville to make one out of pine. Anyhow, I'll have to let you go. You can't do Jake any more good now."

"Mrs. Holderman," he said, "I don't mind sitting up with the body until daylight without pay. I remember a man down at Gussettville whose wife died early in the night like Mr. Holderman. They lighted a candle to burn by her body. 'Blow it out,' the husband said. 'She's dead whether it burns or not' — and he a faithful Catholic."

The originals of this world below the rank of genius are mostly duplicates. Here is a Jake Holderman duplication in Richard Kearton's *A Naturalist's Pilgrimage* (London, 1920):

"Owd Bob was a skinflint farmer in the north of England. At harvest time he refreshed his hands on what an Irishman described as 'tay verra strang of waater.' He died loyal to his principles of thrift, as his housekeeper testified. She sat up and nursed him in his last illness, and on the last night he whispered to her to blow out the tallow dip burning on a little table by his bedside, 'to save the expense.' As the candle was the only relief to total darkness, she refused. Too weak and slight of breath to blow it out, Owd Bob raised the

corner of his quilt and flicked the candle out. Then he chuck-
led and a little after went into total darkness himself."

The Holdermans had no children. Jake had willed half
his property to a sister and half to his wife, with the provi-
sion that if she married again, all would go to the sister. According to law, she had half of the estate, anyhow. She did
marry again — a deadbeat who swindled her out of what she
had.

Jake Holderman was stingy, all right, but he was fair to
other men and he loved a horse named Brown Jug beyond all
money value. He thought nearly as much of him as he did of
his wife, and he thought a lot of her. When the horse was
twenty-four years old, Jake turned him out on the Frio River
bottom. He was rolling fat. John Rigby, at that time inspector of brands for the Texas and Southwestern Cattle Raisers'
Association, knew the horse well, but he did not know that
Jake had given him his freedom. Rigby was in Cuero one
day inspecting three carloads of horses and mares being
shipped by a man from Mississippi. Rigby's eye fell on Jake
Holderman's brown, branded X T. He cut the horse back.

"I bought him yesterday for thirty-five dollars from a
young fellow," the buyer explained.

"If you did, you bought a stolen horse," Rigby answered. "I
have got to hold him for the man who gives the X T brand."

After some argument, Rigby agreed to let the buyer have
the old horse for $65 and thought that high. He had no idea
that Holderman would not part with him at any price. It was
months before he saw Holderman and gave him the money,
explaining the circumstances. "Why," Holderman said
mournfully, "I had turned that brown out to graze for the

rest of his life. I would not have taken five hundred dollars for him. He never failed me. I have ridden him to New Mexico and have shipped him back and forth so as to have him to ride wherever I was. I want you to go to Mississippi and get him from that feller."

"It would cost hundreds of dollars to go there, trace the horse down, and bring him back in a special car," Rigby objected.

"It makes no difference to me," Jake Holderman went on, "if it costs thousands. Old Brown Jug deserves to end his days in peace and plenty. Go after him."

John Rigby both wired and wrote the buyer. At length the buyer replied that while he had a distinct recollection of the horse, he could not remember to whom he sold him but thought a Negro in the Mississippi Delta took him. The horse was never located, and Jake Holderman as long as he lived lamented his loss.

Born in Louisiana in 1849, J. M. Shannon tried out California and Australia before he began raising sheep in western Texas. In 1885 he contracted to fence some of the three million acres of X I T ranch land — land paid over by the state of Texas to a syndicate for building the capitol in Austin. He claimed to have lost $35 a mile on eighty-five miles of fence contracted for at $111 a mile, but Mr. Shannon seldom admitted to making money on anything. He went to Scotland to marry a lass he had met on a ship. For a time they lived on a ranch he built up to a hundred and fifty thousand acres in Crockett County. They finally moved to San Angelo. He owned two smaller ranches besides town property and stock in banks and an insurance company.

Mr. Shannon saved on everything. While living on the ranch, he was especially saving on clothes, sometimes wearing breeches pinned together with safety pins or mesquite thorns. He would wear a hat greasy and shapeless, but his head was always up. One day while he was camped on the Concho River, coffee boiling in a tin can, salt pork broiling on a stick over the coals, a drummer drove up behind a good team. The drummer stopped, and Mr. Shannon invited him to get down and have a cup of coffee.

"Thanks," said the drummer, "I will. I've got a little lunch with me, and if you'll unhitch my horses and water them and stake them out to graze and then hitch them up again, I'll give you a dollar."

"All right," Mr. Shannon said, and began taking care of the horses.

After both men had eaten, the drummer said, "Well, I've got to be going," and Mr. Shannon hitched up the horses. The drummer handed over a dollar. Before he got in his buggy he asked, "What part of this country do you live in, anyway?"

"Oh, out yonder," Mr. Shannon replied.

"What do you do?"

"I just take care of things."

"What sort of things?"

"Well, sheep, cattle, horses, windmills, fences — things like that."

"You must live on a ranch," the drummer said.

"That's right."

"Whose ranch?"

"People call it mine."

"How big is it?"

"Several sections."

"How many cattle do you own?"

"For taxable purposes, several hundred, I guess."

The answers that Shannon gave as to sheep and horses were also based on "taxable purposes."

The next day the drummer had to go to a bank in San Angelo. He knew the president of the bank, and after getting a check cashed, said, "You certainly do have characters in this country. One I ate with up the Concho was dressed like a sheepherder the rats had dragged in. He told me he owned a big ranch stocked with thousands of cattle, sheep, and horses — and he took care of my team for a dollar."

"Why," the banker replied, "that was Mr. Shannon, one of the richest men in west Texas."

An hour later the banker encountered Mr. Shannon on the street and said, "Now, Mr. Shannon, you are a very important man in this country. Everybody knows of your big holdings. Everybody respects you. The way you dress does not fit your station in life. It is not becoming. Why don't you go in that store over there and shell out a few dollars for a suit, some new work pants and a new hat? You ought to dress like a respectable ranchman."

"You mean here in San Angelo?" Mr. Shannon asked.

"Yes. Here and everywhere else."

"Well," Shannon said, "I don't go anywhere else hardly except between here and the ranch. Everybody here knows me and everybody out on the range knows me. What difference does it make whether I'm dressed up or not?"

That fall the San Angelo banker went to Kansas City to borrow some money on livestock notes he held. Just as he was leaving a livestock commission company, whom should he encounter but Mr. Shannon? Shannon had ridden to Kansas City in a caboose behind a train of his own cattle. The lower part of one breeches leg seemed about to fall off. What some cow had discarded from a grass diet indicated that he had slept in his clothes at the stockyards.

"My goodness alive, Mr. Shannon," the banker said, "here you have sold a trainload of steers at a good price and are looking more disreputable than you were the last time I saw you. I just can't understand your not wearing clean, fresh clothes."

"Do you mean up here in Kansas City?" Mr. Shannon asked.

"Yes."

"Oh, pshaw," said Shannon, "nobody up here knows me. What difference does it make anyhow?"

He was not much of a hand for talk. Frank White, who inherited a building and bank stock from Mrs. Shannon, managed for years the Crockett County ranch. One time after Shannon returned to it from a long absence, Frank White pointed out several things he had done not in accordance with instructions from the owner. "Mr. Shannon," he began explaining, "I thought . . ."

Mr. Shannon interrupted, "Frank, there you go thinking again."

He had made a will in 1912 bequeathing "to my beloved wife, Margaret A. Shannon, all my estate and all my property real, personal and mixed, wherever situate." The probation of this will upon his death in 1928 did not annul such stories as one claiming that he left $20,000 to a waitress because she had never even hinted for a tip.

Mrs. Shannon, who died in 1931, left various benefactions to friends and relatives but, carrying out the wishes of J. M. Shannon as well as her own, left the main part of the estate to establish and maintain, in San Angelo, the Shannon West Texas Memorial Hospital, to be open "to every sick person applying for admission," those not able to pay to be cared for free, others to pay.

Since oil and gas, in continuing production, have been found on virtually all the Shannon land, the estate, tax-free, probably amounts to seventy-five or eighty million dollars. The Shannon hospital is quite a memorial to a man who once saved by using mesquite thorns for pins.

5

Caballero Rustico

IN A DANCE HALL, bed-cribs adjoining it, over a saloon, a cowboy might be as brash as a flour peddler running for governor; in the presence of respectability he inclined to be shy. An instinct not unlike that of a wild gobbler held in check any impulse to be familiar. He came out of the Victorian Age. In a country where men were mostly without women, cowboys looked upon females, except the dance hall variety, as sacrosanct. It is a law of human nature as well as of economics that scarcity determines value.

Before fences and settlers took the land over, women were scarce at Doan's Store just south of Doan's Crossing on Red River up the trail from Texas. Here men from ranches and passing trail drivers hitched their horses, asked for mail and bought something. Two young ladies, cousins, who came to live with the Doan family were deft — but not playful — with their hands. Eager for pin money, they let it be known that they would make buckskin gloves at five dollars a pair. Indians from the Territory frequently brought dressed deer hides to the store for barter. The young ladies made a sample pair of fringed gauntlets, doted on by all cowboys.

To get a fit, a man had to have his hands measured. To have his hands measured by the hands of a lovely young woman was divine. Such a proximity of soft female flesh was, in the words of old-style poets, simply ravishing. The young ladies were overwhelmed with orders. Several of the cowboys, after receiving their gloves and going off with them, returned within a few days to order more. They had lost their gloves, they declared. They were actually throwing or giving the gloves away in order to be measured again.

Among frequenters of Doan's Store was Jim Gwindy of the R 2's. He was backward, but one day in the Doan house, after much egging on, he asked Miss Sally Brazale if she would go over to the store with him and take a treat. The available treats consisted of striped stick candy and chewing gum. These delicacies were kept in a case along with sundry toilet articles. It was the day of tucking combs, and conspicuous among the toilet articles was an assortment of the combs.

For a little while the couple stood before the case, observed by two or three grinning cowboys well back against a counter. Then in a low voice Jim Gwindy asked, "What will you take, Miss Sally?"

Miss Sally hesitated a moment, then said, "If it's all the same to you, I'll take one of them tucking combs."

She got the tucking comb. The cowboys snickered, and when the couple withdrew, they exploded. That was the last time Jim Gwindy ever mustered up enough boldness to pay attention to a girl. The other cowboys made life miserable for him. His name became "Tucking Comb" or "Tucking Comb Jim." He died with the name still fastened upon him.

One time when an outfit of Panhandle cowboys came to a ranch where a young lady was visiting she suddenly let it be

Two cowboys of the Nueces River country, southwest Texas, trying to pass themselves off for "dandies." They put on six-shooters for style. (Tintype, 1875.)

known that she had to go home. It would be necessary for her to travel some distance in order to catch a stage. She could ride and the outfit had plenty of horses. The gentlest in the remuda was roped out for her. He was a potbellied plug commonly known as Old Guts, on account of the way his internal organs rumbled when he trotted.

A retiring, even religious, cowboy was delegated to accompany the young lady. He carried her telescope valise and was taking no chances lest a rough trot make Old Guts rumble. Before long the valise came open and female attire scattered over considerable territory. Sight of it embarrassed him and the shying and snorting of his own horse worried him, but he got the things back into the valise. The two rode on mostly in silence, he keeping ahead to avoid conversation. The young lady was not embarrassed, and she did her best to relieve the tension. Finally she took as her theme the horse she was riding.

"He's such a nice fat horse," she said.

"Yes," the cowboy agreed, "he's in purty good condition."

"I like his gait, too," the young lady went on, rising in her enthusiasm. "And he minds perfectly."

"Yes, he's steady, all right."

"Oh, I shall never forget this horse and the ride on him. I must know his name. What is it?"

The cowboy mumbled, "He ain't got no name."

The young lady repeated her question. "I just must know his name," she declared. "A nice horsey like this has some name. I want to call him by his name so he'll know how much I like him. You are trying to deceive me."

Again the cowboy evaded.

A Montana cowboy (1896).

"Come, come," the young lady insisted. "You are putting me off. Do tell me the name."

The cowboy hesitated, stammered. He had no more imagination than a barrel of sauerkraut. He could not invent. He could not lie. He blurted out in a low voice, "Old Bowels."

My father used to tell of a man who came to his mother when he was a boy, not long after the Civil War, to buy "a gentleman cow." In 1869, the proprietor of the Bull's Head Saloon in Abilene, Kansas, then the northern terminus of the Chisholm Trail, had a thoroughly masculine bull painted in red across the false front of his building. People were used to seeing all sorts of bulls roaming and breeding about the town — at that time the only noted cow town in America, but a cry of indignation arose from respectable citizens. Nature might be allowable; in art it was obscene. The picture would corrupt youth. It was an insult to women. A petition was presented to the proprietor of the Bull's Head. He ignored it. A delegation of citizens waited upon him. To paint a bull that wasn't the real thing, he told them, would be absurd and against his principles.

After days of asserting his rights as a free American citizen, he gave in to the extent of having the offending features of the red bull painted out — but they remained visibly outlined beneath the new coat of paint. The citizens calmed down. In another retreat from the forces of prudery, the Bull Durham tobacco people installed a fence plank to hide the testicles of their trademark printed on all packages of cigarette "makings."

Any young woman of fair looks and trim dress going west to teach school had chances to marry. Where ranches were too far apart for community schools, a family here and there

Two cowboys dressed up to have their pictures taken in Dodge City, 1877.

employed a governess. Not long after one arrived at a ranch west of Fort Worth, a neighbor twenty miles or so farther on announced a dance. The family employing the governess took her to it. A fall rain was coming down and she carried along her overshoes. When she left after sunup she forgot all about them. On the following Sunday a cowboy from the ranch where the dance was held showed up and boldly asked to see "Miss Anne." He waited in the parlor and, as she came in, handed her something wrapped in a newspaper.

She opened it. "Oh, it's one of my overshoes!" she exclaimed. "I forgot them, but there were two."

"Yes, I know it," the cowboy said. "I'll bring the other one next Sunday, if you don't mind — and, Miss Anne, I sure wish you was a centerpede."

When another young lady went to visit on a ranch in the same region, young men working on one adjoining agreed with each other to cut cards for the first go at her. A cowboy named Neville drew the highest card. The young lady responded to his "attention." Their daughter told me of this wooing. It was not unprecedented. In Samuel Butler's *The Way of All Flesh* five daughters of an English rector "played at cards" to see which would have first claim on their father's newly arrived bachelor assistant.

In order to introduce Lige Carter I here interject Sam Anderson. His kind ceased to exist long ago. He could not write his own name, had never had occasion to sign it on a check, but he could tell by a brand who owned an animal. He was a Webster on brands. Also, he could draw pictures, especially of horses. About 1894, Jess Presnall put him in charge of a string of steers he was pasturing in the Carrizo Springs country, which is not far from the Rio Grande. Among the horses

A southwest Texas cowboy, in a photographer's studio, 1883.

turned over to him was a brown branded J E S that Jess Presnall thought a lot of. At this time horse thieves were still
now and then hazing stolen horses from one side of the Rio
Grande to the other.

One day Jess Presnall received an envelope postmarked
Carrizo Springs. He opened it. It contained a sheet of foolscap paper on which was drawn in a red fluid that had run
too much to be ink the picture of three riders driving several
horses and leading one branded in big letters J E S. The
horses were crossing a crooked line. Jess Presnall understood.
Bandidos from below the Rio Grande had come up and
stolen a bunch of his horses, among them the J E S brown.
Sam Anderson had trailed them to the crooked Rio Grande,
come back empty-handed, and now was reporting. Somebody
had left a few sheets of foolscap paper at the ranch shack in
which Sam Anderson lived, but no ink. He had used the red
juice of a tuna (ripe prickly pear apple), and with a mesquite thorn for a pen had drawn the picture. Then he had
gone to town, got the storekeeper to address an envelope to
his boss, put the folded sheet inside, sealed it and mailed it.

Aren't writers of words wordy?

Lige Carter couldn't write either, but from reading brands
he had learned to spell a few words, like K I L for Kilmer
and D O L for Dolly. Nobody ever regarded him as either
stupid or bashful. One time while he was riding through a
herd with John Bryan of the T Diamond outfit, they spied a
cow branded A N N.

"That's one of my sister's cows," Lige said.

"One of your sister's cows?" Bryan queried. "What do you
mean? That cow drifted down here from a ranch on the
Clear Fork."

Two cowboys, A. H. (Hi) Webb *(left)* and J. F. Wells *(right)*, who had their pictures taken while driving cattle in South Dakota.

"Well," Lige replied, "A and two N's spell Ann, don't it? One of my sister's beaux branded that cow for her, I guess."

Lige may have been bluffing but he could have cited scattered practices. If some squatter in the open range country had a girl even halfway attractive — and nearly any girl is to somebody — one or more cowboys might "start a brand" for her on weaned calves or mavericks. In the 1880's a settler came into the Clayton, New Mexico, territory with nothing but a rickety wagon, a few pieces of rickety furniture, some pots and pans, six poor horses, and eight children. The oldest was a comely girl. Through the brand started for her by cowboy admirers she soon had a bunch of cattle.

Years after John (W. J.) Bryan became a leading citizen and the leading storyteller of Abilene, Texas, he told me this story. "I was driving a herd through the country when we came to a creek with good water in it. I noticed a wagon camped a little ways down and got a glimpse of a skirt. Some of our cattle were pokey, and Lige Carter was one of two drag drivers. He must have been born with an ambition to be bold. Anyhow, he had it.

"Coming along behind the herd, he got a better look at the skirt than I got. While the cattle were stringing across the creek, Lige pulled off to ride down to the wagon. There, sitting on his horse, he saluted the only person in sight. She, as I later learned, was not cordial; pretty soon he was back at the tail end of the herd, where he belonged.

"The paint horse he was riding distinguished him from other riders. We hadn't gone far from the creek when I noticed Lige easing up on my side of the herd. I looked back and here a man with a shotgun across his saddle was coming in a high trot.

"As Lige, still working forward, came up even with me he said, 'Look at that old devil. He's after me.'

" 'What on earth does he want with you?'

" 'Well, I wunk at his wife just now. I guess she's about his second wife — and he hasn't been married very long. She's shore a purty heifer.'

"About this time, paying the rest of us no mind, the man with the shotgun rode up alongside the cowboy on the paint horse. Lige turned his head so that the stranger could see him full in the face. His right eye was winking like an electric danger signal on a crooked road in the middle of a dark night.

"For a full minute the stranger gazed at him in silence, both riding at a walk. 'What in creation is the matter with your eye?' the stranger demanded.

" 'It s-slips,' Lige kinder stuttered.

" 'It slips!' repeated the stranger. 'Do you mean to say that your eye goes that way all the time?'

" 'Yes, stranger,' Lige explained, 'it's been this way for seven long years. I can't keep it steady even when I'm asleep.'

"The jealous husband looked at him a minute longer, while the winking became, if possible, more rapid. Then a kind of relaxation came over his face and he rode back to his camp and the purty young heifer."

6

Bogged Shadows

FINDLAY SIMPSON was about the last of the makers, inventors, yarn-tellers of the horseback men. Few riders now say, "Tell me a story." They turn on the radio or television and drink down their entertainment out of cans. Even in his time, some matter-of-fact people called Findlay Simpson a liar. The term was and is too harsh, but if it must be used, then, with Charles Lamb, I like "a matter-of-lie kind of man."

He must be an authentic liar. The art of the authentic liar lies in giving homely, realistic details to everything connected with his preposterous inventions. Unlike the bishops of all religions, he does not expect his impossibilities to be believed; he merely expects his ingenuity to be appreciated. His aim is to lie in such a manner that the credulity of imagination will not be straightjacketed by skepticism of the intellect.

Moses Findlay Simpson (1858-1924) flourished among other Irishmen in Refugio County, Texas, back in the days when for them March seventeenth meant more than July Fourth. At that time the Refugio *Timely Remarks* published each week a list of "foreign visitors" to the village — most of them from two adjoining counties. I never knew Findlay Simpson, but one winter I spent a month on the Tom O'Connor ranch where he used to make people merry, and where some of his inventions continue to be recollected with glee. They are the only part of him that has not evaporated from this earth. While he rode the range alone, his artist soul joyed in fabricating something to "tell the boys" when he got in. Then he joyed in fulfilling their expectations.

When it rains and rains on the coastal prairies where Findlay Simpson cowboyed, the ground gets soggy enough to bog a saddle blanket. One day, Findlay said, he was floundering along in the mud on Wild Cat Flats, holding his feet up out of the stirrups to keep from dragging them in the mud when he noticed a buzzard four or five hundred yards ahead of him. It wasn't very high up in the air and it wasn't sailing around. It seemed to be fixed in one spot, and was beating its wings and struggling like a kite at the end of a taut string. It seemed unable to make the slightest progress, north, south, east or west. It acted like a wild colt setting back on the end of an invisible stake rope.

As Findlay Simpson floundered on, he could not take his eye off the buzzard until he noticed a big mud puddle directly beneath it. The closer he got, the more puzzling the actions of the buzzard became. Finally, when he was right under it, he stopped his horse to study out the situation. By now his neck had a crick in it from looking up, but he just had to keep on looking. The sun was straight overhead. Suddenly Findlay Simpson saw what held the buzzard.

There right ahead of him, at a spot to which his horse's ears pointed, was the buzzard's shadow. It was actually bogged up, or down, or in, or whatever is the right way for a shadow to get bogged hard and fast. The buzzard could no more move without his shadow than the shadow could exist or move without the buzzard. A light-footed mouse might have skinned up that shadow, Findlay Simpson said, and got on top of the buzzard. He had never seen a shadow bogged before this, but then, he had never seen the country so boggy.

He spurred his horse, belly-deep in the mud, right through the puddle holding the shadow — and turned it loose. The buzzard flew away, sailing straight for a cloud that it soon got behind.

Before Findlay Simpson died in 1924, he had become a legendary character in the Irish-featured land where he rode and yarned. That was mainly on the O'Connor ranches. He had worked up to be boss under Pat Lambert, and he used to say that Pat Lambert was the most considerate boss he ever knew: he would give every man in his pay eighteen hours to do a day's work in.

They say that one time a cow crowd of O'Connor hands, some white, some black, decided to test out the talking powers of Findlay Simpson. It was early summer and the weather was pleasant. After an easier than usual day's work, the boys got him strung out. They had arranged their pallets so that when a listener became too sleepy to listen longer he could easily awaken the next man, who would egg Findley on. Findlay talked all that night and worked the next day. The second night he kept the relays up, then worked all day. The third night one of the relays went to sleep on him, and then Findlay decided that as nobody was listening he had as well sleep a while himself. He was up with the Morning Star, talking to the cook, when the first hand came to the coffeepot.

He became a kind of court entertainer for parties of young people on the ranch. When the late Tom O'Connor, great-grandson of the Tom O'Connor who founded the ranch, was a young man in camp, he might say at the end of a day's riding, "Findlay, tell me some of those lies. Tell me about the big snow in the northwest the winter you spent up there."

"Yes, it snowed and snowed," Findlay would begin. "The cattle drifted up against the mountains on the south side, and the snow filled up the valleys between the mountains. The cattle were all under it. It held there for six months before it begun to thaw good. Then it melted down so the cattle could walk out. You wouldn't believe they could hibernate that way like bears, but they could. They went into the snow fat, and when they come out they was packing rolls of taller around their tails.

"But I never see anything up in that cold country to what I see here in the big blizzard of 1899. During that die-up hands would take pack horses out from the Melon Creek ranch every morning to bring in the hides skinned off dead cattle. Well, one day I was riding along Copano Creek looking for bogged-up stuff, pulling out cows and skinning as I went. I guess this was maybe a month after the big freeze. Let's see, that was on the twelfth of February.

"Well, over in a little place between some granjeno bushes and a huisache I seen a cow standing. She looked as ga'nt as a gutted snowbird. I pulled over to make sure she was all right. It was troublesome to get through some bushes right next to her, and I yelled so she'd turn round and show herself better. She didn't budge. Then I started in to her, and when I leaned over to dodge a limb, I seen a calf standing by her side a-sucking. It didn't move neither. When I got slap in on her, she still didn't move and the calf didn't neither. Thinks I to myself, 'This is mighty funny. I've heard of the lockjaw but never heard of the lockfoot.' I quirted her on the back, and still she didn't move. Then I got down and give myself a tap with the quirt to make sure I wasn't paralyzed. That cow was as dead as a doornail just a-standing there, and that calf was as dead as a doornail just a-sucking there. When cattle die standing up, it's hard times.

"That winter of '99 was an awful winter on everything, but I don't know as it was any worse on animals in general than the drouth of '86. The creeks all dried up that year and what waterholes were left got so boggy the buzzards were scared to fly over them for fear their shadders would bog down. The country was full of razorback hogs then, and most of them got such big balls of mud on their tails that the weight would draw back everything on the animal clear up to the snout. When you met a razorback face to face, he'd be grinning at you like a Cheshire cat, 'cause his lips were pulled back. Why, the mudballs on their tails drew their eyelids back so tight the razorbacks couldn't sleep.

"Then the critters drunk so much mud they all got pot-bellied. I've seen one of them just a-rocking and a-teetering and a-seesawing on his belly, unable to get his hindfeet or his forefeet either on the ground. There he'd be up in the air, on top of his own belly, his eyelids pulled back by the weight of mud on his tail, and his eyes bugged out till you could have roped 'em with a grapevine. It was a sight, I tell you.

"But talking about mud and water, one year I went with a train of cattle to Chicago for Dennis O'Connor. We got along all right till we left New Orleans and started across the biggest lake there is, I guess, outside the Gulf of Mexico. We'd no more 'n got out on the bridge when I heard the derndest whistling and screeching from the engine a man ever listened to. The train stopped and still the whistling went on. I was riding in the caboose, and I crawled up in the cupola to look out. Then I seen what the trouble was. It was enough to make a man and an engine both whistle.

"It looked to me like all the alligators in the world had crawled up out of that lake to sun theirselves on the bridge. They were laying acrost the tracks and in between the rails and dangling over the ties and every which way. The cow-catcher had plowed up the first ones, I guess. At least, they was piled up ahead of the engine higher than the smoke-stack. Now the engine couldn't budge. The engineer kept a-whistling and the trainmen sorter cleared the pile away. Then we went on a few feet, the engine all the time letting out screeches that would have waked up dead Spaniards in the Refugio graveyard. Why, before we got acrost that lake the engineer had wore out his whistle. Then he wore out his bell a-ringing it. After that we didn't have no more trouble and the cattle sold well in Chicago. But them alligators!

"Still, I don't know as they were much thicker on that big lake than I see them oncet in San Jacinto River. I was taking a herd of T H C cattle east, and it was an awful wet year. We'd been having plenty of trouble. We had to pull twenty or thirty out of a bog they got into in a cut at the Colorado River. Then the Brazos was up on a toot, and the herd got into a mill while they were swimming in the middle of it. We'd sweated at some of the little creeks, and I shore was a-dreading the San Jacinto.

"But when we got to it, the sun was right for crossing — back behind us instead of in the cattle's eyes — and I told the boys to pop their leggins and bring 'em a-stringing. I was back a little from the point, and when I got to the bank I never was more surprised in my life. Them cattle was a-walking across dry-shod, like the Children of Israel a-crossing the Red Sea. They was a-stepping on alligators' backs. Seemed like the alligators had all congregated to sun their backs or something like that. They didn't seem to mind the weight. I guess being so thick that way they kinder supported each other.

"When I come to cross, my horse give a snort, but he took the bridge all right. Still, I didn't feel easy. I knowed if one of them alligators give a flip of his tail so's to hit the nose of some snuffy steer, there'd be a stompede would shake their ancestors. But nothing like that happened.

"The biggest alligator I ever see was in the Mission River, right here in Refugio County. I was riding up it one day looking out for bogged animals, and before I knowed it, the bed was practically dry. Thinks I, 'This is mighty peculiar. I was up above here about three miles day before yesterday and the river was bank-full — fuller'n I ever see it except after a big rain. Now down here there ain't no water at all.'

"Well, I kept a-riding on upstream, my curiosity getting more and more het up. Then I come to the answer of all my curiosity. It was an alligator, a regular giant of an alligator, the Goliath of all alligators that ever lived. His tail had got tangled up in a lot of willer roots on one side of the bank and in pawing and struggling he had evidently hung his snout and forelegs in the roots on the opposite bank. There he was stretched out damning the whole river up, so the water was about to make Refugio a deep-sea port up above and the bed drying up down below.

"I could have killed the critter easy, but I wasn't going to destroy a specimen like that. I just took my axe and cut the roots. But when that alligator got loose, danged if he didn't have to crawl out on the prairie to turn around. The river was just too little for him to operate in.

"He really belonged over in the San Jacinto River. People in this country think they have big mosquitoes and big frogs and big cottonwood trees and all that, but they ought to go over on the San Jacinto. Why, Tom, I remember when you was a boy shaking with a chill one day over on the San Antonio River and getting blue around the gills and imagining you was really having the ague. You'd been tanking up on Grove's Tasteless Chill Tonic. Nobody was heeding my remedy of a glass full of whiskey mixed with the juice of an even one hundred Mexican peppers.

"But I'll tell you again, the chills on the San Antonio River or anywhere else in this western country ain't nothing to compare with the chills on the San Jacinto. Ain't nothing, I tell you.

"One time over there I was riding along kinder out from the bottom when I noticed the leaves of a certain cottonwood tree just a-shaking and a-trembling like they was bewitched. I stopped and looked all around and not another leaf in the whole timber was a-moving. It was so dead ca'm I'd been saying to myself how a storm must be brewing. Still, to make certain there wasn't no current of air anywhere, I spit on my finger and held it up to see which direction any little breeze might be blowing. Not a breath from any point.

"Then I rode straight in to that cottonwood to see what in the creation was causing such a commotion amongst the leaves. If it was squirrels or coons frisking about, the leaves would be shaking just in one place, but they were shaking all over the tree, and it was a big one, high up over all the other trees. Well, sir, when I got there, you'd never guess what I discovered.

"There was the king bullfrog of the San Jacinto bottoms having a chill. He was backed up against that tree and the tears was just a-rolling out of his eyes, he was shaking so hard. And all unbeknownst to him he was shaking so hard against the cottonwood that all its leaves was a-trembling."

About here Findlay Simpson discovered that Tom O'Connor and everybody else had gone to sleep.

7
Talk and Silence

"Blessed are those who have nothing
to say and cannot be persuaded to say
it."

AMONG COW PEOPLE, some — as among all people —
had nothing to say but said it anyhow. Some who had
something to say said it in few words. Others didn't say anything whether they had or not. Many wanted company.

As a girl at Rancho Seco in Nueces County in the '70's, my
mother knew a rancher named Kellet who at times so craved
company that he would ride out to the road from San Antonio to Corpus, which passed only a few miles from his
ranch, and wait until somebody came along. It might be a
freighter. He'd hold him up, prevail on him to turn off and
go to the ranch, where his team would have plenty of feed
and he would have a regular preacher's supper and a clean
bed to sleep in. Kellet had a way of getting people to talk.
He liked talk. He wanted to know what was going on beyond
the county.

He was the opposite of two line riders, or at least one of
the two, who rode in Montana before barbed wire kept cat-

tle in pastures. One summer evening after supper while they were sitting outside the cabin a bellowing came over the air. One said, "Bull." The other said, "Sounds like an old steer to me." Not another word on the subject or any other subject was spoken before the two went to bed.

The next morning the man who had spoken first the evening before brought in the saddle horses, roped out his personal mount and pack horse, and began rolling up his bedroll and putting his clothes in a sack.

"Riding?" the other questioned.

"Yes, too much argument."

The man who had identified the bellowing as an old steer's was left to silence.

I heard this story first from Carl Sandburg. It has traveled far. Two Australians of the great spaces were covering distance together, neither voicing a word, until a solitary bird flew across their path. "Magpie," said one. Hours afterward, while making a fire, the other said, "It might 'a been a crow." "Too much arguing in camp," the first speaker stated. Silence was resumed.

"I don't like a feller that belches up too much," Cole Railston, general manager of the V Cross T in New Mexico, said to me one night on his ranch, where he lived alone. "I think lots of times of old Spotted Tail, Cheyenne chief in the Territory. He could talk a little English. One day he took out on his experiences in getting wo-ha [beef] from trail bosses. He said, 'See boss, hat up, talk much, me get beef. Boss hat over eyes, no say nothing, no get beef.'

"One time Henry W. Porter, owner of the V Cross T outfit, came out from Denver and I took him to the old horse camp where Lou Gatlin was staying. Gatlin had the manners and etiquette of the range down as well as any man I have ever known. Porter was a great hand to ask questions, and while I was out of the house, he began augering into Gatlin. I had given Porter the count of the year's calf branding, but he asked Gatlin how many calves we had tallied.

" 'By God,' Gatlin answered, 'you're paying men to keep tally. I'm hired to work.'

"When I came back in, Porter was trying to whistle and Lou was burning the meat. I could see something had passed between them. Lou afterwards told me what it was.

"Another time when Porter came, full of inquisitiveness as usual about range affairs, I drove him in a buckboard to Gatlin's camp. The sun was maybe three hours high when we got there. I saw a horse with saddle on tied outside. Inside we found Gatlin on his bunk, though he hadn't taken his spurs off.

" 'How's the Beaverhead country?' Porter shot the question.

" 'All right, far as I know,' Lou drawled, implying he had not seen it in a month of Sundays.

" 'How are the cattle over on Willow Creek?'

" 'Didn't notice any dead ones the last time I was in that country.'

" 'How's the grass holding out up this canyon?'

" 'Far as I've seen, holding out all right.' Then, after a slight pause, Gatlin added, 'I might have ridden fully a mile up that way this morning.'

"I knew that Gatlin was always out long before daylight and had probably ridden ten miles out and back before we arrived, but he would not say so.

"Turner was like that too. You could ride with him all

[87]

day, and he'd never take part in talk on any subject, but his eyes were always scanning the range. They never missed anything, near or far."

Of all books on the early West made up of knowledge gained from perspective and firsthand experiences and observations, I rank Captain John G. Bourke's *On the Border with Crook* (1891) as the highest in intelligence, the richest in detail, and the most ample. While on duty to conquer the Apaches, Bourke came to know them as justly as he knew Army men and frontiersmen. He wrote: "Strongest recollection of all that I have of [border] persons is the quietness of their manner and the low tone in which they usually spoke to their neighbors. They were quiet in dress, in speech, and in conduct — a marked difference from the more thoroughly dramatized border characters of later days."

Men living out alone next to the ground, even though associated with a few others, in vast, silent spaces develop silence — a development now blocked by the murder of silence over the air. These men did not like to be disturbed, did not want to disturb others. The silent habit may have been stronger in men without women.

Martin Dodson was out of the old rock and of long shadows. While I was still a boy, he rode away from the Dodson ranch, about fifteen miles from ours, to follow cows in Arizona. He never married. When too weak to ride he came back to his sister Ruth's home to die. This picture of him is from a letter written by Ross Santee, artist and author of *Cowboy* and other true books. After four years in art school, Santee went to Arizona and as a horse-wrangler under Martin Dodson learned about the land and men belonging to it.

"He was the loneliest man and the man of the most contradictions I have ever known. When I first knew him he carried a Bible and a six-shooter. He was gentle with horses, children; his courage was never questioned; he had a biting humor often misunderstood by the men he worked with; he didn't have many friends; he didn't want any, but anyone in his presence respected him. I can hear him now saying, 'Sir?' to someone he didn't like. What he meant was: 'Damn you, say Sir to me.' He was so good at his job and knew it so well he was frequently out of patience with men who, supposedly, should know and did not. With him, if it wasn't perfection, it wasn't right.

"I'll never forget waking up in the middle of the night while we were camping alone and seeing Martin sitting there like an old Indian staring into the fire. I was always sleepy-headed and he had to wake me up. I usually wrangled the horses while he cooked breakfast. I've seen him sit around a fire of an evening with the outfit, very much a part of the group; then instead of shaking his bed down with the rest of us, he'd get on his night horse and ride away — just away in solitude. When we got up in the morning he'd be sitting there by the fire, as alone as the Morning Star, drinking coffee."

John B. Slaughter, a strong, decent ranchman of Arizona, had just ridden out from headquarters one day when he met a stranger who asked the way to "Slaughter's ranch." "It's just over that hill," Slaughter replied, gesturing. The stranger rode over the hill, pulled up, and told a man that he had come to see Mr. John Slaughter. "You must have met him a little while ago," the man said. "He left here on the road you came in on." Slaughter almost certainly understood that the stranger wanted to see him, but he would not say that the ranch was his. He would never have intimated an interest in the stranger's business.

It was taken for granted that if a man cared to reveal his name he would volunteer it. A long time ago while I was trailing down the story of the Lost Adams Diggings in New Mexico, Bela Birmingham, who then got his mail at Horse Springs, told me that in 1889 he helped trail his mother's cattle and horses into the Panhandle of Texas. Soon after she and her father and two sons had made a permanent camp, a stranger rode into it. "We ate dinner," Bela Birmingham related, "and then I joined my older brother in asking the stranger what his name was. 'Jones is the name,' he said. As soon as he rode off, our mother and our granddad laid us boys out for being so ill-mannered as to ask any man his name. 'Maybe a man can't afford to bring notice to himself,' one of them said." In a recent letter Mr. Birmingham added: "I think we lived in the best part of our history. It's gabble, gabble now all the time over TV and radio. We might be better off if we did not have so much of everything, especially of talk."

Billy the Kid was more cow thief than cowboy, more murderer than Robin Hood, but he belonged to the range. In 1881, by shooting two men in the back, he escaped from the Lincoln County jail, where he was held for hanging, rode to Fort Sumner, and in the night walked into Pete Maxwell's room. There he heard a slight movement and asked Maxwell, "Who's that?" The answer was six-shooter shots from Sheriff Pat Garrett. The Kid was dead forever — physically. Maxwell never liked to discuss the killing. He summed it up in these words: "The trouble with Billy was that he talked before he shot. His habit was to shoot first. Maybe he might say something afterwards. Not much."

John Dunn was in his time cowboy, trail driver, stage-driver, professional gambler — without a touch of the sentimentality personified by Mr. Oakhurst of gambler heroism in Bret Harte's *The Outcasts of Poker Flat*. At one time Dunn drove the stage daily from Taos, New Mexico, to a railroad junction, meeting a train. The road was canyon and mountain. One day two men and a woman got into his car — not advertised as modern. The men sat in the back seat, the woman with John Dunn. She was vocal, and every time the corkscrewing road got near enough to the brink of a canyon that she could look down, she'd cry out, "Oh, do be careful." She praised distant prospects.

When the passengers got out at the hotel in Taos, one man asked, "How much?"

"Two and a half," John Dunn replied.

Each man paid and took his luggage. The woman handed over a five-dollar bill. John Dunn put it in his pocket.

"Aren't you going to give me my change?" she asked.

"You don't have any change coming that I know of," he answered.

"You charged those men only two and a half apiece."

"They didn't talk."

In 1871 John Chisum of Denton, also of the Jinglebob ear-mark in New Mexico, turned over a bunch of horses to three hands to drive west. Smith, the boss, carried $2000 in silver and gold to deliver to Chisum's foreman. One of the other men was a half-breed Indian. The third, Ike Fridge, about a

IKE FRIDGE. He was with John Chisum of the Jingle Bob on the Pecos during the days of Billy the Kid. Of another thief he wrote: "We got his horse and saddle and the $2000 he was trying to make away with. Then we proceeded on to the ranch with our horses." (Ike Fridge died in 1926.)

half century later partly wrote down and partly told to a woman snatches of an autobiography significant for leaving things unsaid. In quoting I have restored bits of Fridge's natural language journalesed by the woman.

"Cleburne was just a wide place in the road and when we got near, Smith rode ahead to locate a field to hold the horses in overnight. At dark we were still waiting for him and I sent the half-breed to a house where he got a field. Our leader, we found, had not stopped to ask about grazing. He had lit a shuck, taking the money with him.

"The half-breed and I saddled fresh horses and left the others with the farmer to care for. We rode about eight miles and learned at a house that Smith had passed that way headed north. We took his trail. About midnight, we decided to stop until daylight. Next morning we hit his trail again. He and his horse were easy to describe. Several people along the road had seen him. After pushing our horses hard all day, we overtook Mr. Smith.

"We got his horse and saddle and the two thousand dollars. Then we went back to where we had left the horses and drove them on."

Implying rather than stating and softening fact by understatement either ironic or friendly were more characteristic than bragging. Late one summer, a big sheepman of Montana who also owned cattle moved sheep by the thousands into Canada. Blizzards brought ice and snow. The next spring friends asked if his losses had been heavy. "No," he answered, "I saved some of the dogs and all the sheepherders." It was raining one night when Charlie Russell went on night herd. "He put on his slicker and it made his horse nervous. He got nervous too and directly had to crawl on again."

[93]

Russell's cowboy friend in relating the incident would not say that he got "throwed" by the horse.

The art of succinctness was not uncultivated. A cowman's son, dissatisfied with life on the ranch, persuaded his father to send him to town, where he could benefit from cultural advantages. The family was religious enough to attend church services when there were any. The son was captivated by a minister fresh out of an Eastern theological seminary. He wore his hair parted in the middle; his speech was full of flowers and mists.

One Saturday the rancher came in and the son could hardly wait to take him to services next morning. On the way home from church, he eagerly asked, "Papa, what do you think of his preaching?"

"Too much mane and tail," was the laconic answer.

The usual preacher fitted into the life. After one who understood the meaning of a "fatted calf" had pitchforked the prodigal son into red blazes and toasted him over white-hot coals, a weathered cowman said, "If that son-of-a-bitch don't go to hell, there ain't no use having one."

Before a church was built in the region, a certain Baptist itinerant used to visit ranches west of the Pecos and preach. He would send word ahead that he'd be at a ranch on a certain date, and ranch people would customarily gather there from over a big scope of country to hear him. One time he drove up to a ranch that had been notified and found nobody there at all except a lone cowboy. Word hadn't carried. He was, of course, made welcome.

After supper he said to the cowboy, "I came here to preach. Do you have any objections to our holding services tonight?" The cowboy had no objections. He sat easy — for

W. J. WILSON was called "One-armed" Jim Wilson. He fought Apache Indians when he was with the Goodnight-Loving herd on the Pecos River in 1867. He was not talkative. He kept a lot inside himself.

a time at least — while the preacher stood. He was long-winded and preached for over an hour to the solitary listener, finally ending with this question, "What do you think of my sermon?"

The cowboy hesitated but got out what he had to say: "When we are feeding cattle and drive a wagonload of cottonseed cake somewhere and find just one steer there, we don't unload the whole thing for him."

"I quit shoveling," one cowboy explained the course of his life, "because I couldn't see nothing ahead of shoveling but dirt."

Maybe the cowpuncher who happened to look over Stewart Edward White's shoulder while the latter was reading a novel was not himself much of a reader, but he had read enough to know what goes on in old-fashioned fiction. "What are they doing now," he asked Stewart Edward White, "kissing or killing?"

"If what brains you have were all made out of dynamite," another cowboy passed judgment on a biped by saying, "you couldn't blow the top of your head off."

Economy in talk may be rarer than in art and literature. While Charles M. Russell was learning the life that he put, often with superb economy, into drawings and bronzes, he said: "There are three things I love to hear: the old dishpan banging for chow, a coyote barking, and a wolf howling." His compadre Patrick Tucker said: "There were three kinds of cowboys: those who gave all their money to the dance hall girls, those who gave it to the gamblers, and those who drank it up."

A kind of euphemism was in style, particularly in northern grass country, before families and family talk took over. A

man "died of defective vision"; that is, another man with a
gun saw him first. "They quit breathing" — said of certain
cattle thieves. Two New Mexico cowboys trailed Black Jack
Ketchum, noted badman, into Mexico, were attacked by
rurales, the Mexican equivalent of border rangers, and found
themselves afoot. Four *rurales* followed them. Then, to
quote, "Two of them *rurales* didn't need their horses any
longer and we rode them out." A horse thief was "accused of
finding a rope with another man's horse at one end of it." A
cow country preacher said to his congregation, "Some of your
freshly branded calves don't suck the right cows"; that is, the
calves had been mavericked.

A United States deputy marshal and a helper taking two
horse thieves to Caldwell, Kansas, ran out of grub. At their
hungriest, they sighted a camp on the Chisholm Trail. The
owner of the herd gave them a good dinner. After watching
the prisoners share it, he said: "If I ever catch a man stealing
horses from me, I'll take 'em home, and you can bet he won't
never steal another horse." One winter all the whiskey in a
frontier saloon froze. Bigfoot Wallace said, "People were under the impression that the saloonkeeper had watered it
pretty freely." No region or individual has a corner on a way
of saying. The acid Henry David Thoreau of Concord, Massachusetts, wrote: "Some circumstantial evidence is very
strong, as when you find a trout in the milk."

Some cowmen could put up with having dirt-honest speech
turned into jargon identifying private profit with public wel-
fare. In 1887 the Montana Stockgrowers Association resolved
that an interstate commerce law interfered with the trans-
portation of "our quota of the food supply of the nation." In a
trivial book written by a once honest-speaking cowman

turned salesman I found, right against a straight-out account of an outlaw cow, this slickness: "Success has five ingredients. The first one is honesty; so are the other four." Speech of the soil is often commonplace; it never attempts to transmute the dullness of sun-baked alkali into tin-can brightness.

Comparatively few old-time cowmen encountered by me, either in person or in print, have showed much picturesqueness of speech. The more property they owned, the less picturesqueness, generally, in choice of words. They tended to be plain. I heard one from down in the brush remark: "Some cowboys with outfits on the Plains had an original way of saying things. Sometimes they seemed to be overdoing their language."

Two range sayings express the utmost in trustworthiness: "He will do to tie to" and "He will do to ride the river with." That is, this character will stand hitched until hell freezes over and a little while on the ice. You can trust him to hell and back. If it's work you want out of him, he will pull till he busts a hamstring.

After his first taste of jello a cowboy said, "I'd get as much feed by loping a rough horse against a west wind with a funnel in my mouth." Another time he said, "It's as easy to braid a mule's tail in flytime as to stop a herd drifting with a snowstorm."

Sayings of this kind are based on familiarity with country things. While Charlie Newman, old-time cowman of El Paso, and I were riding with a pack outfit across the Sierra Madre in Mexico, he went to remembering a character noted for always recommending his own possessions. Charlie Newman said, "To hear him talk, you'd have thought they were all red roans and natural-born pacers."

FRIENDLY H. DUBOSE, ex-Confederate soldier (about 1892). He bought cattle to be slaughtered for their hides and tallow on the Gulf of Mexico before there was a market for them after the Civil War. He drove horses to Kansas, ranched, went broke, ended his career as a justice of the peace in a ranch town. He slept in his underwear and shirt; when he got up — before daylight — he put on his hat, lighted his pipe, then pulled on his breeches and shoes. Never garrulous, he was a philosopher. "His looks and my ways would hang any man," he would say of one he did not trust.

Talkative show-offs, sometimes entertaining, often boring, have always bobbed up everywhere. Soon after a railroad reached Abilene, Texas, a trainload of Easterners pulled in for a long stop. They piled out of the cars to exercise their legs and view the West. Lige Carter, who was noted for whiskey-stimulated loquacity, was at the station with numerous townsmen. He had just been taken in charge by the city marshal. "I've got to make a speech to these people," he said to the marshal. "Let me be for a little while." The marshal decided to "let him be," and he mounted a convenient hand-cart for baggage. He "didn't know enough to carry guts to a bear," but he had listened to promoters.

"Ladies and gentlemen, strangers in our midst," he began, "Abilene, Texas, welcomes you. You can gaze over the prairies and see how much room we have to expand. We want you. Stay here and spend your money. Let's all spend all we have. If we spend and spend, Abilene will grow and grow until it is a metropolis. There's nothing to keep it from growing as big as New York. That's all it takes — money. Spend it!"

Cold type cannot convey the enthusiasm of Lige on the subject of spending money. His auditors were convulsed with laughter. One stepped up to the marshal and asked, "How much will it take to pay that fellow's fine?"

"Eleven dollars and a quarter."

"Here it is," the stranger replied, pulling out his pocketbook. "His speech is worth that much."

Some men have always shared Mark Twain's "love of strong effect." It adds to the gaiety of life. Frank Bates, originally from Elmira, New York, and one of the owners of the Spade Ranch, carried an eye-attracting cane, not to walk with but to display in town. After meeting Laban A. Records, one of his men, on business at a hotel — probably the only one then extant — in Wellington, Kansas, he picked up his cane and said, "Let's go out on the sidewalk." Records followed, humoring him. At a wagonload of pumpkins and turnips for sale, Records asked, "Were these apples raised in this country or shipped in?" Bates took pains to answer the question and informed the gathering spectators that the questioner was one of his punchers.

"Where do you ranch?" a spectator queried.

"In the Strip," Bates replied.

"How big is your ranch?"

"Maybe seventy-five thousand acres or something like that," Bates modestly answered.

He was not a boaster. He merely enjoyed attracting notice.

Among autobiographies, *A Texas Cow Boy; or, Fifteen Years on the Hurricane Deck of a Spanish Cow Pony,* "taken from real life" by Charles A. Siringo (1855-1928), exemplifies the diction. Among chroniclers in fiction form, Andy Adams (1859-1936), who drove up the trail and was an intense listener for characteristic speech, makes it, without show, altogether natural in *The Log of a Cowboy* and in other narratives. Charles M. Russell (1864-1926), horse-wrangler who became *the* authentic artist of cowboy life, saturated his letters and anecdotes with special uses of words. Like his spelling, they often seem consciously defiant of orthodox English. Some writers of cowboy life claiming to be authentic have resembled a preacher of the 1930's I knew. He wore a six-shooter under a black coat into the pulpit. I doubt if he had ever seen a hired hand on horseback carrying a six-shooter. He could not have found one in the counties where he carried his.

A few men of open range days wrote in a blend of natural understatement and overstatement. Lee Moore, born in 1856 among original settlers of Williamson County, Texas, drove cattle up the trail and settled in Wyoming as a cowman. In 1923, the Wyoming Stock Growers Association printed a pamphlet of reminiscent letters from its members. I can give only abbreviated extracts from the most rollicky and extravagant, also most reticent, of them all — Lee Moore's. Its originality is not in diction but in his particular way of setting down, without one simile, the minute particulars of experience.

"In 1861, when my uncle Jack Elliott started to the War of the Rebellion, or maybe it was to Mexico, he gave me an old cow and a little calf, and my father gave me a pony and a bridle and a sheepskin for a saddle. My cowboy uniform consisted of a straw hat and long hickory shirt; so at five years of age I was a cattle owner equipped for business, but that winter the old cow died or went to war. As I thought in those days, everything went to the war but women, children and Negroes. As my calf was not a heifer and I was too young to rustle, my herd did not increase during the war. When it was over and my father came home, I owned a work steer.

"My father, knowing my fondness for little calves, gave me one for my steer, and he continued to give me a little calf every spring for my yearling until I was about sixteen. Then I went out of the cattle business by giving the little calf to my sister. The year after he came back from the war, my father had added to my uniform a saddle, overalls, a wool hat, a pair of shoes and had started me out repping [representing his brand at cow works]. Repping in 1866 in Texas was quite different from repping in Wyoming in 1915.

"In those days we did not have 'roundups.' We went on cow-hunts, and the men on the cow-hunt I joined were all cattle owners just home from the war. They went out to see what they had left and to brand up what I had neglected to brand during the war. I was the only boy on this cow-hunt. We had no wagon. Every man carried his grub in a wallet tied behind his saddle; his bed was a saddle blanket under the saddle. A wallet is a sack with both ends sewed up and a hole in the middle to put things in, half on one side of the hole and half on the other. I. P. Olive, the boss, put me on herd and kept me on herd when we had one, and I don't think there was ever a day on this hunt when we didn't have a herd. Also, I carried several extra wallets behind my saddle and a string of tin cups on a hobble around my pony's neck. Whenever the boss herder couldn't hear those cups jingling, he would come around and wake me up.

"We would corral the cattle every night at the house of some owner on the cow-hunt and stand guard around the corral. I didn't stand any guard but carried brush and cornstalks and anything I could get to make a light for men not on guard to play poker by. They played for unbranded cattle, yearlings at fifty cents a head. The top price for a cow or a steer was five dollars a head. If any man run out of cattle and had a little money, he could get back into the game. For ten dollars say, he could get a stack of yearlings. My pay for supplying a light was twenty-five cents per night, or as long

as the game lasted. Every few days the men would divide up
and brand and each owner would drive his cattle home and
come back.

"This cow-hunt continued nearly all summer. In the winter of '66 I started to school. I went two or three days nearly
every month when there was any school. When I wasn't going
to school I was picking cotton or cow-hunting until '69. Father sold his cattle to J. F. E. and F. N. Stiles and threw me
in with the cattle, with the understanding that he would receive twelve dollars a month for my services. As you can see,
I began to slip back, owner to rep, rep to common waddie. I
worked for the Stiles men as waddie, top-hand and then boss
until the spring of 1876. They sold their cattle and me with
them to D. H. and J. W. Snyder.

"The Snyders built corrals and a branding chute on Turkey Creek on the Stiles range and put their brother Tom in
charge. The creek had plenty of water and we headquartered
between it and the corrals.

"We had no tents, tarpaulins, cabins or anything of that
kind. We had a wagon with a cover over it and a little grub in
the bottom of the wagon box, which we kept dry. I had no
bed, but used J. W. Snyder's and when he visited us, he had
the pleasure of his own bed with me in it. It was the best bed
on the job, consisting of a buffalo robe, one suggan, one
blanket and a feather pillow. J. W. Snyder hired a big crew
of men and started me out with a two-horse wagon, a bunch
of saddle horses and some cowboys just from Tennessee and
a few Swedes from Round Rock to gather these cattle and
turn them over to Tom Snyder to hold and road brand. I was
boss of the first wagon I ever saw on a cow-hunt. I had no

check book, one reason being I couldn't write a check, and another, there wasn't a cowman in our part of the country could read a check.

"I want to speak of our grub as it was my starting in at high-living. We had flour, coffee, sugar, beans, bacon and some dried apples from the north in a barrel. The cook had never seen a dried apple and nobody else in the outfit had either. After the cook learned how dried apples swell when cooked in water in a covered skillet, we ate them raw. On this cow-hunt I saw for the first time a cowboy put sugar in his coffee.

"We soon had a herd made up for Tom Snyder to drive north. J. W. Snyder kept me helping receive steers he was buying around. Delivery was at the Olive ranch, and I boarded there except when driving small herds east.

"The Olives furnished coffee, corn meal, salt, whiskey and beef, provided you didn't kill something in their brand. We would sometimes get out of coffee or meal or salt but never out of whiskey or beef. Unknown parties not in favor of the Olive way of doing business slipped up on the night of August 2, '76, and set the ranch on fire and the shooting began. When the smoke cleared away, I was running across the prairie with my life and night clothes and a Winchester handed me by a dying Olive. I don't know whether it was loaded or not, but I was afraid to drop it for fear the attacking party would hear it fall.

"I resigned, and picked cotton the balance of '76. January 1, '77, I rented land and put in a crop. When I got the net proceeds of that crop in my pocket, I started to the Texas Agricultural and Mechanical College at Bryan to finish my education. The habits I had contracted while a cowboy and persisted in following did not meet with the approval of the college officials, and I finished in fourteen days. I hired out as a common waddie to go down on the coast and help drive a herd of cattle to Cheyenne, Wyoming. I decided to stay in Wyoming."

8

Of Imagination All Compact

"The cowboy story differs from any other I have
ever heard, both in extravagance of statement and
manner of telling. The stories relate to anything
and everything that has ever come under the teller's
acute observation."

— Robert McReynolds, *Thirty Years on the
Frontier*, Colorado Springs, Colorado, 1906

ALONG IN THE 1930's, John A. Lomax, collector of cowboy ballads and other folk songs and one of the three
best tellers of character stories I have known, sent me, "for
enjoyment," a typewritten piece sent him by Lloyd Lewis
of Chicago, who, anything but sheep-minded, operated a
sheep ranch in Colorado.

Mr. Lewis wrote: "Here in this day of damned efficiency
is a verbatim transcript, made in 1924, of talk by Tom Ble-
vens, an aged cowpuncher whose knees gave out on him from
too much riding in Texas. The night he turned himself loose
on this 'dream-like concern' he had spent a year watching
the gate of a sheep pasture out in the desert. We were in a
cabin at Cockleburr Springs. He believed his story absolutely, possibly from having told it so many times. It and his
recollection of having been John Chisum's favored boss

sound to me like wish-fulfillment. Was there ever any such place as The Two Minnies?"

Now follows "the verbatim transcript" of what the stiff-kneed old cowpuncher told.

"Well, Lloyd, if you feel anyways funny this evening, I'll tell you about The Two Minnies. That was the finest place a cowboy could be in and it was the most talked of place, I reckon, around the wagons at night all through Texas and the Indian Territory. Lots of times a feller on night herd would be singing 'Rock of Ages' to quiet the cattle while he was thinking about The Two Minnies.

"Outside, it looked like any big city block, and from the time the two Minnies come to Fort Worth in 1873 and put it up in what people called 'Hell's Half Acre' it was the biggest showplace in town for size and character. Pretty soon that part of town got to be Hell's Whole Acre, but the first time I seen it the section was smallish and all anybody talked about was The Two Minnies.

"I seen it first in 1874. I had got back from driving a herd of John Chisum's cattle to the railroad and John says, 'Tom, take a rest. You've been working steady for two years and a foreman gets wore out. Here's four months' wages. Ride over to Fort Worth and get rollicky a spell.' Then he says, 'You've never seen The Two Minnies, have you?' None of the cowpunchers knowed about it then. Later on, when the word got spread all over Texas and the Territory, a man would know what to expect, but in 1874 mighty nigh nobody did. I didn't have any trouble locating the place. I just walked in and seen a hell of a big fine room with cushion chairs and tables to drink off of placed around in front of the bar. I'd been riding three days and I made a line for the bar, but a big nigger, as polite as a basket of chips, stopped me and took my chaps and my gun and hung 'em up.

"I ast fer whiskey and wanted to set 'em up fer the house, but the bartender frowned and drawed himself up. The Two Minnies had the dudiest-looking men they could git. The pins in their neckties sparkled and their hair was combed. So I poured out a drink and says to myself, 'Don't look like you're going to have much fun here' and throwed back my head fer to swallow — but I never got that drink. No man ever downed his first drink in The Two Minnies. When I throwed back my head to dreen the poison down, I seen the ceiling was glass and there was anyways forty girls walking around up there with no clothes. They was playing tenpins.

"They was as fine a-looking women as you'd ever want fer to see — laughing quiet to themselves, and they'd take their turns to bowl and start their roll but the bowling alley wasn't on the glass. It was off to one side. I set down in one of them big leather chairs next to another man where I could take in the whole room upstairs.

"Them women lived up there. Some of 'em was sewing and some reading and some playing guitars. Jest as I got there, niggers in shimmy-soled shoes was washing and polishing the glass floor. Once in a while one of the women would look down into the barroom-and kind of smile and then go on talking with the other girls. Around the edge they had long sofeys and a thousand lamps. It was about as light as the plains before it gets dark.

"They was all plumb stark naked. They seemed like that was the way they'd been born and had never knowed clothes exist in this world, or anyways they seemed to be thinking that clothes was just fer men. There was no women down in the barroom and had never been any. The girls up there was never allowed to come down and no women from the outside was allowed to come in. First time in my life I ever seen a bartender too high-toned to wait on a chippy.

"Them niggers in their shoes with them shimmy-skin soles up there would bring them women their meals and they'd eat with fine manners and wipe their mouths with napkins — I guess of silk anyway — and they'd drink wine out of long glasses and the niggers waited on 'em careful and quiet and hauled stuff up on dumbwaiters fer 'em. All you could hear downstairs was when they'd laugh now and then or play the guitar or do a little singing.

"It was a kind of a dream-like concern. There was velvet curtains all around the room and a feller said that the girls' rooms was behind there somewhere.

" 'You've got to dress like a dude,' he says, 'to get in up there.' He was a rich buffalo-skinner and had knowed the place for a full year. 'There's a regular price for certain hours,' he tells me: 'five dollars up to ten o'clock at night and ten dollars from then on till daylight. You have to get a ticket at the bar and go up them stairs back there. As soon as you open that door, you'll see right in front of you a big feller in striped pants dressed up like Prince Albert. He takes your ticket. You don't pass without handing it to him.'

"This rich buffalo-skinner knew about everything going on at The Two Minnies and was a reg'lar gusher in telling it. The way he put it, 'The girls get half the five dollars and six of the ten dollars and their board throwed in. They don't need no clothes from the time they come here till they go. They get ten per cent on the drinks served in the bar downstairs and their license paid. Then they get to keep half of what's stole.' Poor innocent things wouldn't turn all that in, I guess. The buffalo-skinner said he'd known a girl to lift a thousand dollars off one of these big cotton men that comes up here from Mississippi by the trainload, and ruther than fer his family to find out he'd keep still.

"I told the man it was funny to me, fer they didn't seem like the girls I'd knowed in them rough-and-tumble parlor houses back at San Angelo and Wichita Falls and Eddy — the place named Carlsbad now.

"'Oh, no,' the buffalo feller says, 'there's none of them green sagebrush girls here. They're all from New York and Paris and have got educations. I'll say that fer 'em,' he says, 'they're just as fine a-talking women as you'll ever run across anywheres.'

"Along about four o'clock that afternoon the two Minnies that owned the place come in. They was full sisters and wore Paris styles and had drove up in an open carriage with niggers to drive and watch out behind and open doors and spread dusters over their laps. The two Minnies was smart women. They was French and there were six sisters of 'em all together. The other four run The Four Minnies in Mexico City just like this Two Minnies place in Fort Worth with the same glass ceiling business, but in Mexico City they had more girls — sixty of 'em anyways, living up there. The Minnies would visit back and forth some, but they all stuck to business close. They was in it fer the money. The buffalo man, he introduced me to the youngest one of the two Minnies, Little Minnie, and she said, 'The minute this place begins to run behind, we quit.'

"They come in with their bookkeepers, slick-looking men who went right to the cash drawers and checked up on the bartenders and on the ticket man in the striped pants and put the money in satchels and went out with the two Minnies. Then a new shift of bartenders came on and the girls had their supper with the niggers hurrying around waiting on 'em.

" 'Them two Minnies, they never have anything to do with men that come here,' the buffalo feller told me. 'They're too rich. They live with them bookkeepers. They've got a big, fine mansion up on Tucker's Hill, and you'll only see 'em like you did now, drive up with fast-trotting horses and get the money. This place here is worth a hundred thousand dollars. They brought these pictures you see hanging on the walls across the Atlantic Ocean from Paris. Some of 'em wouldn't do to hang in the church where I was raised.'

"Well, along in the evening about midnight I come back from eating supper and seeing to my horse down in the wagon yard, and everything was changed at The Two Minnies. You had to ring a bell to get in and then a nigger looked you over.

"At night a man wasn't allowed on the glass floor unless he was naked, too. He got more attention paid him, more of the niggers would run to get him wine. It was sixteen dollars a quart, and a ticket to get up there cost ten. More of the girls would run to get him a match or a glass or to play him a tune or insist on him dancing. They had an orchestra of niggers playing Mexican waltzes. They was rollicky but not rough this time of night. They'd just dance and laugh and drink and get old men to betting on a game of tenpins. It was a plumb silly sight to see some old cowman dancing with a ring of women around him.

"It was no place fer a cowboy. He could have more fun in

them sagebrush houses and not have to worry about style. They didn't like cowboys on the glass floor, fer a cowboy would shoot up the place fer fifteen dollars stole off him, while these rich cowmen and buffalo skinners and cotton men would keep still.

"The two Minnies stayed fer eight years till the railroads shipped all the buffalo hides out of the country; then they went away. I was in there a hundred times, I reckon, but there was never no real fun in The Two Minnies, no yelling, no natural person not being toned down. We could have more fun in Frankie Day's place at San Angelo."

On Christmas Eve, 1925, I went to the little shop — harness and shoe repairing — run by old Frank Graham in South Austin. Stepping inside, I saw him hobbling in the back yard, a crutch in one hand and a rake in the other. After we had talked a bit he said he had to rake up some chips. While I did that little job for him, he kept warning me not to get any bones mixed with the chips. After we went in and sat down, I drew him out. All he required was a chance to let his memory weave. Imagine him, a poor old neglected shoe-mender there, dependent upon a crutch, burgeoning on times when he rode a free horse in a pristine world where violence often ruled and he was dominant in the middle of everything. This is what Frank Graham told.

"I came to Texas from Georgia after the Civil War ended. A friend of mine up there had to leave the country on account of having knocked up two girls; if he stayed, he could not by law marry but one of them. I was young and full of juice and pulled out with him. After I got to Texas I began cowboying. In 1875 I made my first drive for Bill Allen, who ranched out from Weatherford. On the way up through the Cheyenne and Arapahoe country, some Indians demanded twelve head of beeves. There were nine of us cowboys, and we told the boss that if he would give us twelve head of beeves or the equivalent in money, we would take the herd through. 'All right, boys,' he says, 'I had rather for you all to have the beeves than them sonabitching Indians. Let's move.'

"We pulled out our six-shooters, pointed them at the Indians, and told them to vamoose. They left. We drove as late as we could see that night and then every man stood guard till daylight. We drove all the next day and that night kept around the herd. Some of us rode out a little ways and slept on the ground with bridle reins in hand until it was time to go on watch. We got about as good a night's sleep as if we had bedded down in camps. No Indian ever did bother us. When we got to Dodge City we had to wait for the shipping pens to be remade or enlarged.

"In all I made eight trips up the trail. Part of the time I was trail boss, always working for Bill Allen. He had cattle everywhere, but I bossed his outfit in Young County, where twenty-two cowboys besides cook and horse-wrangler worked under me. One year Mr. Allen decided to open up a ranch between the North and South Forks of the Platte. We started out with a herd of three thousand heifers for Nebraska. When we got to the South Platte it was up half a mile wide. The other bank was away over yonder and nobody wanted to head for it. I had a little pony that I would trust in any water, and I offered to lead the herd in. I took all my clothes off except drawers and undershirt. Then I took bridle and saddle off my horse and rode in. Other hands pointed the cattle in behind me. For a good way out we could wade, but a little after we struck deep water — and it was just rolling over in sandy waves — the heifers began milling. Milling in midstream is what every cowman dreaded. The outside cattle crowd in and screw the circle up tighter and tighter. I have seen hundreds of cattle drowned that way.

"I had to break that mill of heifers. I just reached over and patted my horse on the jaw and gradually brought him around. He knew what he had to do. Then I rode up alongside the tangled heifers, circled five or six back from the way they were winding, and led off. The whole bunch followed, and after a while I stood on the north shore of the river without bridle, saddle, shirt, or breeches, and three thousand head of cattle under my charge. Not another man would take the water. They managed to get a little boat somehow and crossed over in it, bringing my clothes and some provisions. The horses were swum over behind the skiff, one or two being led alongside. The next day a raft was floated down from upstream, and the chuck wagon was crossed over on it. Mr. Allen gave me one hundred dollars for that day's work.

"I had a six-shooter that I called 'Old Dangy,' short for Dangerous, and I could shoot a prairie chicken's head off anytime I wanted to. I used to shoot their heads off and bring 'em in to camp for our yaller nigger cook to fix up. His name was Sam, and he was good, had cooked before he ever went to working for cow outfits. It had been ten or twelve years since I had seen Sam when one day out in Gallup, New Mexico, I run into him. He saw me coming half a mile away and said to some miners standing by, 'Yonder comes Frank Graham. If he's got that old gun he used to carry, I'll bet fifty dollars he can shoot the necks off of five beer bottles out of six.' 'Haul out yer money, and we'll cover every cent you put up,' two of the miners offered. 'Wait till I see whether he's got Old Dangy,' Sam told them.

"The first thing he asked me when I loped up was if I still had that six-shooter. 'Yes.' 'Then,' says he, 'pull it out and git busy. I've bet fifty dollars you can shoot the necks off of five out of six beer bottles. Do it, and I'll give you twenty-five.'

"I told him I'd have to rest up a bit and get a little something to eat so as to steady my nerves. He hurried me into a saloon, ordered the best they had, and I took a good dram of French brandy. It was dinner time and I ate a good meal. 'All right,' says I then, 'I'm ready. Look at my hand. It's as steady as a team of oxen pulling a freight wagon on level ground.' Instead of shooting five out of six bottle necks, I shot all six.

"New Mexico was a wild place when I went there, and the Apaches were on the warpath. While I was at Gallup, a telegram came from some wide place in the road that everybody there had been killed except one little girl. The telegraph dispatcher sent that telegram before the Apaches got him, but what he said proved to be true. We got an engine hitched to a car and when the engineer slammed the brakes on, the Apaches were still there, dancing and whooping and swinging that little girl around by the hair. I remember the color of it yet. It was gold. We began shooting into them with Winchesters and mowed them down like cane. As soon as the little girl got free, she ran into the arms of the first man she could reach. We sent her to Albuquerque, where she had some relatives.

"The toughest men in the old days seemed to me to be the buffalo-skinners. The railroad-builders and the mining men were tough, too. The cowboys were not bad men. They could shoot, of course, and take care of themselves. They simply wanted to be let alone, and they would stand by each other to the last ditch.

"One night in Dodge City a bunch of Texas cowboys were dancing with the women and setting up drinks in the Red Light. While they were blazing with life, a bunch of half-drunk gamblers and chippies from another Kansas town came in and ordered the floor cleared. They wanted it for themselves. One of the chippies had a little knife, a kind of poniard, and when her crowd undertook to clear the floor, she jabbed it clear through a cowboy's arm. The gamblers pulled their little .32 guns, and the old forty-fives answered back.

"When the smoke cleared away, there were seven men and five women on the floor, all dead. Those Texas cowboys made a line for the livery stable, got their horses, and rode south. Somebody whispered a word to the cook, and the next day about noon the chuck wagon overtook them where they were waiting. Nobody in Dodge City ever knew who those cowboys were, or if they knew, I guess they did not care. The men in that outfit had been inside their own rights. The city marshals were not riding after Texas cowboys.

"Once in Weatherford two of our cowboys got locked up for something they had not done. When Bill Allen heard that his men were in the calaboose, he rounded up his outfit and we rode into town. It was dark when we got there. He went straight to the authorities. 'Now, by God,' says he, 'you turn them boys out of that jail and turn them out damned quick, or there won't be a light left burning in this town.' The jailer could not be too quick in unlocking the doors. That was the way Bill Allen stood by his men, and they stood behind him.

"Because a man was bad was no sign he might not be true as steel when it came to keeping his word with a friend. In 1881 I was carpentering in Caldwell, Kansas. The town marshal there went under the name of John Henry Brown. I knew him as soon as I saw him. Years before I had saved his life. He was swimming the Rio Grande with Mexicans shooting at him. I was on the Texas side of the river, and I had a rifle that made the Mexicans stand clear till he got across. He went under the name of Frank Norris then, and he told me that if ever I needed help and he knew of it, he would be right there. When he sighted me in Caldwell, he kept his distance for a couple of days, but when he saw I was going to stay, he came up, shook hands, and said: 'I am at your mercy. You know my past. A five thousand dollar reward hangs over me in Mexico, dead or alive. Many a man here would betray me for five hundred.' I never knew what he had done in Mexico, but naturally I let out nothing.

"While I was carpentering, rheumatism almost paralyzed my legs. Brown had me carried to the hotel, paid for my keep for months, kept me in spending money and furnished careful attention. Later he, an assistant marshal and two other men murdered the president and cashier of a bank in Medicine Lodge, Kansas, but were captured. Brown tried to get away and was shot to death; the other three were hanged.

"Once in Fort Worth one of my cowhands got on a drunk and was being robbed by a professional gambler. I walked into the saloon and gambling hall and ordered the gambler to return the money. He refused. Then I told him I'd drill daylight through his liver if he didn't hand over the money. The saloon keeper let him know that I generally kept my word. I got the money and took the drunk to camp. When he sobered up, he wanted his money, but a dollar was all I let him have until we were well out of town. I never would give the boys more than ten dollars apiece when we got to town. They generally thanked me later on."

Alonzo Mitchell, a genuine trail driver, some of whose experiences I put into *The Longhorns,* had eyes open for other characters than himself. He seemed sometimes to be less skeptical than credulous. As he told it, on a drive to the ranch of Dudley H. and John W. Snyder on the South Platte with a herd of steers, he began paying particular attention to a very long-legged, long-armed, long-haired cowboy who had anything but a long tongue. He almost never spoke. When riding he had a peculiar way of looping his bridle reins around the horn of his saddle and letting his long hands hang at his sides, touching the reins only to turn his horse. The boys called him Bob.

One man kept pecking at him, throwing it into him. Bob said nothing. Alonzo Mitchell told the bully he had better go slower and not aggravate that long-legged feller too much. But the bully went on bullying. One day at dinner he said something to Bob that brought on more words.

"I've about got tired of your talk," Bob said in a slow way, and then whaled loose and slapped the living whey out of his tormentor. He slapped his hat off, slapped him on both sides of the face and over the forehead. At each slap the skin of the man he was slapping stuck to his hands.

That was all there was to the fracas. There was no more

bullying, but something very peculiar came on the man who had been slapped. The skinned places of his cheeks and forehead would not heal up. They watered all the time. Finally he quit the outfit at a trading post in the Indian Territory. Then Bob told Mitchell that he always hated to hit a man because electricity in his body drew the skin off anybody he slapped or hit. He could not hold his reins on account of so much electricity, he said. He claimed the power to locate water under the earth, and one time on the trip he actually found enough below sand in a dry creek to water thirsty men and horses. He was a lone and lonely man with all that electricity in him, and he never lost consciousness of his own singularity.

"I have been killing rattlesnakes for fifty years. Four measured from eight feet one inch to eight feet three inches in length, with from twenty-three to twenty-five rattles. The biggest I know about was killed by my neighbor, Ira Cockrell, while he was riding with the Three D Waggoner outfit. He was loping to the roundup grounds when his horse gave a snort and jumped sideways so far that Ira lost a stirrup. When he got balanced again he saw that monster rattlesnake r'ared up. He didn't have a thing to shoot with, and not a stick or a rock was in sight. He just takes down his rope, dabs it on the snake and drags him till he comes to a pile of posts, and beats him to death with a post. He cut the rattles off and tied them to his saddle and went on to meet the wagon — thirty-two rattles, as I recall. He gave them to an old professor from the Smithsonian Institution. The snake measured nine foot or over."

Of Imagination All Compact

The above is from a letter by R. J. Barbour, an old-time Texian of Archer City. In response I wrote, "I don't see how a man roping the biggest rattlesnake there is with a regular roping rope could hold it in the loop. I don't see how the loop could draw up tight enough to keep a snake from wriggling through. Anyhow, why didn't the man make a knot in the double of his rope and pound the snake to death? Thousands of big rattlers have been killed that way."

To this Mr. Barbour replied: "The average cowman would have the same thoughts as you. That snake Ira found was too big to be killed with any rope. His rope was smallish and limber. When the loop pulled up, the snake kept wriggling through it until it got to his head. Then it held. The head of a nine-foot diamondback rattlesnake would be as wide as your hand and his neck would be maybe two inches in diameter."

We are on a subject now as unending as Van Sickle's snake track appeared to be. Van Sickle farmed and raised a few shelly cattle on Ferber's Branch and had the kind of reputation that Mr. Fishback of the Sulphurs established for himself when one hot January day a blue norther hit him without a coat. He was riding a horse with speed and bottom and turned him loose for home. When he got there the front legs of his horse were in a lather and the hind legs were frozen. Anyhow, one Monday morning, Van Sickle was two hours late in responding to a summons to appear in court at 9 A.M. Vexed at the delay, for it had necessitated some shift in the order of procedure, the judge fined Van Sickle ten dollars when he came in. Van Sickle protested.

"What excuse have you to offer for such unseemly and contemptuous tardiness?" the judge demanded.

"Your honor," Van Sickle replied, "I was delayed by the track of a rattlesnake."

Exasperated by such a ridiculous excuse, the judge sternly called for an explanation.

"Your honor," went on Van Sickle, "it is the most enormous track a man ever laid eyes on. The sight of it held me spellbound. I followed it in hope of getting a glimpse of the snake that made it. I left it only because of my duty to this court."

The judge would not remit the fine, but when court recessed for dinner Van Sickle continued to talk about the enormous snake track. Finally a lawyer and two other men asked him to lead them to it. Nothing would please him more. Several miles out, on a sandy hillside sloping down to Ferber's Branch, he pointed to the "drag" of a snake. It was distinct, but there was nothing about it to excite anybody familiar with snake "drags."

"Why," the men said, "that snake track is not wider than lots of snake tracks we have seen."

"That may be true," Van Sickle replied, "but, great goodness, look how long it is!"

The way to make a record in snake-killing is to be away off from tape measures or yardsticks and not to have any witness. The Abbé Domenech came to Texas in 1846 and wrote *Missionary Adventures in Texas and Mexico: A Personal Narrative.* He no doubt had precedents. His sprightly account of marvels in man and other forms of nature takes in rattlesnakes. West of San Antonio, the Abbé relates, "a tiger hunter killed a rattlesnake he had mistaken for a dead tree fallen to the ground." He had sat down on it to rest. "The reptile measured seventeen feet in length, eighteen inches in circumference and had twenty-five rings, or rattles." To be factual, the biggest rattlesnakes known to herpetology are of the eastern diamondback species, the largest officially measured reaching a length of eight feet. Next in size is the western diamondback, with an official measurement of seven feet.

9

The Right Medicine

🐂

RABIES FROM SKUNKS and venom from rattlesnakes are not the only evils remedied by whiskey. Nobody knew this better than Governor O. M. Roberts, who wrote the "Jack Rabbit History of Texas" and who taught law in the University of Texas soon after that institution was established.

By the time "the Old Alcalde," as he was called, began to expound the law, he was subject, in wintertime particularly, to coughs, colds, wheezes, phlegms and all other afflictions of head, lungs and passages between that bring the animal "created in the image of God" to the nadir of wretchedness. One cold, damp morning, in this ignoble and depressed state, he stood before his class, eyes watering, handkerchief soggy, voice between a squeak and a croak, his whole body a slump, his mind an utter blank without a single idea, a single fact, a single intimation of intelligence. He opened his mouth and wheezed, "Please excuse me for a minute."

Thereupon he walked out of the room and down the hall to his office, the door of which could be heard to shut. A minute passed, several minutes. Then the Old Alcalde strode back into the presence of his "young jackasses." He strode; he did not drag. His shoulders were thrown back; his head was up; brightness glittered in his eyes. Just as his eagerness was about to explode, a "young jackass" in the front row interrupted him.

"Governor?" he queried.

"What is it, sir?"

"I'd like to ask a question, sir."

"Ask it, sir."

"Governor, don't you think a better remedy could be found for coughs and colds than whiskey?"

"Young man," and the Old Alcalde fairly roared, emphasizing the finality of his opinion with a slam on the table before which he towered, "young man, who in the hell would want a better remedy for coughs and colds than whiskey?"

Back in the days before barbed wire put a Spanish bit on Free Enterprise, Henry Williams was boss for the T X outfit. His range stretched up and down the canyon-cut Pecos River from old Fort Lancaster to Pecos City. The "city" part of Pecos City was not visible; three or four rock chimneys, bleak and deserted, marked the site of Fort Lancaster, as they do today. Cowboys riding out daily from a series of line camps prevented T X cattle from drifting away. They camped in pairs and each morning rode out in opposite directions.

To one of these camps Henry Williams drove up in his buckboard about sundown. He found both riders in, preparing supper. They had frying pan, coffeepot, Dutch oven, bean pot, tin plates, a cast-iron stove and bedrolls, all in a small dugout, roofed with poles and dirt. They were fixed up for the winter. The dugout door, on the south side, consisted of a piece of old tarp that lacked several inches of touching the ground. Despite the camp's open door policy, Henry Williams preferred to sleep outside. He always carried his own bedroll in the buckboard, along with coffeepot, some jerked beef and sourdough biscuits dehydrated by time; he was prepared to be self-sufficient anywhere. After he had hobbled his team, eaten supper, rolled and smoked three Bull Durham cigarettes, listened to the two cowboys express their views on Pecos River water and Carlsbad whiskey and enjoyed — without saying so — a coyote serenade, he unrolled his bed beside the buckboard, pulled his hat over his eyes to preserve his complexion, and went to sleep.

The two cowpunchers went inside the dugout to sleep. In the night one of them awoke the slumbering hills with a yell. A skunk had bit him through the nose. Skunks are always prowling at night for something to eat. To enter a dugout smelling of food was as natural for a skunk as to enter an old badger hole. One summer night when I was a boy, a skunk came up into the open hall of our ranch house and bit into the big toe of a Mexican girl sleeping on a pallet spread on the floor. This was down in the Brush Country of lower Texas, where the worst thing connected with a skunk that people feared was the animal's fire-extinguisher. On west, any skunk that bit a human being was supposed to be a hydrophobia skunk. No cow camp ever conjured up any other horror as horrible as death resulting from the bite of a hydrophobia skunk.

And now in the middle of the night, away out in the middle of the vast and empty Pecos ranges, this T X cowboy had a hydrophobia skunk biting into his nose. Somewhat curiously, the cowboy was called Snort; the episode in the dugout did nothing to change his name. Snort was highly excited at the prospect of hydrophobia; his mate and Henry Williams were too. He rubbed some kerosene oil on the bite but had no faith in its powers to arrest hydrophobia. Hydrophobia was something that galloped; you had to gallop yourself to overtake it. The proper remedy to gallop towards was a madstone, but none of the three men knew where one was. Henry Williams always carried a bottle of whiskey with him for emergencies. He wanted to cheer Snort up and told him he'd heard a doctor say that whiskey was even better than a madstone for the bite of a hydrophobia skunk. Snort listened to the prescription, swallowed a big dose without flinching, and seemed to take a less gloomy view of his destiny.

Henry Williams had heard of a kind of doctor having come to Midland, fully a hundred miles northeast of the dugout camp. No doctor had yet felt the call to settle in Pecos City. The hobbled horses, none too fresh, were brought in and hitched to the buckboard. Snort got up on the seat with Henry Williams. He did not forget to bring his medicine with him. Henry Williams headed for Midland, and before long they saw daylight coming to meet them. As in the old cowboy song, "It was a long and lonesome go." The horses suffered for water. There wasn't any road — just a way. Long before dark Snort had taken the last drop of medicine out of the quart bottle. They made a dry camp, let the horses rest and graze and then about three o'clock in the morning drove on. Snort became more despondent over the prospect of hydrophobia than he had been at any other time. Henry Williams was mightily relieved when, just at daybreak, he smelled coffee boiling and mesquite wood burning and knew they were at the Block Ranch.

Three cowboys were eating breakfast. They said yes, a doctor of some sort had put down stakes in Midland. It was still thirty-five miles or so to Midland. They would bring in a fresh team of horses to hitch to the buckboard. Meantime, they had a quart of whiskey, always reserved for emergencies, and they were glad to help fight hydrophobia with it. In a melancholy, disinterested way, Snort began swallowing it, while Henry Williams downed coffee, steak and hot biscuits. Then, while the fresh horses were being roped and harnessed, Snort staggered out to the pen and sat down, leaning his back against the fence. He was beside a pile of old lumber. As soon as the team was hitched in, Henry Williams called Snort to come on. Snort didn't seem to make any effort to move, and Williams walked towards him with the intention of helping him up.

Just as he got to the old lumber pile, he heard rattlesnake rattles whirring. He saw Snort put a hand out on the ground as if to raise himself up. He saw a monstrous rattlesnake plunge his fangs into the hand. The three Block Ranch cowboys said the only remedy they knew for snakebite was whiskey. That was the only remedy Henry Williams had ever heard of. They all encouraged Snort to take more medicine. He took it.

He acted as if he thought as well of it as the Tennessee moonshiner who had to make a trip down from his mountain fastness and set out with two bottles of whiskey in his coat pockets, two bottles in his capacious breeches pockets, and a jug over his shoulder. After getting het up from walking and toting, he lay down in the shade of a tree and took a nap. When he awoke he moved slightly and heard a loud rattling. Calmly, without moving, he looked and found himself facing the triangular head of an enormous rattle-snake, coiled and threatening. After gazing at it awhile, he said, "You're sudden, I know, but I am as well prepared for you as I'd a-been if you had given me two weeks' notice."

It took all three men to get Snort into the buckboard. Henry Williams started off, just hitting the road in high places. "I didn't know," he later told, "whether that feller Snort would go mad from skunk bite or die from rattlesnake poison. I didn't know what might happen. I jest kept bathing the butts of that fresh pair of horses and they laid down in the collars like a pair of Spanish mules. Snort was cooperating on the bottle right along. About an hour before noon he held it up to the sun to show me it was empty. I grabbed it and throwed it away to lighten the load. That pair of Block ponies was pure buckskin. We got into Midland along early in the afternoon and found the doctor.

"He was a dentist but had practiced some on horses. All he knew to do for snakebite or skunk bite was give whiskey. It looked like everybody in town wanted to provide medicine. We all kinder forgot who was the main patient and whether it was hydrophobia or rattlesnake poison that Snort had to be doctored for. I lost sight of him. In fact, I forgot all about him. I forgot about a lot of things.

"About sunup next morning the weather cleared and I set out to find Snort. I found him in a livery stable stall, asleep. I woke him up to ask him how he felt. He said he didn't recollect having been sick. He wanted to know how he'd come to make a trip to Midland. 'Why,' I says, 'in the first place you got skunk-bit and then you got rattlesnake-bit.' He wouldn't believe it. He wanted to know if a man could get a drink anywhere. I drove him back to the T X dugout. As far as I know, he never did recollect about the bites, and if he ever died I never heard of it. My private opinion is that he took the right medicine at the right time in proper doses."

10

Cooks of the Chuck Wagon

BOBWIRE — cow people do not take to *barbed wire* — had fenced in the plains before Bob Simpson rustled pots. His addiction to literature made him singular; his cooking and his harmonizing with the men he fed ranked him at the top. His memory was so tenacious and accurate that after he became a bank cashier people, sometimes in court, relied upon him for unrecorded facts pertaining to a wide country. He joyed in reciting long passages from "Locksley Hall," *Lays of Ancient Rome* and *Hamlet*. Like children begging for stories, the cowboys often called upon him in camp under the stars, hearing the same passages over and over. Many a man got his first and only introduction to literature from Bob Simpson.

There are no more chuck wagons, though on a few large ranches hands eat seasonally at a truck more likely to transport meals cooked in houses than to be a long-time camp center. The old-time cook of camp and trail has vanished. He left no record. About all I have on cooks came to me by word of mouth, either from a few of them or from men who hired them.

A good one who made cooking his business drew higher wages than anybody else connected with a cow outfit except the boss. In trail-driving days he might draw $60 a month while cowboys drew only $30. A proud young man on horseback would not have cooked for $100 a month. Most seasoned hands had experience in batching, but if an outfit's cook came up missing or was fired, the man who took his job understood it would be temporary. No regular cook wanted "a cowboy for to be." He was usually older, more mature, than the riders. The horse-wrangler often dragged up wood for him, one end of a rope around the wood, the other around his saddle horn. On the prairie he helped gather cow chips; he helped hitch up the horses and break camp.

The cook ate alone, got up earlier than anybody else — except maybe the boss — to prepare breakfast, worked alone, slept alone on sheltered ground under the wagon, might manage a lone nap. A good one kept himself clean and shaved. In the eastern part of Texas he was likely to be Negro; in the Southwest, Mexican. Neither could be the autocrat that many a white cook was, as independent with his wagon far out amid empty spaces as the captain of a sailing ship on the ocean. Of course, the boss was responsible for all the cattle, horses and hands.

Traditional cook crankiness was based on duty and a desire to keep camp in order. Beyond a radius of about sixty feet — the length of the longest roping rope — from the wagon his power ended. No man was supposed to ride up close enough or fast enough to scatter dust over pot, pan, food, or fire. Only the boss could hitch his horse to a wagon wheel. No man could walk in and take a snack, even a cup of coffee, unless given permission, until the cook announced chuck; breakfasting was less uniform. No matter how friendly he might be with the hands, the cook, like an army officer, found avoidance of familiarity helpful to authority. A servitor, he nevertheless dominated. Before the wagon moved, every cowboy was expected to tie up his bedroll and put it in the wagon bed. If he left it on the ground, an accommodating cook might roll it up and carry it; a tough one might leave it behind. Let the owner ride back, pack it in — and learn a lesson.

Bud English, as Cole Railston pictured him, was as "techy" as any cook ever aspired to be. He baked pies of dried apples just sweet enough and the shortening in his tea cakes was absolutely right. That meant that he was not from south Texas, where food for ranch hands, however plentiful, was bleak in comparison with the variety on the plains and on north and west. Bud was never ambiguous.

One afternoon he made up a big supply of cookies, set out a heaping panful for supper, and put some more in a sack for another time. Those in the pan were soon consumed. That night cowboys got hold of the sack and cleaned it. The next morning Bud addressed them as sons-of-bitches. Thereafter the guilty ones had a tendency to gang up on him. One day while he was getting wood, six or eight barged into the forbidden space between the fire and the chuck box. When Bud came back with wood, he said nothing. He left again and was gone several minutes. He returned with a long, heavy pole and threw it into the fire, scattering coals among the gathered hands, who retreated. Then Bud raked the coals up, placed his little box to sit on in the center of the space he claimed, and sat there grinning, boss of his kingdom.

Time went on, the outfit constantly moving. One day they

stopped at a log cabin without roof or flooring and with holes in the walls that you could throw a cat through, but with a good fireplace. The wind was blowing great guns; while the walls were an imperfect windbreak, they were better than nothing. Bud made his kitchen in the cabin. After breakfast most of the hands left to work on a fence. One cowboy named Willis was going to ride somewhere alone. He began pulling on his leggins in the cabin. He got one foot through one leg, but the other foot hung in the other leg and while struggling with it he hopped around, flopping the big leather wing and raising dust.

"Get out of here to put your leggins on and quit raising dust," Bud ordered.

"Put me out, you son-of-a-bitch," Willis returned. He wore a six-shooter. This was in 1902, when a good many cowboys in remote parts of the West still wore six-shooters.

Bud pulled his sawed-off six-shooter out of the chuck box, hit Willis over the head, and knocked him out of the cabin onto the ground.

Willis got up, mounted his horse, and rode to a line camp six or seven miles away where two men with a bad reputation were staying. He counted on their helping him beat the whey out of the cook. When all three came riding back, Bud was sitting in the door with a grin on his face. That grin was often a disguise. Bud was not bothered, but he quit. He told Cole Railston that he could not "afford to bring notice upon himself."

The best cook Cole Railston ever had, he said, was named Tucker. He kept everything in camp, including himself, clean. Once Railston spoke to him about his "even temper."

"I get terribly furious sometimes," he said, "when they hang a clean towel on a muddy wagon wheel."

It was not the custom for an outfit to furnish a community towel or for the cook to wash towels for cowboys to dry on, but Tucker liked to accommodate and ran his chuck wagon in family style. The towel he let cowboys use was his own.

When he left timber for prairie, he always carried wood in his wagon. At times when water covered the flat camp ground, he would, without a murmur, shovel up a pile of mud so that he could build his fire on it above water-level. A good cowboy stayed with the herd no matter what he had to endure; a good cook fed his cowboys no matter what the obstacles. When there was no wood and cow chips were rain-soaked, he might burn bacon to boil coffee. He might commandeer fence posts for fuel.

The absence of water was likely to be more of a handicap than the presence of mud. Out in the dry Pecos country during the famous work of 1885, a wagon boss said to his cook, "Scour your pots with sand and wipe 'em with a rag." "Rags all used up," the cook replied, "but grass'll do."

A cook with an Arizona outfit used to wear a derby. Nobody ever asked him where or why he got it, and, so far as is known, only one cowboy dared laugh at it. He didn't remain. The derbied cook was good. He could hold his own.

Bill Sims, who cooked for the Chiricahuas in Arizona — better known, from the C C C brand, as "the Cherries," the Cherry Cows, or the Three C's — was particular that no privately used fork or spoon be put into a pot of food. One day he saw one of the Boyce men — owners of the Chiricahua Cattle Company — spearing stewed dried apples out of the pot with his own eating fork.

"You go to town, I guess," Bill Sims said to the big owner, "and eat around them fine cafes and talk to society folks and laugh about the manners of poor ignorant cowboys. By God, any cowboy that ever straddled a Three C horse has got more manners than you show. And I'll tell you right now, Mr. Boyce, when you get victuals out of my pots you'd better use the big spoons provided for that purpose. Nobody round here wants to eat out of a pot after you've licked your fork and pronged into it. Damn such manners, I say."

To further emphasize his indignation, Bill Sims picked up the pot of stewed apples and threw them out on the ground — beyond the sixty-foot radius of his kitchen. Owner Boyce did not say a word. He backed down like a little boy caught stealing jam, and after that was strictly on his manners when around the chuck wagon run by Bill Sims.

When any man who draws wages or salary gets so good that he can tell his employer to go to hell, he has realized the dream of independence in every hired man. In no occupation were bootlickers scarcer than in old-time ranching. They were as scarce among professional cooks as among cow hands and bosses.

There was Lin Coates of Montana. The R L outfit, which ran thirty thousand cattle on the Musselshell, was bossed by Jim Cox. He was an A-1 cowman but stingy with grub. When, one spring, he hired Coates for roundup cook, the cowboys were jubilant. They knew his reputation for puddings and other fixings. He was used to buying groceries for his wagon but, with an eye on costs, Jim Cox made out the list.

The morning the outfit was to start from headquarters Lin Coates climbed up on the wagon and looked the grub over.

He jumped down and said to Cox, "You don't need a cook. You ain't got nothing for him to cook. All you need is a teamster." Then he grabbed his coat, which was all the baggage he carried, and struck out across the prairie for Custer Junction, fifty miles away.

O. E. Brewster cooked with pride for George Miller's 101 Ranch in Oklahoma long before Miller's sons, all gone now, made the 101 Wild West Show famous — following the lead of Buffalo Bill's. About 1925, years after he had boiled his last big pot of red beans and salt pork, I penciled down his reminiscences while he sat at leisure in our house and told them. I had become friendly with him in Oklahoma.

"The most men I ever cooked for at one time," he said, "numbered eighty-five. I didn't cook for that many every day, but during one work that lasted for twenty-one days I never had less than forty-five men to feed. The Millers were working a big country east of the Salt Fork of the Arkansas River and were feeding reps from other outfits. When they offered me the job, they said they'd pay a dollar and a half a day and furnish a helper, or two and a half a day without a helper. I took the two and a half. At first men just joining us from outside outfits were coming in to eat at all times of the night. Joe Miller got after them and told me not to try to keep open house all night long. I could generally get to bed by ten o'clock and sleep till three in the morning, when it was time to start breakfast.

"The noon meal, when they ate like starved bears, was apt to be the most rushed. I've cooked many a dinner with the horses still hitched to the chuck wagon. I would drive up to water, trying also to get close to wood. The first thing after jumping down from the wagon I'd shovel me a trench, lay wood in it and then, as soon as the coals were ready, put the meat on — some roasting, some stewing in a pot. That time when I was feeding forty-five men at a single meal, I cooked a calf or a yearling every day, with plenty of beans and potatoes besides.

"Sometimes when I left camp in the morning I didn't know where the roundup herd would be held, only the vicinity, but the men never failed to find me. When there were lots of them, I'd place the vessels containing the food on my side of the fire trench. The men had to file by and reach over the coals in order to dip frijoles and other chuck out of pots. With the heat hitting them in the face, they'd dip fast and not overload their plates. They always got all they wanted to eat.

"There was a big fellow in the country named Theo Baughman. He pretended to be a trail guide but didn't know much. He was a kind of commission agent, too, representing traders in Caldwell, Kansas. Later he wrote a book called *The Oklahoma Scout*, most of it hot air. He weighed three hundred pounds. One day when I had dinner all ready for my outfit of thirteen men, here rode Baughman into camp. I offered him coffee and, believe me or not, he dragged a gallon coffee pot out of the fire, boiling hot and full, and drank it dry.

"A lot of those Texas fellers would drink coffee boiling off the fire that way. They never mixed their whiskey either. When a man ran with cowboys in those days he almost had to drink. I wasn't a drinker and didn't run with them much.

"One time down in the Cheyenne country I had supper all ready when the outfit rode in, and just about the time they started to eat, here showed up three Cheyenne Indians. 'Let 'em have what they want,' the boss said. I was against such doings but followed orders. The Indians hadn't more than filled up when here showed up three more.

" 'Go on, give 'em something,' the boss said.

" 'No, I won't do it,' I said. 'I'm not hired to cook for Cheyennes. I've got just enough food here for the outfit and if the Indians eat it up, the boys won't get any.'

" 'But we've got to treat those Indians easy,' the boss argued. 'If we don't, they'll stampede our herd to hell.'

" 'Well, by God, you got thirteen men and all of 'em armed,' I said. 'If they can't stand off Indians, you'd better quit. I am not going to sit up all night cooking for Indians.'

"By this time four or five more Indians were coming over the hill. They reminded me of buzzards circling in over a dead cow that one has spotted. Three Cheyennes had already eaten, and three more were wading in. 'Get out of here,' I yelled, and I went after them with a butcher knife. 'White man eat first. If anything left, Indian eat.' They moved out and the white men ate. Nothing was left for Chuckaway John.

"When we swam rivers, I caulked the cracks in the wagon bed and then laced ropes back and forth from the bows, making a kind of basket as high as the sideboards. I piled bedding, flour and other perishable stuff on this lacing, a wagon sheet or a tarpaulin under them. It didn't hurt if the bacon, axle grease, lard, and such things got wet. A dry bed and decent chuck was what men valued — not style."

Many a cowboy selected the outfit to work for by the reputation of its wagon. The cook could make it home. If he was good-natured, he applied kerosene oil, kept for his lantern, to any man's cuts and bruises. He usually had a corner in his box for Epsom salts, calomel, arnica salve, Mustang Liniment and quinine. Some Mexican and Negro cooks seemed to be providers by nature. A *cocinero* on La Parra ranch, alongside the King Ranch, led a gentle cow behind his wagon to provide milk for the boss's coffee. He kept a pair of bantam chickens with the wagon and often the boss had an egg for breakfast.

John Young used to tell of a musical Negro cook named Sam. One night soon after starting north from the coast with a herd, Sam left his banjo exposed and a cowboy stepped on it accidentally, demolishing it. The cowboys chipped in and at the first town they came to bought a fiddle. Whenever he got a chance, Sam would pick "Green corn, green corn, bring along the demijohn" on his fiddle. He picked other tunes, chanting the words.

Sam was in glory in a game country. He might have fried wild turkey, antelope steaks and roast calf ribs some night when the hands came in wolf-hungry from all-day riding and fasting. As soon as they unsaddled, Sam would say, "Boys, wash yer faces and comb yer hairs and spruce up lak ye was going to a wedding. I'se got a reg'lar wedding feast prepared. It's a wedding o' dinner and supper. Come 'long, come 'long, while she's juicy and hot."

I can't leave out Frank Smith, the cook who lived on in Ab Blocker's memory. He had saved money and made it breed while he cooked for railroad construction crews in California. He had cooked in Montana. When he began with the Blockers at Austin, Texas, he loaned John Blocker $4,000 at ten per cent interest. Year after year he went up the trail with herds that Ab Blocker bossed. He always sided with him in any difference with a cow hand or with an outsider; he always saw that his own men were fed, no matter how many strangers invited hospitality. Ab Blocker always backed him. "There are no poor soldiers," Napoleon said. "There are only poor generals."

"Once," Ab Blocker loved to recall, "I was talking to Frank Smith in camp about some feller that ought to have been hung before he was born. 'Damn him,' I says. 'Yes, damn him,' Frank Smith says, 'and damn any man that wouldn't burn the shirt off his own back to make a light at midnight to damn him by some more.' Oh, he was loyal."

One early morning in the Indian Territory, before the herd had been thrown on the trail, two strangers with forty or fifty horses came by the Blocker camp. One rode over to the chuck wagon and asked for some bacon, bread, and coffee.

"Where did you get them horses?" Frank Smith asked.

"None of your god-damned business."

"Then it's none of my god-damned business to give you coffee, bread, and bacon. I asked you where you got them horses."

"I don't know as I want to say," returned the stranger, not quite so proud.

"Then I don't know as I want to give you coffee, bread, and bacon," the cook answered back. "I asked you where you got them horses."

"Well, if you have to know," confessed the stranger, "we stole 'em from Caddo Indians and we're headed for Texas."

"Why in the hell didn't you say so at first?" Ab Blocker's cook ejaculated in his most cordial manner. "Get down and gimme that morral and I'll chock it full of bread, bacon, and coffee. Come on and eat breakfast. I'll help any man steal from Indians or the gover'ment.

When Frank Smith loaded his wagon with provisions, the bill had to be charged to "Smith and Blocker." He bought in wholesale quantities and generally inveigled the storekeeper out of a jug of whiskey for a "pilon." This he kept against the rainy day sure to come. Drinking in camp was against the rules, but after a night-long storm of cold and rain during which every man, no change of the guard, rode holding the cattle, Smith doled out to each a half cup of the whiskey. If there was enough, he would occasionally favor the boss. After making his fire and getting breakfast under way, long before daylight, he would arouse him with a cup of hot coffee diluted by half as much whiskey.

"Here, Ab," he would say, "put this under your belt and then call them hard-working devils to get up." Though Irish, he hardly ever took a drink himself. "The memories of that laced coffee will last as long as I last," Ab Blocker used to say.

A good cook left a good taste to linger long. It belongs with memories of riders who stayed with the herd.

11
Old Igo's Bookkeeping

B EFORE THE BIG breakup after World War I, cattlemen who operated on borrowed money were great hands
for "going in pardners." Speculative buyers and sellers, big
movers of livestock, always moving about themselves, inclined more to partnership deals than did settled-down
ranchers who sold only what they raised, culling out aging
cows and bulls. Many money borrowers went on each other's
notes as readily as they threw in with each other to work cattle. Yet they were slow to organize, and for years after they
did combine into cattlemen's associations opposed railroad
corporations for charging high freight rates and packing
houses for, allegedly, keeping the price of cattle down.

Some cowmen stood behind each other out of friendship
beyond business dealings. Los Ojuelos is down country from
Laredo. *Ojuelos* means *springs*. Here was the only natural
watering for long stretches between the Nueces River and the
Rio Grande. Don Eusebio Garcia's people had owned the
hacienda for generations. He owned it free of mortgage. He
never speculated.

His friend Tom Coleman did. His far-spreading Callaghan ranch made the two neighbors. As Captain Bill (William Warren) Sterling tells in *Trails and Trials of a Texas Ranger,* the two men while out in a Callaghan pasture one day got to speculating on the chance of striking oil. In their region no well was yet producing oil. They agreed, as owners of land still agree, that a few oil wells would be mighty handy in helping a rancher pull through drouths, die-ups and panics.

"I'll tell you what let's do," Tom Coleman said. "If I strike oil on the Callaghan, I'll give you a lease on forty acres of proven ground. If you strike oil on Los Ojuelos, you'll give me a lease on forty acres of proven ground."

"Hecho" (it is done), replied Don Eusebio.

The agreement was not put into writing. To be factual, Coleman owned less than a half interest in the Callaghan, though he was wholly manager. In the great slump of the 1920's he went under. About the same time an oil field was brought in on Los Ojuelos ranch.

Now to quote Bill Sterling. "In 1923 I drove Don Tomás Coleman and Don Eusebio Garcia out to look at the Coleman oil wells on forty acres of Garcia land. Don Tomás said that the money he and his family were living on at the time came from wells that he owned through the word of a friend." A few months later Tom Coleman was dead.

A few partnerships included everything that each man made and spent. "How do you and your pardner keep your accounts straight?" a banker asked a cowman. "Oh, it figures out about square, I guess. Jim smokes and I wear socks."

For years the bother of keeping books as much as sending checks to the Internal Revenue Department made little owners as well as big ones grumble at the income tax. Generations coming on now will never know, except by hearsay, how simple account-keeping used to be. In 1895 the Supreme Court declared an income tax unconstitutional. In 1913 an amendment to the Constitution vetoed the Supreme Court veto and the income tax began operating. It was as mild as a sucking dove. Before that anybody who kept books kept them for his own benefit and not for the benefit of the government. Few farmers and ranchmen bothered with ledgers except to keep up with hired help.

Back in trail-driving days Ike Pryor got him a bookkeeper at $60 a month and a set of ledgers. He had cattle by the tens of thousands on the trail, was grazing other thousands in three or four states, owned stock in loan companies, was doing big business. He became, in fact, a businessman at a time when few cowmen were.

John R. Blocker was not, though he had as many herds on the trails and owed as much to livestock commission companies and banks as any other cowman. One fall, after Ike Pryor had figured out neat profits over the year's business and was feeling mighty pleased with himself, he met John Blocker.

"John," he said, "you ought to get a bookkeeper. I've tried out one this year. You have no idea how much trouble it saves and how much help it is to a man's business."

"Maybe so, maybe so," John Blocker replied. The next day he changed vests but forgot to take his account book out of the old one's pocket. He was put out considerably when he missed it and could not square accounts readily with a trail boss back from Kansas. A day or two later he had trouble locating the stubs of a checkbook. He went over to the Alamo Business College and hired on part time a young man about to graduate. He had no idea of opening an office, but he arranged for a table and a chair in the quarters of a livestock commission company with which he did business. He gave the young bookkeeper six dollars, told him to buy all the ink, pencils, pen points, paper and account books he needed, and said he'd meet him after breakfast the next morning.

The young man was on hand promptly, his office supplies wrapped in brown paper.

"Now what do we do?" John Blocker asked.

"First thing, I'll have to make out an inventory of your assets," the bookkeeper responded.

John Blocker itemized the cattle he had at the Piedra Blanca Ranch in Mexico, the she stuff he had in different brands, each mortgaged to a separate loan company, at the Chupadera down in the brush country, the steers he was wintering in Montana, and so on.

"We ought to put in the saddle horses and wagons and land too," the bookkeeper suggested. Then he discovered that some of his employer's business was on a partnership basis. He had to backtrack on various entries.

"My name is on all the notes anyhow," John Blocker said, "and so there's no use being too particular about the pardnerships."

"It's these notes and liabilities that we've got to go into now, Mr. Blocker," the bookkeeper informed him.

"Oh, never mind the liabilities," John Blocker said, getting up and making a sniff as if he smelled coffee. "The banks and loan companies always notify me when interest is due and I have to renew a note. I'll be contracting for more stuff soon, and I'll let you know so you can put it on the books."

John Blocker felt the little account book in his vest pocket and wasn't sure he had done a wise thing in hiring a book-keeper.

The late Herbert L. Kokernot of San Antonio — a civilized cowman and businessman — gave me the following account of bookkeeping without books. In the year 1900 he went to Lubbock County to buy out the Iowa Land and Cattle Company's holdings. The land was only loosely fenced and was watered only by the Yellow House Canyon, along the meanderings of which it lay. Intermixed with it were forty sections controlled by Green Igo and James R. Kerlin.

As he intended to put down wells and otherwise improve his range, it was to Kokernot's interest to get control of the forty sections. Igo and Kerlin knew this as acutely as he knew it and held out for a stiff price. They had been in the country a long time, having come there when the nearest trading point was Colorado City, more than a hundred miles to the southeast. The nearest railroad to Lubbock was still a hundred miles away, at Canyon.

In 1903 a banker in Lubbock secured an option on the forty sections controlled by Igo and Kerlin and advised Herbert Kokernot to come up if he still wanted to buy.

Kokernot lost no time, rode as far as he could on the train, and then finished the trip by stage. He wanted to close the deal at once, and arranged with the banker to take up the option and get the two cowmen into the bank. They lived within reach of Lubbock.

When they came to the bank and saw that their buyer was Kokernot, they had a wilted look but were ready to fulfill their contract. Kokernot was to pay $3 an acre for the forty sections, all in Kerlin's name, and $20 around for his bulls and cows, calves thrown in, and $12 around for heifer yearlings. Kerlin was to move his steers over into New Mexico, along with five or six thousand cattle that Igo owned and was not selling.

But Igo and Kerlin were not at all equal owners in the property to be conveyed. Before Kokernot could settle with them, each separately, they had to settle with each other, and they told him he would have to do the figuring for them. Neither could read or write; neither could figure except in his head, though it turned out that each had a mighty good head. They had been partners for twelve years, and during all that time neither had put down a figure on paper, balanced debits and credits, come to any kind of settlement with each other.

Kokernot got them off in a back room at a table, took pencil and paper, and after an understanding of their agreements with each other began to set down figures. He took up their accounts year by year, calling first on Igo for his memories and then on Kerlin. Neither contradicted the other a single time; each confirmed the other on every item. For some years there were twelve or fifteen items to put down; for other years twenty or thirty.

In 1891, as the non-bookkeeping story unfolded, Jim Kerlin had under lease several sections belonging to the Iowa Land and Cattle Company and four leagues of school land belonging to San Augustine County. His leases were at the rate of 3 cents an acre per annum. He owned a few isolated sections of land. He controlled some other land that was rent free, having in all between sixty-five and seventy thousand acres. He had seas of grass but owned only three hundred head of cattle to eat it.

Thus he stood in 1891 when he made a trade with Green Igo to pasture five thousand stock cattle at the rate of 75 cents a head for each animal taken out in any given year, the rate to apply to the increase of Igo's cows as well as to the original stock. If Igo kept a cow on the range for ten years and then sold her off, he would pay only the 75 cents; for any yearling or other offspring of hers that he sold off he would pay the 75 cents. His brand was I G O.

Kerlin was as short on money as he was on cattle. Igo was as long on money as Kerlin was on grass. Igo had agreed to furnish money for paying the land leases, also for purchase of any land that Kerlin made during their partnership, also for running expenses. At the same time he sold Kerlin five hundred cows on credit at $12 around. Kerlin was to pay ten per cent interest on all money owing to Igo, compounded annually. Finally, Igo was to have bed and board at Kerlin's ranch house, paying $10 a month.

Igo liked fried chicken and encouraged Kerlin to buy a few hens. In the year 1891 — as the accounts were pulled up out of memory for settlement in 1903 — Kerlin bought a dozen chickens, including a rooster, for which Igo advanced the money. He bought a new saddle and some saddle horses, paid for by Igo. He bought a section or two of land, for which Igo advanced the money.

At the end of the first year, according to the agreeing memories of the partners, Kerlin owed Igo around $9,500. Interest on that at ten per cent would be $950, which, added to the principal, made a debt of $10,450 to start the year 1892 with.

In that year Igo took out six hundred yearlings, credited Kerlin's debt with $450 for their pasturage and advanced money for the purchase of some more land at from $250 to $350 a section — the average price, less than fifty cents an acre. In that year also Igo bought some pigs for Kerlin in Colorado City, also four loads of groceries and about a hundred spools of barbed wire, also two bolts of calico desired by Kerlin's wife.

Thus, adding and subtracting for each year and totaling up the interest, Herbert Kokernot made out the accounts from the memories of the partners. One year when Kerlin drove a herd of yearlings to Canyon for delivery, Igo paid off all the hands. Another year, he bought lumber to add a room to Kerlin's house. Igo kept advancing money for Kerlin to buy sections of land. And all the time old Ten Per Cent kept on working as unsleepingly and as unswervingly, day and night, as the Big Dipper swings around the North Star.

Finally, they came down to the year 1903. It was August 10 when Kokernot made out his checks to the two men. Igo's was for approximately $75,000. Kerlin, who had title to all the forty sections of land — twenty-five thousand six hundred acres at $3 an acre — got a check for around $12,000 — just about the value of the cattle he delivered to Kokernot.

In his talk Igo never referred to himself in the first person. He always said "Old Igo." Invariably he called James Kerlin, his partner, "Honey Jeemes."

After Kokernot had signed the checks and handed them over, he said, "Well, Mr. Igo, what are you going to do with all that money?"

"Old Igo," came the reply, "is going back to Kentucky, where he was born and bred. He's going to buy hisself a little house, some yaller-legged chickens and a barrel of whiskey. He's going to set in the shade and eat them yaller-legged chickens and drink that whiskey out of the barrel in a tin cup. Yas, sir, Old Igo's going to enjoy the fruits of his labors."

Himself a part of the chronicle, Herbert Kokernot went on, "I rushed back home to beat the check to the bank and called on my banker for a loan of $50,000. 'When are you going to want it?' he asked. 'I've already spent it,' I said, and to my relief was given a note to sign.

"I was very busy, away from home all the rest of the summer. In September I went to the bank and found a balance of around $75,000 in my favor. The Igo check had not come in. Another month passed and still it had not come in. I began to wonder if something had happened to Old Igo. The grass on the south plains had been cured by frost before I got out to Lubbock. There I ran into Igo the first thing.

" 'What are you doing with yourself?' I asked.

" 'Old Igo is doing jest what he said he was a-going to do,' came back the reply. 'Old Igo's been to Kentucky.'

" 'What has Old Igo done with that check for $75,000?'

" 'Old Igo hasn't had no need fer that money. He's still got it.' "

From his inside coat pocket he pulled out a stout wallet worn at the edges, soiled from sweat and dirt. The check lay between a stack of bills. He extracted it. Holding it between two fingers, he assured Herbert Kokernot, "Don't be skeered Old Igo's going to lose it."

About December he cashed it.

Grandpa Dubose used to sum up the abilities of a man by saying he could "read, write and recollect." Old Igo could merely recollect. In addition to his partnership business with

"Honey Jeemes" Kerlin, he managed the adjoining Z Bar L Ranch for Major W. W. Watts of Kentucky. According to a written contract with Major Watts, he got $10 a month, "jest to keep Old Igo in terbaccer and things like that," and ten per cent of the grazing rights of the Z Bar L range. He bought and sold the Z Bar L cattle.

When he bought a herd, he customarily topped out ten per cent of the best cattle, paying for them himself, then branded them in his I G O brand and turned them loose with the others, in order to graze the ten per cent of Z Bar L grass to which he was entitled. When he sold cattle branded Z Bar L, he sold his also, giving the buyer the customary ten per cent cut. Inasmuch as his own cattle were the tops to begin with, one was seldom cut back.

Finally Major Watts got tired of this kind of management and let Igo go. His new manager did not get along so well. Cow thieves lurked over the ranges waiting for a chance to grab. The Z Bar L ranch house of logs had numerous bullet holes in it. Showing them to Kokernot, Igo laughed. The shooters were pecking after Major Watts, he said. After a year or two of experimenting with other managers, Major Watts got hold of Igo again.

"Green," he said, "you have topped my cattle. You work yours at my expense. You steal from me in every way, direct and indirect, that you can get around. If you will promise not to steal in any other ways than the ways I'm used to, I'll take you back as manager on the old basis of $10 a month and the use of ten per cent of the range."

"Major Watts," Igo solemnly answered, "Old Igo can't make no promises not to steal, but tell you what. Old Igo will promise to make you more money than anybody else you can get and to keep the damned thieves off your cattle."

Old Igo went back as manager for the Z Bar L. He didn't keep books of any kind. He recollected.

12

Man and Horse

MY FATHER BEGAN trading in horses when quite young. He drove horses to Kansas, sold others off his own ranch to be shipped east. In the early 1880's he turned to cattle, mostly steers. He rode good horses, cared for them well, but seemed as I remember to have little sentiment for them, unless for a pair of bay buggy horses named Snip and Snap, for a Thoroughbred stallion named Dandy, and for Old Baldy, the horse on which three of his children learned to ride. He generally sold off saddle horses grown too stiff to run cattle on. To me, making a plow horse out of any honest cow horse, especially one stove-up from thorns and knocks received in brush work after cattle, seemed — and still seems — heartless, callous, unimaginative. When as a boy I protested against selling off certain horses to plow for Mississippi share-croppers, Papa replied, "Never marry yourself to a horse."

He was public-spirited, generally kind to animals, but had no sense of obligation to the shiftless or the unruly among men or horses. Had he known William Wordsworth, he might have read aloud "Ode to Duty" — Stern Lawgiver! — to the Sunday school he established in a schoolhouse on the ranch. He did not believe in sparing the rod. I remember a balky horse named Hippy that he threw down with a rope at a live oak tree in front of the crib and lashed with a cow whip. This stubborn animal of Spanish blood turned out to be the best-bottomed cow horse I have known. He never balked again.

A young Mexican named Policarpo came to our ranch from down the country — down towards the Rio Grande — one fall looking for work. He ate in the kitchen, slept in the commodious barn, was not much interested in working, got $15 a month — standard wages. Papa sold him a gray *potro* he fancied — for $15, as I recollect. He called the *potro* Catarino Garza, the name of his hero, which dates him. In 1891 Catarino Garza undertook to raise, from the Texas side of the Rio Grande, a revolution against President Porfirio Díaz of Mexico. He was chased out of the country by American cavalry aided by Texas Rangers. Richard Harding Davis got near enough to the chase to put a touch of it in *The West from a Car Window*. When in 1904 I went to Alice, Texas, to live with my grandmother while going to high school, Grandpa Dubose, her husband, took me with him in a buggy one Saturday to Palito Blanco, a Mexican rancheria about fourteen miles away, where Catarino Garza had established a revolutionary newspaper and where his widow still lived. We saw her at dinner. It was said that she had not been outside the yard since his disappearance and that she was still expecting him. She wore a black mantilla over her black hair.

It was several years before my romantic encounter that Policarpo roped his *potro* named Catarino and managed to put a *bosal* on him — a half hitch around his nose — and to stroke his head. Papa said he was spoiling the horse, would

A vaquero of the Brush Country, southwest Texas, 1937.

probably try to put diapers on him. One day while the *potro* was in the pen with some other wild horses, Policarpo, unable to rope him by the head, decided to *mangana* — forefoot — him, thus throw him down and get a hackamore (headstall) and saddle on him. He cast his loop while the horse was running past, caught him by the forefeet, brought him to the earth — and broke his neck.

Papa had a horse-breaker named José María gentle any *potros* he expected to keep. Pockmarked, heavy-set, he would come to the ranch, lead a *potro* away with a hackamore, and in a few weeks bring him back, bridlewise and no longer pitching under the saddle. The horse had been staked out — tethered — most of the time and looked ga'nt. The horse-breaker received five dollars for his services. One time he broke the neck of a *potro* belonging to me and did not receive anything for his services.

A man's sentiment for an animal does not determine his character. In O. Henry's "The Theory and the Hound," a sheriff from Kentucky must decide which of two Americans selling coconuts in a certain tropical port tortured and killed his wife in Kentucky. While he drinks with them, a house dog comes in. He kicks it. One of the men objects vehemently. "Hound-lover and woman-killer," the sheriff says as he handcuffs him.

Billy the Kid had a strong feeling for a horse named Don, which in 1881 he stole in order to flee a death sentence and rode to Pete Maxwell's house in Fort Sumner, New Mexico, ten hours away. He considered that he had ruined the horse for life and got Maxwell to promise to pay the owner for him and care for him permanently. In the very room where he and Maxwell talked, Sheriff Pat Garrett killed Billy the Kid. Not long afterward Maxwell sold his ranch and all the cattle and horses in his brand, range delivery, to a combination of cattle companies.

One of them, the New England Live Stock Company, was managed by Jack Potter, who headquartered near Fort Sumner and who told me this story. Only after the trade was closed did Pete Maxwell recall his promise to keep Don. Jack Potter could not see his way clear to release the horse but agreed to keep him in his own mount. Don's looks had not been impaired. He was good to ride so long as he was not pushed. Jack Potter soon had him hanging about camp, asking for sourdough biscuits and winning the favor of cook and cowhands. He kept him for six years until water from a strongly mineralized spring killed him. After all, Billy the Kid's regard of a horse was a momentary whim.

A Wyoming rancher named Tisdale showed Owen Wister another kind of whim. This was in 1891, eleven years before Wister's *The Virginian*, most famous of all cowboy romances, came out. A chapter in the novel sets Tisdale down, under the name of Balaam, as a brute, but his brutality is modified. The facts are detailed in a journal published in 1958 under the title of *Owen Wister Out West*.

When Tisdale's horse gave out under him on a chase up and down mountains after a pair of runaways, he "dismounted and kicked his poor quiet beast . . . He kicked its ribs, its legs, its jaw," and "red foam" ran from the bit. Finally he mounted and started on, beating the horse with fists and heels. It could make no headway, stopped, too weak to move. "I saw Tisdale lean forward with his arm down on its forehead," Wister proceeds. "Suddenly the horse sank, pinning him to the ground. He could not release himself, and I ran across to him and found only his leg caught. So I lifted the horse and he got his leg out. I asked him if he was hurt. He said no and got up, adding, 'I've got one eye out all right.' The horse turned where he lay, and I caught sight of his face, where there was no longer any left eye, but only a sinkhole of blood."

Joe Neal of Live Oak County favored Rattler, the gift of a dead friend. Rattler had a very gentle disposition. Neal would not allow any other man to ride him, though he seldom rode him himself. One day a neighboring ranchman sent over to borrow a horse for a visiting lady to ride. His own horses were all too skittish. Neal was away. John Rigby, his boss, sent Rattler. Two weeks later Rigby was at the neighbor's ranch and noticed Rattler standing under a tree with a wet blanket on his back. He raised the blanket and saw a big rising on the horse's loin. He lanced it.

"Rattler's back hurts," the lady, who had come out, said. She did not know that the low seat of her sidesaddle had caused what might become a setfast.

"I'll take Rattler home and cure him," John Rigby said. He staked Rattler on bottom grass near his camp. Before long Joe Neal came prowling around and saw the horse. "A lady done that," Rigby explained.

"Well, if a lady done it, it's all right. A lady can have anything of mine she wants and you did right lending her Rattler."

But the lady had fallen in love with Rattler. She wanted to buy him to take back to New York. He was not worth more than seventy-five dollars. A hundred would have been high

His face as yet unmarked by life, he thinks it will be easy to ride anywhere. (Picture made in San Antonio in the 1880's.)

for him. She offered five hundred. Joe Neal merely said, "The horse is not for sale. A friend gave him to me."

Horse intelligence is a fact, but no horse can think. Taking a shortcut across a pasture instead of following a road around it does not require thought; it requires the judgment exercised by a mule in corkscrewing up and down mountains instead of trying to follow a beeline across them. The bee instinct is for its own mode of travel; the equine instinct is for another. I have seen a stallion's instinct for a mare hang him in a barbed wire fence, one foot cut half off. Instinct is not reasoning; an earthworm has instinct. "A horse ain't got much sense. A mule has more sense. A mule will take care of you as well as of himself." William Faulkner made this observation after a horse threw him, injuring his back severely, not long before he died in 1962.

Domesticated horses come to people more for something to eat or for something else they desire than out of affection. Their loyalties and hunger for human companionship are not nearly so marked as in dogs. If Sonny, a Kansas ranch boy, took an ear of corn into the pasture, Eagle would come to him at once, eat the corn and accept petting as gently as a post. If Sonny took a bridle in one hand and an ear of corn in the other, Eagle would gallop away and keep on evading approach. The horse was finally given to a family who kept him in a forty-acre pasture with a milch cow. Every evening two little girls would coax Eagle into the pen and then ride him double to drive in the cow. Then he was always given a generous supper of oats. The reward brought him in. Before long he figured out the false motion in getting it: about five o'clock he by himself would drive the cow into the barn and then wait for his oats.

Cow People

Dandy, our Thoroughbred stallion, was a gentleman by nature, elated under new, clean, bright harness, proudstepping whether hitched to buggy or under saddle. He had a winsome disposition. We were all fond of him. Sometimes he had corn for breakfast and supper when no other horse got it. One day my mother missed Henry, the youngest son of the family, probably not more than two years old at the time. She looked outside and saw Dandy shoving him with a hind foot out of a stall in which he was eating hay. Henry had toddled into the stall. Dandy didn't want to step on him or hurt him. A vicious horse might have kicked the little intruder. Dandy showed gentleness and intelligence in merely shoving him out of the stall, but from my understanding of what thought is, he did not think. Thought that liberates the minds of a few individuals and meets change is beyond either charity or cunning.

In tradition the cutting horse comes it proud over all other range horses. He has "cow sense" as well as horse sense, keeps calm, never excites cattle. "As smart as a cutting horse" runs an old phrase of the range, meaning as smart as a Philadelphia lawyer and a little smarter than a steel trap. An extra-smart cutting horse "can do everything but talk Mexican," and he understands that. He's as quick as greased lightning; he can turn on a two-bit piece and give back fifteen cents in change. "If we were cutting yearlings out of a mixed herd," Arthur Howard of the Shoe Bars used to tell, "all I had to do was show Old Harvey the first one. After we brought it out, Old Harvey would go back and bring out the others, one by one, until the herd was clean. I never tried it, but I wonder if he wouldn't have worked just about as well if I had stepped out of the saddle and let him cut by himself. He was so proud

[162]

of his skill that he didn't like me to pull on the bridle reins. If I did, he'd shake his head to say, 'No butting in' — just as any good hand does not want to be told to do what he is already doing. I never got off Old Harvey that he didn't turn his head and nudge me on the shoulder as if to say we had done a good job."

An understanding rider can transfer confidence to his horse, pump power into him; the horse can do the same for a rider. When a man brags on his horse, he may be bragging on himself; on the other hand, when he brags on himself, he may be ignoring what is due his horse. Joe Merrick used to give a cutting horse credit for being able to count. He said that every time he worked an animal out of the herd, Red Bird would give a little nicker. One day Merrick bet that Red Bird would bring out a jack rabbit dodging around in the herd — something as rare as a headless horseman. "I rode him in," he said, "showed him the rabbit and made a motion or two after it, the same as starting out a cow. Then I pulled the bridle off. Red Bird worked that jack rabbit clear of the herd without stirring up the cattle at all."

George Bosler of Nebraska won distinction as owner of the Bosler Blue, a steel-blue cutting horse. One spring Buffalo Bill Cody brought a jug of corn whiskey to a roundup and got somewhat hilarious with Bosler. Several owners were cutting their cattle out of the main herd and holding them in small bunches. Bosler asserted that Old Blue knew his owner's brands and did not need anybody to guide him in picking out a Bosler animal. He rode him into the herd, pulled the bridle off, and hung it on the saddle horn. Old Blue walked around among the cattle until he came to a big wild steer wearing Bosler's brand. Then he began to ease it out toward the cut. The steer didn't want to leave the herd, at the edge turned back to fight. "Old Blue sprang at him, threw his head across the steer's neck, and with shoulder against the steer pushed him out and over to the Bosler bunch." The roundup men stopped to watch the performance, all agreeing that not another horse in the world could do what they had seen. A good cow horse was worth about fifty dollars. Dennis Sheedy, one of the noted cowmen of the West, offered Bosler one thousand for Old Blue and was turned down.

Nobody could now have the experience Asa Jones has had with horses: the horses no longer exist; uses for them have vanished. He used to buy and sell them from south Texas and Mexico by the thousands. He has ridden hundreds and has broken more young ones than most cowmen have ridden. He would be lost without a pocket knife. In a hospital at eighty-three he pulled out his pocketknife to carve a steak. Born in 1880, he was rustling for himself and his mother by the time he was fifteen. When seventeen, with six dollars and a little change in his pocket, he headed his horse for the far West. After riding over six hundred miles, he got a job under Barnes Tillous on the Quien Sabe Ranch south of Midland, Texas — then a cow village.

They got to camp about dark. Tillous roped out a little black horse with white face and feet and said, "This is Polecat. He's your night horse. You'll have to get that big Negro over there to help you saddle him." There were about 125 horses in the remuda. Asa, small in size, kept close to the campfire until the last man rolled into his suggans. Then Asa spread down his saddle blanket and wrapped up in the one thin south Texas blanket he had brought tied to the back of

MARCUS SNYDER, Texan, ranching in Montana, 1947. Descendant of noted cowmen and trail drivers, he knew cow nature as well as he knew the cattle business, was at ease in the financial world, was at home on a horse.

his saddle. A norther was blowing and there was no shelter from it.

About two weeks later Rufe Moore, general manager, drove into camp in a buckboard, carrying a big roll of bedding. To quote Asa Jones, "He was a typical old-time south Texas ranchman. We all sat around the campfire after supper, joking and laughing till finally every hand but me turned in. Mr. Moore rolled out his bedding and was arranging it on the ground when I got my blanket and saddle blanket out and rolled up by the fire. Mr. Moore asked, 'Kid, is that all the bed you have?' I said, 'Yes, sir. But I don't need a lot of bedding.' Then he asked me if I had been with the outfit ever since it started and I told him I had.

" 'And none of them has ever asked you to sleep with him?' he asked. I said, 'No, sir.' He looked surprised and said: 'Then, by God, you crawl in with old Rufe Moore. He's got enough bed for two and no kid sleeps cold in this outfit.' Believe me, no kid was ever more grateful for a good night's sleep, and from then on I shared his bed and I love him to this day for that kindness."

In 1915, as Asa wrote me, he bought a string of Spanish horses from across the Rio Grande and put them on his Bullis Gap Ranch in the Big Bend country. One was a little, ornery-looking, cat-hammed, slab-sided three-year-old brown. By the next spring he had filled out somewhat, and when the vaqueros went to breaking horses they said he was the meanest of the lot. He bit, kicked, and pitched like flashes of lightning. He would snort when he saw a man walk into the corral with a rope. If while saddled he saw a stray rider coming or saw anything else out of the ordinary, he would snort in the same way. That's how he got the name Snorter.

Mexican vaquero on a dun horse of Spanish blood. (San Antonio Viejo Ranch, southwest Texas, 1939.)

Asa Jones never paid much attention to him until he and some other men were running wild range horses to pen them. His horse played out, and while he was falling behind a young cowboy riding Snorter caught up with him. Snorter was not panting. He was still not broke to the bridle and wore a hackamore with reins attached to it.

"Let's change horses, if you don't mind," Asa Jones suggested.

They changed saddles and Asa got on the little bronc. Guiding him with the hackamore, he took out after the wild bunch, ran them down and headed them for the pens. "That little bronc seemed to know as well as I knew what we were doing and to be proud of helping do it," Asa says. "When we got in that evening, I told the boys to cut Snorter into my string of saddle horses. After that very few cowboys ever saddled him or rode him."

As soon as Snorter was bridlewise, Asa began cutting cattle on him. This was long before one could call him a "gentle saddle horse." For a long time he would try to kick and pitch every time he got a chance. But "when he felt me solid on his back," Asa says, "he was the most biddable horse I ever rode. I was handling thousands of cattle at this time, and before long I was using Snorter only as a cutting horse. All you had to do in a herd was to show him the animal you wanted cut out. After that you could take the bridle off and close your eyes. He would work the animal to the edge of the herd without exciting the other cattle and deliver it to the cut.

"The year he was broke I married. Ten years later he was one of our family. In 1926 I was operating a spread of two hundred thousand acres, leased from the University of Texas, north of Sierra Blanca. One day my wife was on

Snorter at the tail end of a herd of steers we were rounding up. Not far from where she was riding, a big wild steer broke away for the brushy hills. Snorter darted after him. Mrs. Jones couldn't hold him and thought he was running away with her. She stayed on him, and after he had got around the steer and brought him back to the herd, he quieted down again into the gentleness of a lamb."

Another time at a roundup Asa Jones put his nine-year-old son, George Asa, on Snorter to help hold the herd while it was being shaped up for a buyer. Every time an animal broke away on his sector of the herd, Snorter would go after it and bring it in. After a while the buyer said to Asa Jones, "Is that kid back yonder yours?"

"Yes."

"Well, he's the best little cowboy I ever saw."

"I didn't tell him," says Asa, "that it was the horse and not the boy — the best cow horse and the best cutting horse either of us ever saw."

Years passed and Snorter was back on the ranch in the Big Bend, a large part of it fenced to hold sheep. When he got too stiff to cut on, Asa Jones set him free on a green mountain seep where he could always get fresh grass. One day while helping round up sheep, Mrs. Jones, riding behind the herd, saw Snorter coming. Whether he recognized her or not, he trotted alongside her mount. Then if a sheep turned back or veered off, Snorter got around it and put it back into the flock. He followed to the pens and then returned alone to his seep. At the age of twenty-seven he died on a trail leading from the seep to water.

"I never passed his bones without tears coming to my eyes," Asa Jones says.

There were, and still are, plenty of pitching broncs on ranches and plenty of bronc-busters, but rodeo displays of fiercely bucking horses, often trained to buck, by professionals give many spectators a false conception of the harmony between a good ranch hand and his mount. Many a professional rodeo rider would not be at home on any lone prairie or in any mesquite thicket. For all that, the contest between rider and bad horse belongs to range tradition.

Booger Red's baptismal name faded out of the popular mind, maybe out of his own. Before rodeos became organized, he went about the country with a wagon carrying bedding and grub and with a helper or two driving or leading several horses. He stopped at towns, barbecues, wherever an exhibition of riding might pay. I saw him at Georgetown, Texas, about 1906, while I was going to college. The fee for spectators might have been as high as fifty cents. I forget.

The firsthand narrative that follows came to me from Joseph J. Good, who matured as a Texas ranch hand and in time took to preaching and religious healing, California style. He was at the Fort Worth Stock Show about 1898 when he saw the horse and the man. At that time the arena was a patch of prairie on which some corrals had been built. The spectators were in buggies, on horses, on foot. There were no stands of seats. When a horse was let out of the corral, he had the whole country to pitch in.

Suddenly a dappled gray horse about fifteen and a half hands high, weighing around a thousand pounds, that had been roped inside the corral broke through or over the plank fence and was out where everybody could see him. But the

I. D. SCOGGINS, Snyder, Texas. Unlike present-day oil-rich cowmen of the country where he ranched, he voted the Democratic ticket all his life and respected the President. He was also director of a bank. His start with cattle was as a driver of oxen.

roper held on to the rope and with help soon choked the struggling horse down. Then a saddle was put on him while he was held down, men rolling and pulling him around so that it could be girthed up. A very young man, just a boy, got into the saddle, taking the reins as the horse was allowed to rise. In a flash the gray was upright. In another flash he had "bogged his head" and was pitching as hard as a cornered tiger fights for life. His motion was one jump forward and the next jump a zigzag in which he writhed all the muscles of his body.

That close-coupled body — short back, rounded hips, beautifully proportioned neck and legs — was magnificently muscled. The sun brought out the dapples in the animal's sleek gray. His mane and tail flowed with his powerful movements. His head, broad between the eyes, bore little resemblance to the jug-heads of some demented outlaws. He looked like a top cutting horse — except for the whites of his eyes.

As he pitched there on the Fort Worth prairie he seemed to put increasing power into his fierce zigzags, but the boy on his back kept a perfect seat, pulling hard on the reins for maybe forty feet. Then, as suddenly as if he had been shot by a bullet, he dropped down over the gray's left shoulder. By the time he reached the ground the gray had plunged forward far enough to kick him a full blow in the chest. He seemed with one movement to step on him and to kick him.

Among explanations that followed, one was that the left stirrup leather broke, another that the string lacing the stirrup leather broke. The way the rider fell indicated that something beyond the action of the horse had detached him suddenly from his firm position in the saddle. It was about

BOOGER RED (on the right, 1924). He made a record as a wild horse rider. With horses, a wagon and a helper or two, he rode over Texas and Oklahoma in the early part of this century, giving exhibitions.

ten o'clock in the morning when he fell. A horse-drawn ambulance took him to the hospital. The killer horse was caught and taken back to the corrals. The show went on. By eleven o'clock the rider was dead. During the morning the reputation of the gray horse spread — and grew — among the spectators milling around the arena. It was rumored that no man had ever been able to ride him to a standstill, that he had thrown them all, that this was the twenty-third man he had killed.

Among the riders present was Booger Red. He was approaching the peak of his riding career, though he was to be much more widely known. Certain men now approached him and asked him if he would ride the gray that afternoon. He said he would if they would make up a purse. The sun was straight up when four men on gentle horses started riding among the people with big Stetson hats held out for contributions. Dimes, quarters, half-dollars, silver dollars — dollar bills did not then circulate — were pitched into the hats from all sides until better than two gallons of silver had been collected.

Whatever the amount was, Booger Red earned it that afternoon. He mounted the gray near the corral. As soon as he was turned loose, the "man-killer," as he was now being called, started out in the one-jump-forward and zigzag-lunging style that had brought him victory a few hours before. After he had gone forward about a hundred yards in this way, he changed his style and went to fence-rowing. After the one-jump-forward, he would make a twisting turn first to the left and then to the right, bringing the side of his body within the turn so low that had Booger Red loosened his leg grip his foot could have almost touched the ground. Booger Red did not loosen anything.

When the gray started fence-rowing, he was headed east. After a jump in that direction, he would pitch crossways, headed north, and then twist back to the east and the next time pitch crossways to the south. He kept this up until he had pitched around and over maybe ten acres of land, covering much of it twice. The crowd followed the pitching horse, keeping back far enough not to interfere. He did not seem to notice them. All his attention was on the man fixed to his back and quirting him at every jump so as to keep in rhythm with his motions.

The gray made one last lunge and then set out on a bee-line run for the corral. "I was standing near the gate," Joseph J. Good wrote in the narrative he gave me, "when the horse of his own accord stopped right at it. Two men seized his ears, bridle and headstall and held him while Booger Red got down. Booger was so drained that he had to lean against the fence. The horse had pitched himself blind. He was led away, and I never heard what became of him. The worst pitching horse I ever saw and the best rider I ever saw were together that afternoon."

13

The Drouthed

FLORIDA GRAZES more cattle than Arizona, but what long ago came to be called "cattle country" is a land of not only little but varying rainfall. Land averaging twenty inches a year may get less than ten inches one year and thirty the next. Lots of cattle country averages no more than fifteen inches. Some good soil in desert spaces may be irrigated to grow feed, but the water comes from precipitation somewhere.

Nick Dunn, who belonged inside and out to ranching before barbed wire was invented, used to say, "With one good name and two good rains, I can borrow enough money to buy all the cattle in Nueces County."

Owners of ranches purchased with money from oil, gas, factories, city business and the like are not among the drouth-marked. Air-conditioning may erase the mark on town-dwellers in arid regions, but air-conditioning does not make grass grow. Flying cloud-seeders, Hopi Indians ceremonially dancing for rain while holding rattlesnakes between their teeth, Christians kneeling to pray for rain, all have proved no more effective than setting up a rain gauge in the Sahara Desert would be.

Charles M. Doughty's *Travels in Arabia Deserta* says more about lands and peoples of drouth than tons of scientific reports and myriads of novels heroizing "hard-bitten men." "It is a land that eateth up the inhabitants thereof," Doughty wrote. "I pray that nothing be looked for in this book but the seeing of a hungry man and the telling of a most weary man. The sun made me an Arab, but never warped me to Orientalism." Doughty was a great human being and a thinking scholar from moist, misty, green England. Wandering for what seemed an interminable time with Arabian nomads over their deserts, he was made into an Arab, not by human association, but by "the sun," by drouth.

Newspapers published in farm and ranch territory west of the 98th meridian headline dollar estimates of drouth and rain. The effect that prolonged drouth has upon people who live with it, resisting and shriveling in harmony with the vegetation of the land, cannot be measured by figures. Feed, mobility and other factors now prevent big die-ups, but not the effects of long unrelenting drouth upon the inner life. Look at the faces of people who belong elementally. They may not be sculptured by thought. They never evidence easy success. They reveal a profound chastening.

One drouth endurer of the 1890's had all his cattle mortgaged and no mortgage-holder was able or willing to advance more money for expenses. Every morning he sent his men out to skin dead cattle; every night he received a tally on the hides brought in. As regularly as it came he would say, "Thank God the hides ain't mortgaged." He could sell them for expense money.

One year down in the Brush Country the prickly pear wilted until it was moistureless. Singeing off the thorns with pearburners made it eatable to cattle but it became more and more foodless. Cattle were dying. There seemed to be no grass anywhere to move them to. Oscar Thompson had got his notes renewed; two or three times with increasing unwillingness one bank had advanced meager sums for running expenses.

He owed everybody he could owe, and everybody he owed was dunning him. For more than a year he had been unable to pay the Hebbronville merchant who supplied groceries, harness, kerosene for pearburners and other necessities. Merchants of ranch country in those days sold on credit — until their own ran out. One day Oscar Thompson drove to town, put his team in a livery stable and boarded the train for San Antonio. Maybe he could get one more advance from his chief mortgage holder. Anybody who saw him get off the train four days later would have sensed his failure. It was dark when he reached the ranch.

"I guess I better eat a little something," he said in a dispirited voice to Juan, the man cook.

"All right." Juan's voice was also dispirited.

Mr. Oscar went into the dining room, dimly lit by a kerosene lamp. The table was set. The water in the bean pot was too clear to be called bean soup. There was a little warmed-over cornbread. There was nothing else.

"Why didn't you cook salt pork with these beans, Juan?" Mr. Oscar asked, not in a reprimanding tone.

"*No hay.*" (There isn't any.)

"The coffee, Juan."

"*No hay.*"

"*No hay,*" Mr. Oscar echoed. "I told you before I left to hitch up the wagon and go to town for a load of groceries."

"Yes, Meester Oscar," Juan replied. "I hitch the horses to the wagon. I drive to the store. The owner he say he cannot sell without pay. You give me no money."

"All right, Juan," Mr. Oscar said, "all right. Everything has come out even. No grass, no water, no provisions, no sale for cattle, no money, no credit. For the first time in my life I see everything come out even — exactly even. No nothing."

The habit of scanning far away out in glaring sunlight gives the eyes of the scanner a different look from that of indoor lookers, whether at books, test tubes, counters, or customers. A man dry-farming or grazing livestock is always looking for rain signs. If no cloud is in sight, the hue of the sky, the phase of the moon, the direction of the wind may mean something.

George West, the biggest cowman in Live Oak County, could see a long way down the road, but he could not tell how long a drouth might last. He was a steer man, buying steer yearlings every spring and holding them until they matured. No "baby beef" for meat-eaters in those days, and a yearling was not a beef. During the great drouth of 1886-87, the George West ranch, on the Nueces River, was stocked with longhorned steers. The whole country had been fenced. There was no grass over which to drive herds to a railroad for shipping to northern grass. People in the Southwest did not at that time buy hay to feed cattle. A panic had killed all active demand for cattle.

The Nueces quit running; water stood only in holes. As grass, all dry, became less and less, steers went to dying. Mr.

George West equipped his hands with axes to carry on their saddles and told them to knock or chop off and bring in the left horn of every dead steer found. He had the horns piled in a stack next to the woodpile, keeping count of them. Many were very long, some wrinkled at the base by age. The stack grew taller and taller. Before the drouth broke the piled up horns numbered about three thousand, each representing a dead steer. Many carcasses in brush had not been found, even if dying bushes and mesquite trees, all dropping sparse leaves, left the bare ground more visible.

George West used to sit at night on the great mound of horns and scan the sky for a sign of rain. He had a saddled horse kept tied ready for him at night as well as by day. After scanning the skies from the elevation of horns, he would ride out on the ranch, listening to the coyotes barking at the carcasses on which they ate, listening to the silence, brooding, looking up at the skies with the quiet eyes of desperation. On all sides of his ungrassed land other land-dwellers, women as well as men, were watching for signs.

Drouth, like other soul-searing experiences, tempers a human being, brings him to accept what is. During one of the worst of drouths, George W. Saunders, for years president of the Old-Time Trail Drivers of Texas, said, "I'm just trying to keep bad from getting worse."

If they have water, cattle can survive for a long time on scant feed. When in 1906, the R. J. Dobie family moved from the ranch to Beeville, Texas, twenty-seven miles east, my mother said, "I'll never again have to listen to the bawling of thirsty cattle." No animal sound is more distressful, more agonizing, especially to an owner. Cattle never died of thirst with us as they did on the Tol McNeill ranch joining on the

Cowboy of Matador Ranch, northwest Texas, 1932. He was raised in the saddle, in a land frequently of little rain. Drouths and adherence to duty have marked his features.

west, on the Avaran Perez ranch farther on, and on many another ranch whose owners, unadapting to fences and lowering water levels, had not bored deep wells, put up big windmills, and with mules and scrapers dug pits in draws and mounded up earthen dams to hold water.

A cowman from the lower country whom I met in San Antonio in the late summer of 1924 said that he could not sleep. All night long in the hotel room he was hearing cows — more than a thousand that he owned — back home bawling for water. For decades cattle have brought prices that justify the cost of wells, enormous earthen tanks and dams across draws over the most arid lands.

Willie Hinnant lives on the ranch where he was born, cornering the ranch on which I was born about the same time. He remembers by date all the drouths of his lifetime, can give the day of the month as well as the year of many a rain. He likes to talk about rains. I have never known a man tempered by drouth to be loquacious; yet in time of drouth most drouth-stricken men talk about it and about other drouths; also, about rains.

"Dry."

"The lizards are drying up."

"I never saw it worse."

"You're apt to yet."

On a front gallery, facing south, two ranchers sat in silence for a while, looking out and away. A spasmodic flurry of wind made the windmill turn over about six times, and then it was motionless.

"Whirlwind," the first cowman commented, without bothering to gesture, for he knew the other had noticed.

"Seems to me I never heard dry weather locusts sizzling at

such a high pitch so late in the fall," the other commented.

"People say fall don't begin till the equinox," the first remarked.

"September is a fall month," the other said, not argumentatively. "It ought to rain in September."

"I guess we all ought to do things we don't do," was the only rejoinder.

"Reckon it would make any difference on the weather if we did do them?"

"Not a bit. There's not a truer saying in the Bible than the Lord sends rain on the just and the unjust alike. It pours down out in the ocean where neither the just nor the unjust exist. Elrich Dobie says that if it would rain on the land of the unjust what's left could be watered with a bucket."

"Joe," the first cowman spoke, "I'm looking for a sign."

"Well, Tom, you seen any?"

"No, but Bill Noble was by here yesterday and said a Mexican working for him said a rooster had been crowing earlier than usual for three mornings. He claimed that is a sign of change in the weather. I guess he just wanted to cheer Bill Noble up."

"It couldn't change to any drier. The President's calling for a change, I see. Talking may get it for him. It won't for us."

"I'll tell you, Joe," the cowman named Tom went on, "I don't put no more stock in these signs than I put in planting potatoes according to the moon. Still, signs are a kind of comfort sometimes. They're like the promises of politicians. They don't fool you, but they feed hope. When you're skinning cows that die bogged down in mud, you notice any coyote howling after sunup. That's the oldest sign of rain I know. I wouldn't bet a rusty fence staple on a coyote's knowing any more about when it's going to rain than I know, but his howl reminds us that it's never too late to hope."

"Even when it rains," Joe concluded, "we are not satisfied. You remember the pair of cowmen on Noah's Ark, along with all those other pairs. It rained for forty days and forty nights, and when the ark landed on Mount Ararat, the cowmen went out to look for good grass country for their pair of cattle. They could see the flood waters boiling down below them.

" 'It was a regular gully-washer here,' one said.

" 'Grass'll come along fine,' the other said, 'if we get another rain before a drouth sets in.' "

Dillard R. Fant, a great operator in his day, used to walk the floors of his Santa Rosa ranch at night, talking to himself. He'd say in a kind of moan, over and over, "My, my, ain't it dry. Oh, oh, oh." Then he'd whistle a long-drawn-out whistle, followed by groans and moans. Finally he'd call to the Mexican cook, "Pedro, a cup of coffee."

One time during a drouth that seemed unending, Jasper Miller, another character, went to visit him at the Santa Rosa. The Fant family was living in Alice. After the cowmen had talked about dry weather past and present for hours, they went to bed. Dillard R. Fant was soon up again, walking the floor. Jasper Miller heard him walking and carrying on and after a while got up to join him. They walked in opposite directions up and down the ranch gallery, and every time they passed each other Dillard R. Fant would say, "Jasper, don't you reckon it ain't ever going to rain again?" Finally he varied the saying with, "Well, Jasper, we'll break one drouth anyhow." He went into the dining room, got two clabber goblets, filled them with half whiskey and half water.

The Drouthed

One time two men from where the frogs holler went west of the Pecos River and took up four sections of state land. One soon surrendered to the perpetual drouth and went back to where it rains. The other stayed three years, proved up his title, and then went back home. There he met his old-time friend.

"What's the news out west of Pecos?" the friend asked.

"Oh, nothing much. Dry as usual — and the damned fools out there are still talking about when it's going to rain and expecting it."

People do not believe in praying for rain as much as they used to. Knowledge of scientific facts spreads, but feelings contrary to knowledge linger. My father was a praying man. Every night, as soon as Mama had, with the help of son, daughter or Mexican girl, washed supper dishes, he held family prayers, reading first, by light from a kerosene lamp, a chapter in the Bible and then kneeling down to pray aloud, all other members of the family kneeling also. But though the grass usually needed it, I never heard Papa pray for rain.

One cold, drizzly winter day we children grew tired of being shut in. We wanted the clouds to break so that we could break for the outdoors. My sister Fannie and I stood at the window looking out and said a rhyme learned I know not where:

> Rain, rain, go to Spain
> And never come back again.

Repeating and repeating, we said the rhyme faster and faster. Papa walked in, stood for a minute listening, then said:

RICHARD J. DOBIE (1858-1920), my father. (Picture made about 1908.)

He was a straightout cowman, always wore a white shirt at work as well as on dress-up occasions. He preferred not wearing a necktie to church and sometimes followed his preference. When working cattle he wore a white handkerchief around his neck or over his nose, folded masklike, to keep the dust out of his nostrils.

Around 1900 he bought good steer yearlings every spring, taking a cut, for $10 a head. When he shipped grass-fat steers, three or four years old, he hoped they would "hit a four-cent market." One hundred dollars for a good yearling is now a hard-times price.

Papa never wore boots or spurs. He wanted a horse with energy that could go from before daylight until long after dark. He would not allow any hand to rope his cattle, though some were wild. He was religious. I never heard him pray for rain or high prices for cattle. I remember hearing him sing to a herd of yearlings we were driving after dark in order to reach the ranch that night. The songs were hymns — "What a Friend We Have in Jesus," "Shall We Gather at the River?" and others. During the times of cowboy songs, plenty of cattle heard hymns.

Papa and his ancestors had been Democrats since the time of Jefferson, but Grover Cleveland was the only Democratic President he lived under until Woodrow Wilson was elected. Yet his daily prayer was for a blessing on "those in authority over us," meaning particularly the President of the United States of America. Another prayer was: "So teach us to number our days that we may apply our hearts to wisdom." He was a great hand to sit on the front gallery after supper and, seemingly, meditate. "Let the words of my mouth and the meditations of my heart be always acceptable in Thy sight" was one of his prayers. He was in my youth the only rancher I knew who cultivated flowers — chrysanthemums, cape jessamines, roses, violets — in a ranch yard.

I thought he did not spend enough money, not realizing until I had finished college that he did not have it to spend. "Make all you can, save all you can, give all you can" was one of his maxims. He finally bought a car, a Buick, but never learned to drive it. He economized in town by driving one horse to a buggy instead of a pair. He was as much at ease in the saddle as on a buggy seat. He invested in a store building that he rented, but belonged essentially to the ranch and silences. He and my mother wanted all six of their children to have a college education, not necessarily to make more money, but to be the opposite of "yahoos." He had a quiet, caustic contempt for all pretenders and braggarts. "Be a man or a mouse or a bob-tailed rat" was one of his sayings; i.e., stand up and be yourself.

"Children, don't say that. We need the rain." He positively *knew* that nothing we could say would have the least effect on the weather, but he *felt*. To this day, contrary to common sense, I dislike hearing anybody say, "I wish it wouldn't rain."

Belief in the power of man to call down rain by prayer goes back thousands of years. After the people of Elijah the Tishbite had turned to the worship of Baal, he, still faithful to the Lord God of Israel, climaxed his prophetic career. "There shall not," he said, "be dew nor rain these years, but according to my word."

No grass or planted grain grew in the country. The brooks all dried up. Then, in the third year of the drouth, Elijah put four hundred and fifty prophets of Baal to the test. They took a bullock and he took a bullock — he all alone, one against four hundred and fifty — to sacrifice. The Baal prophets butchered their bullock and put the carcass on layers of wood and then called and called louder upon Baal to set the wood on fire. No fire came.

After they gave up, Elijah made a stone altar, laid wood on it, put his butchered bullock on the wood, and, to show that there was to be no sleight-of-hand work, dug a trench all around the altar and poured twelve barrels of water into it. Then he called upon the Lord God. "The fire of the Lord fell, and consumed the burnt sacrifice, and the wood, and the stones, and the dust, and licked up the water that was in the trench."

Now it was time to break the drouth. Elijah told the idolatrous King Ahab that it was going to rain. He sent a servant to look towards the sea from the top of Mount Carmel. At

ALBERT RACHAL, about 1900. He was supposed to have crossed more cattle over the Rio Grande than any other cowman. His principle was to "rachal 'em out" and get them to the Territory (the Indian Territory, now Oklahoma) as soon as possible. If it rained, good. In drouths and die-ups, he kept steady and silent.

first the servant did not see anything, but at the seventh look he cried out: "Behold there ariseth a little cloud out of the sea, like a man's hand."

King Ahab hardly had time to drive his chariot out of flood danger. "The heaven was black with clouds and wind, and there was a great rain."

Everywhere in lands of little rain, eyes still look away off over yonder for a little cloud no bigger than a man's hand.

One time after people had gathered in a schoolhouse to pray for rain, somebody started a discussion over the power of prayer on the weather. A ranchman who would never have been called a chatterbox said: "I don't mind praying, but I can tell you right now it won't do a damned bit of good as long as this dry wind stays in the west."

At another prayer-for-rain meeting, five young men who did not approve of the preacher's stand on prohibition entered wearing rain slickers. They sat down on the front bench. The preacher was outraged. When he heard tittering his outrage mounted. He ordered the slicker-wearers to leave. One said, "We just came prepared for the rain."

The late Captain William M. Molesworth, who ranched up the Nueces River, used to tell of a neighbor named Chappy Moore, noted for prolonged and chatty prayers to the Lord. The more people there were at a table and the hungrier they were, the longer Chappy Moore's blessing. One day he rode up the Molesworths' just in time for dinner. The host, knowing his intimacy with God, did not fail to call on him to ask the blessing.

"Oh, Lord," Chappy Moore began, "while I think of it, I sent Juan out into the Vara Dulce pasture this morning to bring in a cow with a wormy calf. When I saw them two days ago, I was in a buggy and couldn't doctor the calf. That's a terribly brushy pasture, and a little water is left in a tank where she ranges. I guess she'll bog down pretty soon unless you see that Juan finds her. You can count her ribs, she's that ga'nt, and her hocks knock together when she walks. I'm afraid she drank last night and is hid out in the brush now. I'd appreciate it, Oh Lord, if you'd take the trouble to direct Juan to this cow. She's a brindle with the left horn kinda drooped. If Juan don't doctor that calf, the screwworms will kill it.

"Now we thank you for the plentiful and tasty repast the good sister of this household has provided. Bless her and may all who eat of her cooking be properly thankful. Thou hast given us many things to be thankful for, Oh Lord, but I'll tell you that nobody is thankful for the drouth you are visiting upon the people of this land and their cattle and horses and other livestock. A lot of the cattle are past suffering. They are dying. Water is playing out in every direction. The wind won't blow. The windmills can't pump enough water to supply the roadrunner birds. We humbly call upon you to end this drouth and send us rain. When I say rain, I mean rain. One of your little drizzle-drazzles won't fool us. It's time to get a soaker. We need a fence-lifter and a gully-washer. We want to see the ground covered with green. Amen."

In dry weather all signs fail, people say. "The only sure sign is an old Indian sign," my mother used to say — "black all around and pouring down in the middle." The only

proven prophecy in drouth is that every dry spell ends
with a rain.

When it finally comes, people — men more than women —
will walk out into it, bare-headed, in shirt sleeves, arms
stretched out, eyes shut, head thrown back, mouth open,
soaking in the wonderful rain. They will walk around in an
uplift of thankfulness. If they don't live by a creek, they will
— unless on the flat plains — go to where they can see the
water flowing. Within three days what looked like dead roots
will be sprouting, green blades will be shooting up around
the wooden stools of bunch grass. If wet weather holds on a
little while, millions of grass and weed seeds hidden in and
on the dirt will be coming up. Some seeds of plant life belonging to arid lands always keep themselves in reserve. I have
seen a desert on which seed had not sprouted for nine years
turn into bloom.

When it rains, animals understand that grass is coming.
Understanding by instinct is sometimes more beautiful than
understanding through reasoning powers. Horses out in the
pasture will dash about as playfully as if they were colts.
Calves will chase away from the cows. Deer and other wild
animals are likewise quickened.

All the lightning that I have in all my life seen flash and
race, whether in sheets or forked lines, has been beautiful.
All the thunder, near or distant, earthshaking or a low mum-
ble, has been music to my ears. Rain may not accompany
thunder and lightning, but it is promised. Coming together, they give life one of its climaxes.

"When the earth answered like a sounding board in a deep
fertile roar, and the world sang round you in all dimensions,

all above and below — that was the rain." So wrote Isak
Dinesen in *Out of Africa*. Then, "the grass was me."

No journey from any Main Street to Fifth Avenue in New
York, from any province in equatorial Africa to Parisian
Champs Elysées can mean more to an eager traveler than the
change felt by a man of drouth-perished soil when rains at
last fall upon it.

14

The Right Tempo

ONE WINTER EVENING in a late year of the nineteenth century the boy who long ago became the past tense of me sighted a wagon drawn by two horses approaching our house at a tempo in harmony with the coming of dusk. In those times the sight of a horseman, a buggy, a wagon, of any human being was an event.

The driver proved to be Mr. Dan Shipp of the Shipp ranch, ten thousand acres stretching from the Nueces River to the east fence of our ranch. While he and Papa were unhitching the horses, to be fed and then turned into the little horse pasture, I saw in the wagon seven mesquite posts, maybe not more than five feet long. Each had been hewed with an axe to a flat surface on one side at one end, and incised with a number: 7, 8, and on to 13. Mr. Dan Shipp was setting mileposts in postholes between two and three feet deep alongside the public road running from Dinero on the Nueces River to Ramirenia thirteen miles west. This road crossed our Long Hollow pasture; Dan Shipp had turned off it to drive a mile and a half down to our house to eat supper, spend the night, and go on early next morning. A spade and a crowbar for digging postholes and an axe for cutting brush were in the wagon.

I knew this road well. There were only five gates on it and not a house excepting at the extremities, beyond which the ungraded wagon road twisted on east and west. Dinero consisted of a little store with a post office in one corner and the owner's house about two hundred yards away across the road. Ramirenia consisted of a similar combination of store and post office with four or five Mexican *jacales* across the road. One could usually ride the thirteen miles between the two places without meeting a soul except in cotton-picking time, when hundreds of Mexicans — passports then being unnecessary — strung across the country to cotton fields to the east and then later back to the other side of the Rio Grande.

Mr. Dan Shipp knew how many feet were in a mile; he had measured the circumference of a front wagon wheel. He sat over the off-wheel to drive and could look down on it. He had wrapped a piece of rawhide around the rim at a spoke to which a white rag was tied. Rawhide wears out very slowly. As his team pulled the wagon along on the road at a slow walk, he counted the revolutions of the wheel. When enough had been made to cover 5,280 linear feet, he said "Whoa!", got down, dug a posthole and planted a post with the correct number on it facing the road. At some spots he would have to cut a bush or prickly pear away to clear the ground. He had spent one day coming west from Dinero, counting the revolutions of that front wheel and setting six mileposts. The next morning he drove back to the public road and resumed counting the revolutions of the front wagon wheel. It took him all day to put down the remaining mileposts. Two of them were in rocky caliche, a little hard to dig. He spent the night of the

The right tempo, or The Wild West in Reserve, by Will Crawford. "He never stood when he could sit or sat when he could lie down."

second day somewhere around Ramirenia, probably with Mr. Hughes, an Englishman who ran the store there and had a Mexican woman as consort. The third day he drove back empty to the Shipp ranch on the Nueces.

That was when a mile was a mile. People who watch horse and relay races may have some conception of a mile, but in an age when an airplane circuits the earth between sun and sun, no traveler can have much conception of a mile. He doesn't travel either; he is merely transported. I remember when it took us all of a long July day until after dark to drive a herd of steer yearlings from the Nueces River to the pens at our ranch — seven miles. I remember another time when it took me half a day to drive a small bunch of yearlings, tired, hot, hungry, thirsty, weak, just two miles.

For a while we got our mail at Dinero, and I rode horseback once or twice a week to get it. I knew certain places where I'd seen deer cross the road. I always remembered them. I knew two glades where quail — bobwhites — were plentiful. I knew an opening in the brush where I nooned once in a wagon and let the horses graze. I knew a hollow live oak tree off the road a bit where buzzards annually nested and the little buzzards could not fly away until they had turned from whiteness to blackness. If I approached too near they would puke, making me understand the common saying, "puke like a buzzard." I knew where I was almost sure to see a paisano running down the road, though I might see one anywhere. If it had rained, I could expect a certain caliche hill covered with ceniza bushes to be turned by their sudden flowers from ashen grey to almost solid lavender. After Zane Grey, whom I never read, wrote *Riders of the Purple Sage*, people began calling ceniza "purple sage"; it's no more sage than honeysuckle is. I knew where sandy loam gave way to gravelly soil and juajillo thrived.

I always enjoyed seeing cattle eat juajillo leaves. I knew where the redbirds, migrating from the north, were thickest in wintertime. Certain mesquite trees and certain live oaks along the road were personalities to me and were cherished as friends. Yet I don't think that everybody who rode those ways saw particulars.

When we drove a buggy or a hack to Beeville, the twenty-seven miles took all day unless in winter, when the sand might be packed by rain. Then there were muddy places. The horses knew every good shade on the road. They would be sweating and panting from pulling the vehicle through sand and when they got to a good shade beside the road would stop whether you said whoa or not. Then we could get out and walk around. If it was spring, we could enjoy the phlox and Indian pinks. Halfway between the Nueces and Beeville were a cotton gin and a store with three or four farmhouses around. The official name of this place was Clareville. The Mexicans called it Los Llanos (The Prairies). Another name for it was Ten Miles. From there on every mile was an individual. Seven miles from Beeville the road made a right-angled jog to go round a small pasture belonging to a ranch on the hill. Five miles from Beeville was the Bouce Franklin ranch, one pasture of which was prairie. I never pass it now without remembering a camp there one night with a herd of yearlings.

Henry Miller of Miller and Lux, the biggest cowmen ever to operate in California and on north, said: "A man with any sense will not run his horse down trying to bring back a calf that has run off. He knows it'll come back by itself after a while for its milk."

"Slow now, slow," a foreman of the V Cross T's said to cowboys racing to get around cattle. "They'll lie down before long and then you can get them without running them."

Many a cowboy expert at riding broncos and roping would, if left to indulge his joy in action, run more fat off a bunch of cattle in one day than they could gain back in a week. Every good cowman knew, and still knows, that cattle thrive only by eating, drinking, grazing, traveling slowly in contentment. One test of a trail boss was ability to water a herd of say three thousand cattle at a river so that each drank all it wanted and was then ready to graze or trail out on a full stomach. A boss who could not put flesh on his cattle while driving them a thousand miles over grass was not a good cowman. It is the tallow on a cow brute that pays; anything that takes it off means loss in price.

Bird Rose, manager of the big L 7 outfit in South Dakota, rode only horses that carried their heads low and padded along evenly. He would not allow a man riding a high-headed, bit-chewing, snorty, nervous horse around a herd of his cattle. "They are like human beings," he said. "Go after them roughshod, and they react accordingly."

Some cowboys might shoot up a town — until the town marshal took them in. Let one try running and shooting for fun around cattle managed by a genuine cowman and he would get fired quicker than you could say "Jack Robinson." Despite all Westerns, TV's and movies, the cow country tempo was the tempo of Sam Galloway in O. Henry's ranch story "The Last of the Troubadours."

Sam wasn't much of a cow hand. "He never sat up when he could lie down; and he never stood when he could sit." It was a sheepman who provided him a cot under a hackberry tree on which to recline and play a slow tune on his guitar, or just to recline. The sheepman's cook, a Mexican without any Latin in his Indian blood, brought him a cup of black coffee whenever he called for it and sometimes when he did not call. No troubadour was ever more welcome in a French castle of the twelfth century than Sam Galloway was on a bleak ranch down toward the Rio Grande in the late nineteenth century. He wore a six-shooter when he rode, but laid it and belt aside whenever he rested. He kept his energy in reserve, but when the time came could use it — as anybody who reads the story sees.

An authentic Zane Grey hero speaks in "a stern, grim tone," never walks out a door if he can jump through a window, and shoots not one but two six-shooters. In the 1920's while Zane Grey was manufacturing Westerns at a jet-propelled rate, I spent a few days in the camp of Dr. A. V. Kidder, archaeologist. He was excavating the ruins of an Indian village on the Pecos River in New Mexico. Some time before that, he related, he was, while working in an Arizona canyon, awakened one night by what sounded like the clatter-wheels of hell — yelling, shooting, shod horse hoofs running across rock, whips popping, lariats hitting against leather. He slipped on shoes and stepped out of his tent. The moon was full. Just as he emerged, a cowboy dashed up and stopped. Kidder recognized him as a pick-and-shovel excavator who had been in his pay a short time back.

"My goodness, John," he asked, "what is going on here?"

"A damned fool named Zane Grey has hired us to make local color," the cowboy replied, "and we are doing our best to make it."

The only moving picture I have ever seen true to the tempo of handling cattle was *North of 36,* based on Emerson Hough's novel by that name — a romance of driving a big herd up the Chisholm Trail. I saw it late in 1924. Often in recollection I see the lead steer, Old Alamo, a mighty longhorn, dun in color, standing at the edge of a lake where the other steers were standing, watering. They looked serene, as cattle at water naturally are. Those in the picture had been furnished by Bassett Blakeley from herds on the prairies of the Gulf Coast in the region of Houston. To be sure, there was a stampede, but the picture furnished views of the herd quietly grazing along and strung out in a long line behind Old Alamo.

This was a silent picture. In 1938 it was remade into a talkie. I read in a newspaper that it was being shot on La Mota ranch, in the Brush Country of Texas. I knew this ranch and its owner, Mrs. Amanda Burks, very well. She had gone up the trail — before it was fenced across — in a buggy with her own cattle. I was in Los Angeles, California, when the newly made picture was released. Walking on a street, I saw a sign announcing it, "now running." I bought a ticket and went inside. I wanted to see the 𐌀 and the 𐌁 brands on La Mota cattle. I wanted to be back home. I looked and listened through the entire film. The only glimpses of the cattle I got was while they were running like scared jack rabbits. I tried another cattle picture or two. Had I not known better, I might have concluded that a herd bound for the Blackfoot Indian

Agency on the Canadian-Montana line crossed the Rio Grande in a run, slept in a run, grazed in a run, drank in a turmoil, and never quit running over the entire two-thousand-mile trail.

Oh beat the drum slowly and play the fife lowly . . .
Oh, it was a long and lonesome go
As our herd rolled on to [New] Mexico.

All cowboy songs sung to cattle were long and lonesome in tune. A man loping or trotting could not keep the tune. It was timed to a slow walk and was meant to quieten all hearers. After John A. Lomax, his son Alan collaborating, revised and enlarged his *Cowboy Songs,* I remarked to him that while he was adding Negro songs to the collection he might have included some camp-meeting songs. They certainly were sung to cattle. Andy Adams tells of an old Texas Longhorn that always got up from his bed and stretched out his neck when at night he heard the long-drawn-out notes of "Jesus, Lover of My Soul."

In 1889 a frontier preacher named Butterfield was holding services back in the woods of east Texas. Not a song book was available. He had exhausted himself on "Jesus Saves" and "Almost Persuaded." It was time for sinners to move up to the mourners' bench, but it takes the right tune to draw them. Now, at his climax, Butterfield was talking without that drawing power of mournful song to back him up. Suddenly the dearth was relieved by a son of the open range singing all alone "Oh, Bury Me Not on the Lone Prairie." Its strains have "a dying fall." Mourners came up and gave themselves to Jesus. "It's the spirit of the song that counts and not

The coal oil lantern belongs on the mantelpiece as the fiddle and bow belonged to a cowboy named Bev Greenwood. Despite his sober looks, he could make "Turkey in the Straw" dance. (Photograph by Erwin Smith in the early 1900's.)

the words," the singer said after the meeting ended. He had seen cattle quieted down by the slow sad sounds of "Bury Me Not" as well as by "Lie Down, Little Dogies."

The right tempo goes back to a fiddle tune without words called "Lizard in the Sun." "Livy, you've got the right words but the wrong tune," Mark Twain said to his wife when he heard her repeating swear adjectives he had poured out on badly laundered shirts. He did not know she was near enough to hear him.

Country people everywhere used to go by sun time, not railroad time; they went by what country Mexicans call *el tiempo de Dios* (God's time), not *el tiempo oficial*. Santa Anna's soldiers were taking an afternoon siesta on San Jacinto Bayou when Sam Houston's army slew and routed them in the battle that made Texas a republic. Many of the Texans were siesta takers also.

Jack Helms ranched in a country where it takes fifty acres to support a barren cow. One summer, though, it rained. His cattle were fattening on the sparse but green grass. Prices were better than strong. He took the train to El Paso, bought himself a new pair of boots and a phonograph for his wife and children. He had no trouble getting his note extended at the bank.

After the papers were signed the banker asked, "What are you going to do, Mr. Helms, when you sell your yearlings this fall and have all that money?"

"I'll tell you what I am a-going to do," he said. "You know there's no place so comfortable for a nap as in the shade of a waggin. I keep mine in front of the house when I can, but seems like somebody is always using it. If we get one more rain and if the price for cattle holds up, I'm a-going to buy me an extry waggin. I'm a-going to put it right there in front of the house and nobody's a-going to disturb it. Every day after dinner I'm a-going right out there and spread my quilt in the shade under it and take a nap."

A man is rich in proportion to what he can do without — comfortably. This is not the philosophy of get-richers of any age or business, but it was the philosophy of many a rancher away out from the strife of getting ahead.

Beatrice was born under a star that danced, and she danced with it, but the speed of man is no more that of light than is the speed of his fellow earthworm. Men have invented an atomic bomber, but no man can ever absorb its speed into his own body. Human energy pulses with desire to rise higher and travel faster; hence the thirst for strong drink and swift movement; but the tempo of all earthborn is the tempo of the earth itself. A raging hurricane may lash a sliver of it, a volcano may spew up some inside matter, but the tempo of the earth sustaining its bipedal nurslings is of growing grass, ripening corn and drifting leaves.

We behold expanses of glaring electric lights. We become fascinated and terrorized by torrents of headlights rushing along speedways in the night, but the light that burns under the stars with the tempo of mother earth is that of a lone campfire.

A long time ago I was a boy riding with my parents in a hack on a dirt road west of the Nueces River. For hours we had not met a single traveler or seen a human habitation. Darkness came, and then away down the slope we saw a little fire, no bigger than the fluttering blaze of a match. It was beautiful and in the emptiness all around it was a mystery. Slowly, as we approached, it grew a little larger. It was beside the road, on Agua Dulce Creek. My father stopped the horses to speak. A lone camper was cooking supper in a skillet beside a coffeepot. He asked us to get out and have something. With thanks and a good-night, we drove on. I have smelled a mesquite fire in darkness before I saw it and felt a harmony. The tempo of earth-men,

> Rolled round in earth's diurnal course,
> With rocks, and stones, and trees,

has seemed to me more pronounced in mature, even fading, cowmen than in springy cowboys out for a high-heeled time.

The time came when Joe Wolfe began to weaken, and his ridings-out became shorter and shorter. Every morning, just the same, rain or shine, he'd saddle his horse. If the flow of juices inside him or the sun-flow outside were not congenial, he might not pull up into the saddle at all; but as surely as the sun rose his saddled horse stood tied to a fence post near the front yard gate, waiting for him to mount. The time came that even when he rode out, he seldom got farther than the shade of a big live oak on the creek. Here he would sit in the saddle or on the ground, equally comfortable, and look at a turtle sunning himself on a log fixed in the water or at a cow that after drinking stood in water half up to her knees switching off flies with her tail. He enjoyed the buzzards in the air and their shadows on the ground.

One morning after Joe Wolfe had a hard time lifting the saddle to the horse's back, he tried to pull himself up into it and could not. Somehow he was unable to get the horse to stand right against a log that he could step on and thence

ANDY MATHER of Liberty Hill, Texas, in 1928. He was one of the mustangers who chased the Pacing White Stallion.

have a shorter pull into the saddle. He just couldn't get into the saddle. He stood looking at it a long while. Then he lay down on the ground in the shade to rest, his heart beating too fast, fast, fast from the exertion. When he got up he did not feel right, but he went over to his old gentle horse and tried again to fork him. He simply could not. He could pull the saddle off. He did and left it on the ground for somebody else to pick up and hang by the hornstring on a peg in the shed. He led the horse to a gate opening into the horse trap, took the bridle off and stood for a while with one hand on the horse's neck. Then his hand dropped.

Old Gallo stood still a minute longer; years ago he had been a bright red, the color of a red rooster (*gallo*); in those times he bore himself with the pride of a red *gallo*. Now he was gray in color and movement. When Joe Wolfe turned him loose that morning Gallo walked to a smooth place, and following a custom begun when he was released with a sweaty back, lay down to roll. He could not roll over but got up and lay down on the other side. After he got up he walked to the shade of a hackberry tree to rest a while before grazing out.

If Joe Wolfe said anything to Old Gallo, nobody heard him. He made his unsteady way into the house, pulled his boots off, spurs still buckled on them, lay down on his quilt-covered bed and after that never spoke a word. One son got him to take a chew of tobacco, but it brought him no comfort. From his bed he could through the door see the foot of the stairs. This son brought in his saddle and girded it up on the banisters, took a rope from the horn of it to Joe Wolfe's hand. Joe Wolfe smiled a little but said nothing. Then after a while he died.

15

Loyalties

"I wish I could find words to express the trueness,
the loyalty to their trust and to each other of the
old trail hands. I wish I could convey in language
the feeling of companionship we had for one another." — CHARLES GOODNIGHT

"Their faithfulness and loyalty to their outfit cannot be described. They were to their outfit what a
good mother is to her family." — GRANVILLE STUART

WHICH IS MORE to be desired in a judge, adherence
to law or loyalty to a friend? Bob Castlebury, of Vernon, Texas, who told me the story, had no doubt as to the answer. Many people — more in the United States than in England — put loyalty to an individual ahead of loyalty to law,
to society.

In 1888 Bob Castlebury and a twenty-year-old cowboy who,
having worn out his original name, called himself Dodge,
were helping move ten thousand Laureles steers, owned by
the Laurel Leaf Cattle Company, from south of Red River,
in Texas, to a range on the Canadian River in the Indian Territory. The steers were cut into three herds, and Bob Castlebury and Dodge went with the first. A Scot named Richards,

who had been in America only a short time, was boss. The Laurel Leaf was British owned.

The fellow who called himself Dodge was expert with rope and gun and was a horsebreaker. To an extent he savvied the cow and was without qualification full of vinegar. One night while he and Bob Castlebury were on guard a range bull kept trying to get into the herd. After running him off again and again, Dodge pulled his Winchester out of the scabbard — for he carried a saddle gun as well as six-shooter — and put a full magazine of bullets into the animal.

"Scotty" Richards heard the firing during the night and at daylight saw the dead bull. He was as mad as a wet hen. "Go on into headquarters and get your paycheck," he ordered Dodge. "I'll let you have one horse to ride and will divide your mount among the other hands."

This talk was in camps, while most of the hands were eating breakfast. Dodge swept his eyes over the crowd and said: "Boys, I like all of you, but the first man that gets on one of my horses I'm going to shoot off. I am not going into ranch headquarters — not yet. Mr. Scotty, you are not going to send me in. I'm going to send you in. I'll give you ten minutes to crawl on your horse and light a shuck." Scotty Richards knew that the young man meant what he said. He remarked that he didn't need but five minutes.

The outfit elected one of their own number boss and grazed the cattle on north. Government orders forbade turning cattle loose on the Indian reservation land but said nothing about the rate of a herd's progress across it. The Laureles steers moved about as slow as a street musician forbidden by police to stop on a corner. It took the outfit seven weeks to graze from Red River to the Canadian. The steers fattened, and once in a while one was cut out for the Indians to keep them pacified.

B. Hopkins, Laureles manager on the Canadian, said nothing to Dodge about his high-handed treatment of Scotty Richards. He made Dodge responsible for all the saddle horses on the ranch. He put the other men to gathering fat beeves and riding down lobo wolves.

That winter some of the Laureles horses drifted a hundred miles or so down into Texas. With the opening of spring, Dodge drifted after them. One day while he was riding in the vicinity of where the town of Panhandle now stands, he came upon two men in a stalled buggy, one of the buggy horses dead. He did not know either of the men; all he knew was that they were stranded a hundred miles from nowhere.

"Just stay here awhile," he said with unconscious irony, "and I'll let you have a horse." Then he rode away.

The men in the stranded buggy were C. C. Wells, district attorney, and G. A. Brown ("God Almighty Brown," as Temple Houston dubbed him), district judge.

After an hour or so Dodge was back. "I think my horse will work in harness," he said. "He's purty gentle." He unsaddled the horse and, with very little help from the upholders of law and order, hitched him in.

"Now," he said, "I'll thank you to take me and my saddle to the horse I am going to ride."

"Where is he?"

"Oh, out yonder."

"We didn't know there was a ranch anywhere in this country," one of the law and order upholders remarked.

"There's not."

Dodge did the driving and soon had his saddle horse pulling evenly. Finally, over a rise, he halted, in sight of a bronc tied down. "There's my horse," he said. Not long before coming upon the stranded buggy, he had seen a bunch of Laureles horses on the prairie, had ridden back to them, run onto a green bronc, roped him, and tied him down. Now he took his saddle out of the back of the buggy, carried it over to the bronc, cinched it on him, swung into it and rode away. The district judge and the district attorney drove on to wherever they were going and disposed of the borrowed horse according to directions of their benefactor.

Dodge knew that he could not work range horses on a green bronc not yet bridlewise. As soon as he got this one under control he rode back to the Laureles ranch, caught a seasoned mount and, with another cowboy to help, returned for the estrayed horses.

After staying on with the Laureles Company for another year or so, he quit and went over into Greer County, now in Oklahoma but then a part of Texas. Here he had a difficulty with the tax assessor, stood up for his rights, killed the tax man, and was put in jail. He broke out of jail, rode to friends who would go his bond, and in time, with capable legal counsel, appeared for trial in the town of Mangum. The case was strong against him; examination of the witnesses dragged through several days.

An observer might have noticed that as the case progressed the judge kept looking more and more intently at the accused. If the accused had any particular interest in the judge, he did not evidence it. The judge was G. A. ("God Almighty") Brown. Not long before he was to make his charge to the jury, he, at a convenient recess, stepped over to Dodge and asked him to come into his office, just off the courtroom.

"Your face keeps looking more and more familiar to me," he said. "Where did I see you?"

"Ain't you the man," Dodge replied, "that the buggy horse died on?"

"And you are the man who roped that bronc and gave your own saddle horse to us?"

"Yes."

"Well, that's a horse on me," the judge closed the interview by saying.

The defense lawyers were mightily shaky until they heard the charge read to the jury. Then one of them said to the other: "Great Scott, God A'mighty Brown's made enough loopholes for a dozen reversals."

As a matter of fact, the jury cleared Dodge and no reversal was needed. Dodge worked up to where he owned a good herd of cattle. Then he went broke, got into the oil business, made half a million dollars, speculated most of that away, and died on his fruit farm in the Rio Grande Valley — a solid citizen.

"The way old God A'mighty Brown acted," concluded Bob Castlebury, in telling the story, "just showed what was in the man. Any real man will stick to a friend."

Here is an instance of the sticking from Earle E. Butler: "In 1896 I was ten years old. We were ranching in Oklahoma Territory, which was admitted as a state that year. My father shipped his cattle every fall from Hominy Post (Osage

Junction). One day while he was gone, two men rode up to our house. Their horses, both bays, were out of this world in splendor. Their clothes and saddles matched the horses.

"One man dismounted and came to the door and rapped, hat off. The other remained mounted, holding the first man's horse. When my mother went to the door he said: 'Madam, my abject apologies for coming here. We know that Mr. Butler is shipping cattle from Hominy Post. We are hungry. Could we get something to eat and graze our horses?'

"My mother replied: 'Come in, gentlemen. My son will show you where your horses can graze. Certainly I shall prepare you some food.'

"They staked their horses, and one man stayed with them while the other ate. After the second man finished, he placed a twenty-dollar gold piece on the table. Mother handed it back to him and said, 'We don't accept money for food. My husband would not like for me to take it. Any rider who stops at our house is always welcome.'

"The man bowed gravely, repocketed the gold piece and walked out. The two rode away. The next day about noon the sheriff and five deputies rode up. My mother fed them. The sheriff asked if we had seen two men riding big bay horses. My mother replied, 'We have not seen anyone.'

"After the sheriff's posse left, I said, 'Mama, those two men here yesterday rode big bay horses.' She said, 'Yes, I know, son, but I am your father's wife. I do not have time to be sheriff also.'

"Our ranch was on the Arkansas River. Along in the spring while cattle were bogging in the quicksands, those two men wanted by the law came again. They camped in the river bottom. For about a month they pulled cattle out of the quick-sands and helped on the roundup. My father said they were fine cowhands. When the work was over, he told them to come up to the house for a settlement. 'We do not want a dime, Mr. Butler,' they said. 'We were weak from hunger. Your wife cooked us a fine meal and turned down our money.' Then they rode away."

This incident came to me from Miss Lillian Gunter while she maintained the Cooke County Free Library at Gainsville, Texas. Her uncle Jot Gunter ran cows but made his fortune buying land script, and selling land after population gave it value. He financed the Gunter Hotel in San Antonio, head-quarters a long time for cow people all over southwest Texas.

One day one of his men named Wright, managing a ranch in the Panhandle, received a telegram from the big owner. It had come by way of Dodge City, Kansas, some two hundred miles north of Amarillo. The telegram read: "Come at once. Sherman. Jot Gunter."

"I took out on the best horse I had," said Wright, "and made it in to Sherman in six days and a half. I would have got there sooner but couldn't get grain for my horse till I reached what is now Wichita Falls. When I rode into Sher-man, I put him in a livery stable and made right over to Jot's office. 'Wright,' he says, 'the town is full of purty girls. You see my buggy and team out there. Get right in and take a lit-tle sashay around with some purty girl.'

"Well, I thought to myself, this is a fine come-off! I've nearly killed the best horse Jot Gunter owns riding to Sherman from the Staked Plains day and night, only to find when I get here, there's nothing to do but take some gal I never seen and don't want to see buggy riding.

"After a while Jot took me down to the saloon he favored, the best in town, where he always drank with eastern buyers and his cowboys. It didn't make no difference to Jot who he treated, he treated him the best he could. After we got down there and a barkeep waited on us while we sat at a table sorter off to one side, Jot says: 'The fence-cutters are cutting my fences all to pieces, and I can't get nobody here to stop them. I've sent for you.'

"No, I didn't have to kill anybody. Of course, if Jot had ordered me to kill a man, I'd a-done it. I'd a-killed for him if he'd said to. We just had one little run-in with the fence-cutters. Then I was free to ride back to where I belonged."

Without trying to define loyalty and without wish to analyze the many components going into it, I quote one sentence from Polonius:

> . . . To thine own self be true,
> And it must follow, as the night the day,
> Thou canst not then be false to any man.

However, every man follows his own interpretation of what being true to himself calls for.

In 1882, Joe Erricson, a native of Sweden, nineteen years old, hired himself to help fence the far-spread S M S ranches in west Texas. In time he became range boss over seventy-five cowboys, twenty-five thousand cattle and five hundred saddle horses. Then he married a lady who found ranch life far from attractive. He quit the land of grass and silences

JACINTO DE LOS SANTOS (Hyacinth of the Saints). In 1920 he was
bossing the fence-building and tank-scraping outfit on the J. M. Dobie
ranch down in the Brush Country of Texas.

and moved with her to pavement and noises. Six months later he showed up in the office of A. J. Swenson, part owner and manager of the S M S's. "Andrew," he announced, "I'm lonesome." "Lonesome, Joe. For what?" "For the ranch. If you have a place for me, I'm coming back." A. J. Swenson put him in charge of the Spur Ranch of about half a million acres. There he lived and worked the remainder of his life. When he died in 1931 he had ridden S M S horses for nearly fifty years.

In August of that year he was confined to the house that was his home, but was still keeping up with ranch affairs. One morning he called a man in and told him to hitch his pair of bays to the buggy and drive him to where a herd of S M S cattle was being worked, a few miles away. When they arrived at the edge of the roundup grounds, he gave the driver a sign to stop. The buggy top was down. He rose to his feet, one hand on the dashboard, and stood in silence gazing at the cattle and the riders. Then he turned his head as if to look again at the Caprock in the hazy distance. Without a word he sank to the seat from which he had risen. He was dead.

Joe Erricson was loyal to the Swensons, loyal to his work, loyal to the S M S tradition. His loyalties seemed to depend upon following the life inside himself, the only kind of life he got satisfaction from — ranch life. He had to be true to himself.

Loyalty is more pronounced, it seems to me, in individuals not ambitious for themselves than in those who are. It is marked in certain hirelings without hope or intention of rising in the economic scale to be employers. It is more noticeable among postmen than among corporation heads who interpret grasping greed as "free enterprise." In the United States of America, ambition is generally regarded as a virtue; in Mexico, I have time and again been warned by a Mexican: "Look out for him; don't trust him; he is *muy ambicioso.*"

I heard the name and the story of old Ablos around 1930 on the King Ranch. A paragraph in Tom Lea's history of the King Ranch, based on much research, leads me to believe that time and the creative processes of living memories transmuted Ignacio Alvarado into Ablos. If a story brings out truth, why let facts interfere with it? This is how I heard the story.

One spring in the 1880's Captain Richard King of the vast ranch that bears his name had already sent several herds up the trail to Kansas and had the last herd gathered, "shaped up," ready to go. It was made up of big steers, all in the Running W brand, freshly road-branded with the K W.

Ablos, the most efficient and most valued *caporal* (boss) of the ranch, was to take it. He had been trail boss for years, but now, his outfit all ready, he had not appeared. For a day, two days, three days, the vaqueros loose-herded the steers by day and held them on bed-grounds by night. Still there was no Ablos. It was said that he was away in San Diego on a drunk. Young Richard King, very young, was in a stew.

"What on earth," he said to his father, "do you mean by putting up with that old drunkard? Let's place another man in charge and get the herd moving."

"We'd better wait a while longer, I guess." Captain King measured out his words.

A caporal (cow outfit boss) of the King Ranch.

"Just an old drunkard," young Richard insisted.

The captain kept on waiting and a day or two later Ablos showed up. "I am ready," he said. He took over the herd and left. The property under his charge was worth many thousands of dollars. He was as much the master of it as a captain at sea is master of a ship. He must rely upon himself. For many weeks he would have no one to report to or account to.

After the herds had been on the trail for two or three months, Captain King and his son Richard traveled to Dodge City, Kansas.

"How did you make the trip?" would be the question asked of each trail boss as he arrived.

The first one said: "We had much trouble at the Cimarron. The cattle milled in the water and several drowned."

The second one said: "It kept raining and storming all through the Indian Territory. My cattle stampeded every night for two weeks. I am short."

Indians had run off the third man's horses, some of them not recovered.

And so it was with each of the half dozen trail bosses. At length Ablos appeared. He had started after the others and had steadily lost time. "And how did you make it through, Ablos?" Captain King asked.

"Oh, *muy bien, señor*. No trouble anywhere. All was pacific all the way. We came along *despacio, despacio,* slow, slow. I picked up 136 K W cattle lost out of other herds. We are 136 cattle long. And look how all the cattle have gained in weight! Look how contented they are!"

Captain King turned to Richard. "Now you know why I wait for that old drunkard Ablos."

Years went by. Captain King had died. His son-in-law,

R. J. Kleberg, was managing the great King estate. Ablos was still the king of *caporals*. One day a herd was to be moved. Ablos had been notified to take charge of it. The herd was "shaped up," ready to move. No Ablos. One day passed, two days. No Ablos. Then his son appeared.

"My father says to tell you he cannot come," reported the son.

"Why?"

"He says he is sorry, but he has to stay at home to die."

At the rollicky 1924 gathering of the Old-Time Trail Drivers of Texas in the Gunter Hotel in San Antonio, two fiddlers and one guitarist from Bandera County kept "Rye Whiskey, Rye Whiskey, I Wish You No Harm," "Turkey in the Straw" and other such tunes, many with words, going day and night out in the lobby. At the first big meeting upstairs two Negro trail hands were formally introduced. George Glenn had been present the year before and wore a badge. While the sheriff of Gonzales County was enforcing the fact that none of Al Jones's people had ever been in jail, a veteran of the Civil War got to his feet yelling, "Why ain't my nigger got a Trail Drivers' badge on? Put one on him, I tell you!" It took five minutes of milling and hunting to get him a badge. Then both were voted life members of the organization, "without dues." The president said, "These men were pioneers like us. They always knew their places. They were faithful. We love them."

Al Jones had driven up the trail thirteen times, four times as boss, white men, Negroes, Mexicans all under him. George

AL JONES, old-time Negro cowhand. He went up the trail to Kansas and beyond with Texas cattle thirteen times, four times as boss, with white men as well as Negroes under him. (Picture taken at meeting of Trail Drivers of Texas at San Antonio, 1924.)

Glenn had, for me, the story. I put it down in his own language.

"I was born in 1850. In 1870 I went up the trail with Mr. Bob Johnson. He'd raised me, you know. Everything wuz all right and we wuz all happy till we got to Abilene. That was the end of the trail. Then Mr. Johnson took sick and died. We buried him, and after that it took three months to get the cattle delivered and things straightened out. Meantime word had come fer us to bring the body back to Texas so it could be put in the ground next to Mis' Johnson's. There wan't no way of sending the body on the train. We all had a talk about what to do. Mr. Bob Johnson's brothers couldn't none of them bear the idea of driving his corpse back. They asked who'd volunteer to drive it. I said I would.

"I had a new Studebaker wagon and a good pair of mules, and I set out alone. It wuz a thousand miles, they say. It took me exactly forty-two days and nights to make the trip. I had a bottle of medicine and would drop a little out of it on the box every morning. I couldn't smell anything, but the wild animals could, I guess. All the way down they'd be crossing the trail right in front of me and follering along behind. At night I slept on the box, and many a night I woke up to hear 'scratch, scratch, scratch,' on the wagon bed. I'd pick up a stick and knock on the wood and whatever it wuz would go 'way. Right at the head of the box I had the money for the cattle we'd sold. Gold, and it wuz safe enough."

"George," I asked, "were you afraid of ghosts?"

"No, sah, I wasn't a-scared of no ghosts. He'd been my master and raised me. I loved him and I knowed no ghost of his wan't going to bother me. But after that trip I never went back up the trail. I'd done 'sperienced enough."

GEORGE GLENN, Negro cowhand, at meeting of Trail Drivers of Texas, San Antonio, 1924. About 1870 he drove alone a wagon containing the coffined body of his boss a thousand miles from Abilene, Kansas. to the Texas coast.

Cow People

In "The Hired Man on Horseback," Eugene Manlove
Rhodes has the last word on staying with the herd — loyalty
epitomized.

But Lefty does not leave them and Lefty tries once more;
He is swinging the wild leaders in toward the northern shore.
"He'll do to ride the river with!" (Bridging the years between,
Men shall use those words again — and wonder what they
  mean.)
He is back to turn the stragglers in to follow the leaders
  through
When a cottonwood snag comes twisting down and cuts the
  herd in two. . . .

— A brown hand lifted in the lashing spray;
Sun upon a golden head that never will be gray;
A low mound bare until new grass is grown —
But the hired man's herd has crossed the Cimarron.

16
Within the Code

SOMEHOW, DURING the period of "manifest destiny," people of the West, especially manifest males and journalists, began bragging on themselves as "rugged individualists." The idea developed that sheer ruggedness made them more individualistic than men to the east had ever been. Boiled down, this individualism, however pronounced in conduct, was as short on thought as the doctrine of free enterprise in the middle of the twentieth century has been short on free intellectual enterprise.

The rights of freedom, of thought, speech and print were believed in so intensely by so many people while the nation was being formed that some states would not adopt the Constitution until the Bill of Rights was added to it. Even in the present age of conformity, Benjamin Franklin the skeptic, Thomas Jefferson the freethinker, and Abraham Lincoln committed to no dogma remain the foremost representatives of American freedom and individualism.

Before Western individualists of ruggedness reached their climax, the village of Concord in Massachusetts had emitted more ideas on personal independence than all the spaces

GUS BLACK. Between 1875 and 1882, while delivering herds of cattle to Nebraska and Wyoming, he noticed near camp one evening a pair of horns that had slipped off the head of a dead cow. Governor Bush of Wyoming was to inspect the herd next morning with a view to buying it. Gus Black told a cowboy to rope a yearling. Then they managed to fix the cow's horns on its stubs. When the governor saw the animal, he said it was a runt steer four years old or better. Gus Black said it was just a yearling. The governor said he'd bet a thousand dollars it wasn't short of four years old. Black took him up, roped the yearling and pulled off the horns. Then he told the governor to keep his money. He built the first barbed-wire fence around one of his own pastures in Maverick County, which joins the Rio Grande. When he died in 1935, many an old-timer said, "We've lost a real friend."

west of the Mississippi have yet generated. In "Self-Reliance," an epitome of much that he had to say, Emerson saw individualism deep in the mind and spirit, the essential character, of every human being. "The Duty of Civil Disobedience," by Henry David Thoreau, Emerson's fellow Concordian, enlarged and deepened the philosophy of individualism beyond the concept of any man "standing up for his rights" with a six-shooter. Thoreau stood against contributing to a government that upheld slavery and invaded Mexico, and in accordance refused to pay his taxes. As a result he was jailed. Visiting him in jail, Emerson asked, "Henry, why are you here?" "Why are you not here?" was the reply.

Thoreau walked sixteen miles from Concord and back to hear Emerson speak, but he would not walk to Harvard to hear the preachers. "I had rather listen to the chickadees than the D.D.'s," he said. When he himself lectured now and then, he habitually stipulated that anything he might say from the platform was strictly nobody's business but his own. He never allied himself to any man, any woman, any property. However his ideas may have approached, on one hand, anarchy, he understood that values attached to privacy and individual rights belonged to America. They were English and Scotch before they became American.

As the South grew more isolated and more violent in defense of slavery, it banned freedom of speech on that subject. Open query on the "peculiar institution," and increasingly on other subjects, ceased to exist in the South before the Civil War. That war freed poor whites as much as it freed black people.

The six-shooter code of the West, especially in Texas, was derived mainly from the South. Here duels were fought between gentlemen — except when a Sam Houston retorted to his challenger: "I never fight downhill." When William Alexander Percy of Mississippi, poet and author of a revealing autobiography entitled *Lanterns on the Levee,* early in this century entered the Sorbonne in Paris, he, "to please" his father, took lessons in fencing. From where else in the United States would a father have prescribed swordsmanship? Southern gentlemen had come to use pistols, rather than swords, in duels. Many non-gentlemen of the South excelled with Bowie knives. Some Negroes used razors. The razor wielders, the pistol duellers, the Bowie knife cutthroats were all above the law. For them the code of "rights" was strictly personal.

President John Adams defined the government of the United States as one of law rather than of men. In regions of sparsely populated spaces controlled by cow people, application of law could be markedly personal.

Ash Upson, who wrote *The Authentic Life of Billy the Kid,* published under the name of Pat Garrett, whose sixshooter ended the Kid's existence, was for a time justice of peace at Roswell, New Mexico. He had been married and divorced and as a justice he hesitated to marry couples, had no confidence in the outcome of such joinings. Against his judgment, he married a cowboy and a woman who appeared before him. He wrote out a marriage certificate — and put it in his desk. Some weeks later the cowboy appeared to complain to Justice Upson that his wife stayed in bed every morning until after sunup, would not cook the kind of grub he liked, refused to help him work cattle. He wanted a divorce. "You don't need a divorce," Ash Upson said. "The day I married you I sized that woman up. I never sent the marriage certificate in to be recorded." He drew it out of his desk, tore it into bits, and concluded: "You are now by law just as free as you were before marrying. Go back to the ranch, take the bridle off that woman, and turn her out to graze where she came from."

The ballad of "Silver Jack" came from some sophisticated writer and not from working men. Its setting is a camp of Michigan lumber cutters, but John A. Lomax heard it in cow country and put it in his *Cowboy Ballads*. Its burden is conformity versus free thinking.

A fellow in camp by the name of Robert Waite, tonguey and "what they call a skeptic," said hell was a humbug, the Bible a fable, and the Saviour "just a common man." Silver Jack yelled, "You're a liar, and you've got to take it back."

> They fit for forty minutes
> And the crowd would whoop and cheer
> When Jack spit up a tooth or two,
> Or when Bobby lost an ear.
>
> But at last Jack got him under
> And he slugged him oncet or twicet,
> And straightway Bob admitted
> The divinity of Christ. . . .
>
> Then someone brought a bottle out
> And kindly passed it round. . . .
>
> . . . And the spread of infidelity
> Was checked in camp that day.

I have never heard of a cow country shooting over religious beliefs. More attention was paid to nonconformity in eating than in creed. "A fine-haired kind of man" named Allsup came to central Texas while the land, except for a few corn patches, was unfenced. He married a woman determined to take care of him and invested about $500, all he had, in eighty-five head of "she" cattle. In the spring following, cattle owners gathered for a week's cowhunt, to brand calves and gather big steers to sell. Allsup joined in. His horse was weighted with a pair of enormous saddle-pockets stuffed with two large, round loaves of bread his wife had baked, a boiled ham, and sugar to sweeten his coffee.

Picking up cattle as they worked a strip of country, the men nooned at a creek. They made a fire, set a pot of coffee to boil and, with green sticks for skewers, broiled meat they had brought along. Tomorrow they would kill a fat calf. Each had cold biscuits in a black, greasy wallet. When they sat down to eat they noticed Allsup about thirty steps off to one side eating a slice of ham with lightbread and putting sugar in his coffee. That evening they penned their cattle at a ranch down the creek and camped. Allsup again ate apart.

At daylight next morning two youngsters were pretending to sharpen their knives on a grindstone made from sticks and one of Allsup's round loaves of bread. The horseplay and laughter roused Allsup to curse the boys and threaten to whip them. "You better ca'm down and do as other people do, if you want to raise cattle around here," the leader of the cow crowd advised him. He took to eating broiled beef at the common campfire.

Men dressed pretty much in the same kind of boots, shirts and breeches, though not so uniformly as modern rodeo performers, few of whom would know how to work cattle. They were especially intolerant of innovations in hats. A tenderfoot's derby might be snatched from his head, tossed up high and perforated with six-shooter bullets.

John D. Talley was eighty-five years old when I came to know him at Austin, Texas, in 1938. He had been reared on the frontier — by gentle parents, had ridden with wild riders and gone up the trail with wild cattle. In his later years at least, he always looked as if he had just stepped out of a bandbox. He was a gentleman in speech and manners, and a superb storyteller. One story he told sums up the code of blood and ethics in the Old West.

"In 1880 I went up the trail with a herd of Ellison's cattle. Jack Robinson was boss. We had hard luck with hands all the way. Two got crippled so they had to be sent back, and two others quit.

"We were shorthanded in the Indian Territory when one evening just before supper a man rode up. He wore extra-good clothes, all clean, six-shooter and a belt full of cartridges. He was on an extra-good brown horse and carried a Winchester in a scabbard. Whatever clothes he carried were rolled up in his blanket with a slicker over it, tied behind his saddle. Of course we asked him to get down, eat supper and spend the night. He said his name was Will Hardin.

"After unsaddling, he led his horse about a hundred yards off, fastened a pair of Mexican rawhide hobbles around his front ankles, and turned him loose. The next morning the horse was close to where he'd been left. Hardin took the hobbles off and fastened them in a rung on the side of the chuck wagon. Jack Robinson picked out from the remuda five horses for him to ride. Every evening when he caught his night horse he would also lead out his own brown, hobble him and turn him loose a little out from camp. Then next morn-

DOLPHUS LOWE (called Dolph Lowe) was another big operator in
the Brush Country below San Antonio. During open range days his
father lost heavily by buying out brands of cattle on an estimate of
the number in a brand instead of counting them. Owners were generally generous on numbers in estimating — except for taxes — cattle
in their own brands. Marked by his occupation as well as by time.

ing he would take the hobbles off, fasten them into the wagon rung, and put his horse in the remuda. He was quiet all the time, and he was a good hand.

"Our boss had a kind of flunkey in a Negro hired as a regular hand. In a way he was, but he washed Robinson's clothes, saddled and unsaddled his horse, brought his coffee to him before he got up, and so on. Trail bosses with body servants were about as scarce as hen's teeth.

"One evening after Hardin had been with us about a week, he brought his brown horse up to the wagon to hobble him. The rawhide hobbles were gone. Robinson's night horse was hobbled a short distance away. Hardin turned to the Negro, and the Negro admitted he had taken the hobbles and put them on his boss's horse.

" 'Get those hobbles and bring them here and be damned quick about it,' Hardin ordered.

"The Negro obeyed. 'Now,' Hardin said, 'I never bother anybody else's property or poke into anybody else's business, and I want my own property left alone.'

"About three evenings later the hobbles were missing again. Robinson was lying on his pallet part way under the wagon and his Winchester was leaning against the wagon wheel.

" 'God damn your soul,' Hardin said to the Negro, 'I told you to leave those hobbles alone. Now get them off that horse and bring them here, and if you ever touch them again, I'll make a sieve out of your insides.'

"He added some other strong words. I will always believe that Robinson had put the Negro up to taking the hobbles. Anyway, the Negro acted as if the boss would back him up.

" 'I ain't going to take no sech talk from nobody,' he said, and started to reach for his six-shooter, which hung low on his hip.

"Before he got the gun out of the scabbard, he fell back dead with three bullets through his heart. I never saw anything swifter in my life than the way Hardin got his gun out and pumped the lead. Later on we looked at the bullet holes; you could have covered all three with a saucer. They had come almost as one.

"At the shots, Robinson jumped up and reached for his Winchester.

" 'Stop,' Hardin ordered. And Robinson stopped.

"Hardin was backing into a position so that he had the whole camp in front of him. The horse he had been riding that afternoon was still saddled. He had roped out his night horse and his private mount from the remuda and walked up leading all three.

" 'Mooney,' he now spoke to the cook, who was a white man — a decent fellow — and he spoke calm and polite. 'Mooney, will you please get my hobbles off that horse out yonder?'

"Mooney went to get the hobbles. Meantime, his eyes covering everything, Hardin changed his saddle to his own horse. 'Thank you,' he said to Mooney. 'Now, please hand me my blanket and slicker out of the wagon.'

"Mooney laid the blanket and slicker, neatly rolled up, over Hardin's left arm. Hardin tied the roll behind his saddle and asked, 'Will you kindly bring the money that Mr. Robinson owes me?' Mooney got it for him. Then Hardin began to back off, leading his horse with an arm between the reins. We could see his fingers working, putting fresh cartridges into the six-shooter.

"About a hundred yards from the camp, he turned his back to us, mounted and rode to a little rise. There he stopped, turned his horse to face us, waved, yelled, 'Adios, boys,' and rode on south.

"Nobody had said anything during all this time. There were two other Negroes in the outfit, and they were scared to death. They wanted to quit but were afraid of Indians, and we persuaded them they were safer with us than they'd be trying to get back to Texas by theirselves. There was no reason for them to fear us white men. We got along with them well. They were good hands and good men. They would not touch the body of the dead Negro. We dug a shallow hole with an axe and the long-handled spade the cook used for moving coals. We wrapped the body in a blanket and covered it up. The next morning we left the place without marking the grave.

"Robinson didn't say what he thought. The rest of us thought Hardin had done the right thing. He had tended to his own business and left other people's business alone."

At a gathering of the Old-Time Trail Drivers of Texas in San Antonio in 1926, I heard a man named Folts tell this incident. One fall in the '80's while he was working with the Continental Cattle Company on the Plains along the Texas-New Mexico line, gathering beef cattle, the cook came up missing. Everybody had to have food and somebody had to prepare it. First one cowboy and then another cooked, each doing his worst in hope of being relieved, but nobody complaining, for whoever complained would have to cook.

One noon while the outfit was eating dinner on the prairie

near a lake, a stranger rode up. Somebody told him to get down. He wanted to speak to the boss. "There he is over there," one of the men pointed.

He walked up to the boss and said, "I'm looking for a job."

"Can you cook?"

"Yes, my middle name is Cook."

"Well, you're hired," the boss said. "What'll we call you?"

Evidently appreciating the nicety implied in the question, the stranger replied, "You can call me Bill."

His worldly goods were in a flour sack tied behind his saddle. He untied it, unsaddled his horse, and turned him loose with the remuda, which was out not far from camp. Then he tied a fairly fresh flour sack around his waist for an apron and flew into his new job.

The men all left. When they got in for supper they found well-cooked meat, well-cooked sourdough bread, beans just right, stewed dried apples for dessert, and all the plates, cups, knives and forks clean and in order. Of course, nobody bragged on the cook; that would have been unethical.

The next day at noon while most of the men were eating, only two or three holding the beef herd, the cook who called himself Bill said out loud to the boss: "Who's in charge of this chuck wagon?"

"Why, you are, of course," the boss replied.

"I'm glad to hear it," said the cook. "I thought I was, but wanted to be sure. And now," he went on, turning to the cowboys, "you fellows have heard. When I came here nobody seemed to be in charge of the wagon, and everything in it was a mess. The horseshoes were mixed up with the rice, the axle grease with the lard, and the sugar with the salt. I'm getting things in order and propose to keep them in order. If anybody from now on wants anything out of this chuck wagon, let him ask me and I'll get it, but I don't want anybody at all going into the chuck wagon for anything at any time."

The cook didn't talk grouchily; he just laid down the law cold and plain. Nobody said anything, at least right then. The hands roped out fresh mounts and left, most of them to hunt cattle, leaving three men to hold the herd. The steers were loggy with grass and water, and so the men on herd went to "riding one horse"; that is, while waiting for the cattle to move, they got together on one side to chin.

One of them, young and green, hadn't been out in the cowboy country long. He was dressed out of Sears, Roebuck and Company's catalogue. He said to the others, "I don't like that bullying talk from the new cook."

One of the others said to him, "That's not bullying talk. All good cooks are cranky and, anyway, any cook worth a damn runs his own chuck wagon."

"I don't care," the young squirt said, "I'm not going to let this one come in and run any rannicky business over me. I'm going down there and call his hand."

One of the other men advised, "You could get into trouble, you know, butting into another man's business."

But the ambitious young cowboy socked the spurs into his horse and galloped right up to the chuck wagon, raising a dust that wasn't calculated to make him welcome. He threw the bridle reins to the ground, jumped up on a front wheel of the wagon. The men's duffle bags were generally carried in the bed toward the front. The young man reached as if to pull out his duffle bag. He hadn't more than bent over till the cook reached too. He pulled out a six-shooter and shot, and this young cowboy fell back on the ground dead.

The horse wrangler wasn't very far off with the remuda. The cook waved his hat to him. The wrangler, who had heard the shot, began driving the remuda in. The cook roped out the horse he'd ridden up on the day before, saddled him, tied his flour sack of possibles behind the saddle, and rode off.

Folts stopped the story at this point. I asked him, "What did you all do?"

"Why," he said, "we didn't do nothing. We figured that young fellow had made a mistake in not tending to his own business and needed a lesson."

"He got it a little late to make use of it," I said.

"Somebody else could make use of it," Folts said, "and maybe so still could."

A cook's wagon was his house, and more than three hundred years back in the Elizabethan Age Sir Edward Coke, in a pronouncement on the Common Law, declared a man's house to be his "castle and fortress, as well for his defence against injury and violence as for his repose."

One time a cow outfit camped on a river within a hundred yards or so of a nester and his family. They seemed to be living on fish, game and milk from three cows. The chuck wagon cook bought a big tomato can of buttermilk from the nester's wife, set it down beside his flour sack and had his back turned washing his hands when one of the cowboys idling in camp sneaked over, lifted the can to his mouth and drained it.

When the cook found the milk gone he said nothing, walked to the nester's camp and paid out another nickel. He was determined on a batch of buttermilk biscuits. He set the can down by his flour sack exactly where he had set it the first time.

"I'll kill any son-of-a-bitch who drinks this buttermilk," he remarked as he turned away to put wood on his fire.

The cowboy who had dared once dared again. A minute later the cook discovered his loss.

"Who drank that buttermilk?" he demanded.

"I did," the guilty cowboy answered with a kind of sneering bravado.

The cook walked to his bedroll, drew out a six-shooter and shot the intruder dead. He had a private mount in the remuda and a saddle in the wagon. When the remuda came in he saddled up and rode away.

In 1925, Joe Burdette, then night watchman for Oklahoma A. & M. College at Stillwater, where I was head of the English Department, told me something that adds to the lesson. Along in the '70's while he was driving up the trail for the Wiley Brothers from north Texas, one of their hands quit and the boss hired a Mexican vaquero in his place. The other hands didn't like this vaquero but he was needed, and no special trouble came up until the herd got into the Wichita country. From here on is Joe Burdette's own relation:

"We made camp on Cow Creek, and had to hold our cattle there for quite a spell. One day when we rode in for dinner, we found the Mexican already eating. He'd left his horse loose and it had grazed off some distance. When the Mexican got done, he walked up to a saddled horse that belonged to one of the boys still eating and said, 'I believe I'll just ride out and get my horse.'

" 'You stay off mine,' the cowboy ordered.

"The Mexican says, 'I'll be back in one minute.' He pulled up into the saddle on one side and fell off on the other. We moved camp four hundred yards off anyhow, and the cattle grazed all about that Mexican's body for a week. . . . Hell, no, we didn't put him underground. We didn't feel any call to bother. And you know, the buzzards never did light on the ground where he laid and nary a wolf ever touched him.

"Sometimes a man had just one chance to tend to his own business."

Hen Baker got a job with the Schreiners on the Guadalupe River up country from San Antonio. He went up the trail with a herd under Gus Schreiner, who sold wagon and horses with the cattle and brought the men back to San Antonio over the new railroad. Before taking the stage to Kerrville, a town then pretty much owned by the Schreiners, he wanted to treat "the boys" to a meal at the Menger Hotel. Robert E. Lee slept there.

They sat down at a table, everybody careful of every movement. A handwritten menu brought by a waiter was passed around, the novelty of it more pronounced to the guests than what it offered. All waited for Mr. Gus Schreiner to order first. He ordered quail on toast. Hen Baker was next to him. He looked at the waiter and said, "I'll take that too and, if you don't mind, I'd like some coffee."

Long afterwards Hen Baker used to tell of this dinner at the Menger Hotel. "And you know," he'd say, "when the waiter brung in that quail on toast it warn't a damn thing but a little old pa'tridge on a slice of scorched lightbread. No meat and not a thing fried."

JULIE MOODY in 1932 at the age of seventy-six. He was range and trail boss for the R2 outfit from 1882 to 1893.

One night while I was standing in the lobby of the Blue-bonnet Hotel in Kerrville a stranger introduced himself to me as fireman of the hotel. Since I wrote stories about his kind of people, he said, he'd like to tell me one on Hen Baker. Hen had quit horsebacking much, was getting along in years and was taking on odd jobs when the Kerr County grand jury indicted him for killing a man with a pocketknife. At the trial he took the witness stand in his own defense. His testimony, spoken to jurymen as his equals, follows.

"You all know about the picnic and barbecue on the river. A big crowd was coming from town and all the ranches around. Somebody had to show the drivers where to put their buggies and wagons and tie the teams and saddle horses too, so as to keep the grounds clear. The boss asked me to take charge of this business.

"I took my place right where the road goes between two big trees and showed everybody that drove up how to pull off to one side or the other and find a good place to tie up. The underbrush has been cleared away out there, you know. After the crowd gathered, some fellers were sashaying around considerable on horses when this man from Bandera rode up. He was purty well lit, and I could see he was packing a gun on his hip. He got down and says, 'I'm the Bull of the Bandera Woods and I hear you're the King of the Kerrville Cedarbrakes. Let's see who's the best man.'

"I says to him, 'I'm busy here. Over there right now a horse some fool didn't tie up right is setting back. I got to tend to him. Go on off.' I stepped over and tied the horse right, but the Bull of the Bandera Woods kept on pestering me. Finally I got rid of him before he started any real trouble. I think he got with a couple of Bandera *compañeros*.

"The crowd didn't break up till late, and I stayed till the last vehicle had cleared out. It was clost to sundown when I got back to town, and I was plenty leg weary. I stepped into the Mint Julep and was leaning against the bar taking my drink easy when Bandera come in the door. He was three sheets in the wind and his eyes looked like a pair of calf nuts floating in a bag of blood. But he was purty steady too.

" 'Uh, I see you're here,' he says.

" 'Come over and have a drink,' I says.

"He comes over and stands up to the bar beside me. I had straightened up and moved a little so that he was to my left. The barkeeper pours him a drink. He swallers it at one gulp and puts the glass on the bar. Then he folds his arms and roosters me in the ribs just like that."

Here Hen Baker folded his arms and jabbed his right elbow into the ribs of an imaginary target. Then he ended his testimony:

"I didn't have my six-shooter and so I had to cut his throat."

Hen Baker grew up where and when it was considered unbecoming any man to use fist or knife in combat. In saying "I didn't have my six-shooter and so I had to cut his throat," he was apologizing for a breach of etiquette. He had tried to avoid trouble; the troublemaker had violated his privacy and insulted his person. Laws and courts ruled the land, but Hen's code of ethics went back to times when a man relied on himself to take care of insulters. The jury's verdict was "Not guilty."

Cow People

On many men who rode horses around cows six-shooter culture did not take any more than Shelley's poetry takes on the majority of college sophomores — though Shelley took on me. In 1925 I chanced upon an old Texas trail driver named Branch Isbell. My mother and her people knew him when he was a gay cowboy down in Nueces County. During talk something about six-shooters came up and I asked Mr. Isbell if he wore one on the trail to Kansas. "No," he said, "I never buckled on a six-shooter anywhere. I figure my life has been saved several times by not having one handy. No gunman ever bothered a man without a gun, and a man without a gun shore wasn't going to bother a man with one — if he had any sense. I never felt undressed or out of place without a gun."

Branch Isbell had plenty of company of no-gunmen. My Uncle Frank Byler was driving a herd of his own horses to the Kansas market by the time he was twenty. One year while passing through the Indian Territory he and two other hands rode to a pool in an opening among trees. While their horses were drinking, one of the men noticed a cottonmouth moccasin swimming close to the bank.

"Frank," he said, "you got a six-shooter. Shoot that snake's head off."

"I know I can't but I'll try," Uncle Frank said, drawing the six-shooter from its holster.

He aimed and pulled on the hammer, but it would not cock. He looked at it and saw that rust and dirt had clogged trigger action. He hadn't shot the thing for months before leaving Nueces County, never had shot it much, and hadn't removed it from the holster during maybe two months of rain, mud, and dust on the trail. He took that six-shooter by the barrel and threw it at the moccasin and watched it sink in the water and mud.

"Nobody that can't shoot a six-shooter has any business carrying one," he said as he rode off.

Mark Twain, in *Roughing It,* characterized "road agent" Joseph A. Slade of Montana as "at once the most bloody, the most dangerous, and the most valuable citizen that inhabited the savage fastnesses of the Rocky Mountains." He was "valuable" because "the world was richer for the loss" of several thugs that Slade put an end to. Society probably suffered no loss when Hen Baker put an end to the Bull of the Bandera Woods.

Charlie Ross took the name of Gannon after a certain "difficulty"; he had killed in what he considered self-defense. He stayed in practice. He would ride a horse at full speed along a fence, hitting every post center. Yet he was a trusted cowman, wore a money belt, and one time carried as much as $25,000 in it. He had long wanted a certain ranch of good valley and hill grass land walled in by rough mountains fantastically beautiful. The setting talked to him, but the owner would not sell. Years went by. He was managing a company ranch for pay when he heard that the land he had kept on wanting was for sale. He rode to see it again. The hills and valleys still grew grass and the mountains still guarded them, but something in him had died. The ranch was no longer beautiful to him.

The time had come for him to quit. He rode back to the ranch he managed. The owners, he realized, were no longer

JOHN TOWNS, rancher of Gonzales, Texas. He drove "mossyhorns" (steers up to ten years or more in age) wilder than the Wild West while cow towns in Kansas were coming into existence.

satisfied with him. The very day he got back, a new man
came to supplant him. In no time he was showing his authority. I do not know why Gannon did not leave at once.

On the following Sunday morning — it was in midwin-
ter — the new manager walked into the bunkhouse where
Gannon and two cowboys loitered. He began by raising hell
at their not cutting ice so that cattle could get to water more
easily, though there was plenty of running water free of ice.
He included Gannon as a common hand.

He went too far. Gannon raised and shot five bullets into
his heart. After a while the two cowboys asked if they might
remove the dead body. "Yes."

They stayed outside somewhere. Before long they heard a
single shot. Listening at the closed door, they heard agonized
breathing and then silence. They went inside and saw that
Gannon had shot himself in the temple a fraction to one
side of the fatal spot. He had kept his plume bright — according to his code — until the very last shot. It was time to
quit.

Gannon and other men of six-shooters in this series of narratives were not considered murderers. Perhaps Gannon was
by some called a killer, but he was not in the professional
killer class, like Wyatt Earp and Billy the Kid. Any killer for
property was beyond the code of "standing up for your
rights."

In July, 1939, Walter Lorrance, a range man of free grass
days, enlightened me at Vernon, Texas, on killings. He had
worked for Cal Suggs in the Indian Territory.

"I helped bury three men Suggs killed," he told me. "He had a little graveyard close by."

"What did he kill men for?" I asked.

"Because they needed it, I guess." He continued: "One time I saw him reading a newspaper on the front gallery. I went up to him and said, 'Mr. Suggs, that man you shot a while ago in the back yard ain't dead.'

" 'The hell he ain't,' Mr. Suggs remarked.

"He went around the house. I heard a shot and he came back and finished the newspaper. The next time I looked at the man he was dead."

Every morning, according to Lorrance, Cal Suggs would empty his six-shooter into trees for practice and then load with fresh ammunition. If a gun made the least bobble, he would give it away. The government grass on which he held his cattle was a no-man's-land. He kept an arsenal of rifles and six-shooters at the ranch. There he ate alone, six-shooter in his lap, back to wall, facing the opening. He habitually came in to eat after the men working for him had eaten and left the room. He slept light. One rainy night while sleeping in a cabin with him, Lorrance was startled by a shot. "What's the matter?" he asked. "Nothing, I'm just a damn fool," Suggs replied. He had awakened suddenly to see light, for the sky had cleared, through a chink in the logs and had shot at it.

After his Indian Territory days, Suggs moved down on the southern plains of Texas and had no need for a private graveyard. He offered the choice of three prizes to the girl graduating with highest grades from the San Angelo high school: a car, a diamond, or a year off at college. He told

"Cap" Yates, then young, "If you ever want a wife, pick only the one who chooses a scholarship." Until he was dying, nobody knew that Cal Suggs had a wife and three children in California. He sent for his wife to watch him die. She and the children got his property.

In 1886 a trail driver up from Texas to Montana decided to homestead a section of government land. He filed on it, built a cabin, got control of two or three adjoining sections, bought about a hundred head of cattle, watched out for them while living on his claim until he had almost "proved up" his title. Two or three men working for a big owner whose cattle used government land made a practice of interfering with squatters, but times now seemed quiet and the Texas man set out on a long trip. He was delayed, had been away for weeks, but as he rode to his cabin in the night he kept telling himself that he still had two more days of grace before any claim-jumper could move in.

According to custom, he had left the door unlocked. Some man needing shelter and food might come along. After unsaddling, he walked through driving snow. As he opened the door, he sensed warmth from a fire, though it had died out. He smelled the smell of cooked food. He lit a match. In the light a man raised himself from his bed, asking in a rough voice, "What are you doing in *my* house?" For answer, the proper owner nearly clubbed him to death with his pistol and then dragged him outside to die. The next morning two riders took the body away.

Perhaps the squatter was not surprised when the sheriff came and arrested him. He was indicted for murder and put on trial. "I had a right," he claimed, "to put out any man trying to take my property." Fighting the case cost him his cattle and land. The big owner who had bothered him all along had put the preemptor, a hired man, in his cabin.

Cowmen who interfered with squatters were relatively few. Many helped the squatters. Very few chose to hire killers for ranch work. I have heard of only one professional killer considered a good cowhand.

Intolerance lingers more steadily than tolerance progresses. In 1318 four friars were burned to death by orthodox Christians for wearing the sackcloth-and-ashes frock introduced by Francis of Assisi instead of the uniform ordered by their superior. Also, the objects of intolerance shift.

In a drawing entitled "Painting the Town" by Charles M. Russell (about 1898), wild-riding, wild-shooting cowboys scatter every living thing on a saloon-dominated street — dogs, chickens and a Chinese who has dropped a basket of clothes and is moving so fast that his queue sticks straight out. The Chinese cooked and washed clothes in cow towns of Montana. To some cowboys and other he-men of the Far West, any Chinese was supposed to afford fun. This kind of fun made Mark Twain boil with indignation. "The Chinese," he wrote, "are a harmless race when white men either let them alone or treat them no worse than dogs. . . . Only the scum of the population on the Pacific Coast ever abuses or oppresses a Chinaman — only they and their children; they, and, naturally and consistently, the policemen and politicians, likewise, for these are the dust-licking pimps and slaves of the scum, there as well as elsewhere in America."

Lincoln A. Lang, a civilized gentleman from the East, came

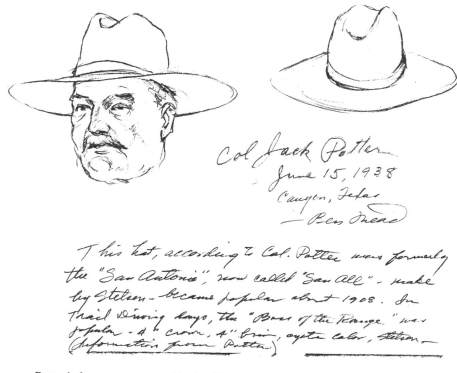

Col Jack Potter
June 15, 1938
Canyon, Texas
— Ben Mead

This hat, according to Col. Potter was formerly the "San Antonio", now called "San All" - make by Stetson - became popular about 1908. In Trail Driving days, the "Boss of the Range" was popular - 4" crown, 4" brim, oyster color, Stetson - (deformation from Potter)

Potter's hat was not too big for him. He was a trail boss at eighteen, managed a big outfit in New Mexico for years, ended up writing about range characters and experiences. One time he got me dead drunk on pure foolery.

to North Dakota in early days and eventually wrote a book entitled *Ranching with Roosevelt* (1926). One summer evening after supper, he relates, he and two other men were sitting outside their cabin facing the gate. Just beyond it passed a seldom-traveled road. At sundown a dilapidated wagon came up, very slowly pulled by a wornout old bay plug on the nigh side of the wagon tongue and on the off side by a tall, stoop-shouldered, limping, long-bearded man dressed in buckskin, his hair hanging down over his shoulders. Wagon and team looked fantastic beyond reality. The viewers knew that no man would hitch himself in a horse collar because he wanted to. They walked to the gate.

The stranger stopped, disengaged himself, and wanted to know "where I'm at." They invited him to pull in, unhitch, turn his horse loose and eat supper. Nobody asked him a single question. He ate ravenously. After a while he asked in a low, disbelieving voice, "Many like you-alls in these parts?" He evidently wanted to talk but before stringing out, he added, "Notice you-alls don't ask no questions."

He hailed from South Carolina and from the time he got out of the Confederate army had wanted to go west. His preferred occupation was hunting and trapping. He carried a muzzle-loading rifle in his wagon. Over a year back he had headed for good hunting country in Idaho that he had heard of. He had wintered in Illinois, supported by a job. Crossing a river in Iowa, he had lost his off horse in quicksand. Nobody would sell him a horse for what he could pay. So he hitched himself to pull with the remaining horse. From there on, except on the Sioux Indian reservation, he had been taken for a crazy man. Avoiding towns made his road longer.

[254]

Now three ranchmen urged him to rest awhile. They found him a horse, but he would accept it only on condition that he work out its price. Then he drove on for the hunting grounds of Idaho. At any ranch he had come to in all the Dakota country, Lincoln A. Long concluded, "he would have been taken in, treated like a man, and helped on his way."

A cowboy of the more than semi-arid ranch country along the Pecos River once said: "A world big enough to hold a rattlesnake and a purty woman is big enough for all kinds of people."

17

Having His Own Way

IN SOME YEAR before World War I, my Uncle Frank
Byler went to a ranch in lower Texas owned by a descendant of an Irish colonist. He was buying steer yearlings
and stayed all night. Long before daylight the next morning
the two men were in the kitchen drinking coffee boiled on a
wood stove. There was a pot for Uncle Frank to pour from
into a cup. The ranch owner took a big can off the stove and
drank from it directly. He liked his coffee hot.

He had lived for years with a wife to whom he did not
speak, nor she to him. He did not sleep with her. Whether
they ate together I do not know. In those times divorces
were rare among country people. The rancher and his wife
were Catholics and divorces were especially rare among Catholics.

It is easy to report on coffee drinking. It is easy to report
a chasm between two people. What went on in the minds of
these two about life is a blank. Historians may analyze personalities, but the personal seldom extends beyond the un-
ceasing progress of history. Dorothy Scarborough's novel *The
Wind* gives the cutting effect of constant dry winds on the

nerves of a woman, but it scants interrelations between human beings. When it was published, chambers of commerce of west Texas, where the novel is laid, protested against it. Autobiographers of the cattle country may afford glimpses of character, but no more than fiction do they reveal the inner lives, especially in relation to each other, of men and women belonging to ranches.

I know what Jim Callan thought about a man who leaves a pasture gate open. He found a gate on the outside fence of his ranch open, found the man who, driving horses, had left it open, and shot him. Many ranchers shared his views and approved his action. He talked in public with skill. I do not know what ideas he held on the rights of human beings. At a convention of cowmen, I heard him tell this story.

Back in the days of sparse settlements, a preacher drove his buggy up to a ranch one evening. After an invitation to stay all night, he said he had come to hold services in the vicinity if a meeting place and a congregation could be arranged.

"Before we settle on anything," the rancher replied, "I want to know straight out whether you are a cowman's preacher or a sheepman's preacher."

The preacher was a little cautious, but he hadn't seen any sheep, and he couldn't smell any sheep. "I'm a cowman's preacher," he answered.

"In that case," the cowman said, "I'll send three men out tomorrow to cover the country for fifteen miles around, and Sunday morning people will gather at Pecan Crossing on the San Saba River to hear you."

This was Friday evening. Early Sunday morning the preacher and the rancher's family got in a hack to drive to the preaching grounds. The hack was a little crowded; the cowman preferred his own company anyhow, and rode horse-back. Looking at cattle he saw in easy reach of the road (just a pair of ruts through the grass) somewhat delayed him, and by the time he tied his horse and walked up to the brush arbor where services were being held, the preacher was already well along. He was starting to read the best-known passage of pastoral literature in the world, as prologue to a sermon that he considered fitting for people whose lives depended upon grass and water.

"The Lord is my Shepherd," the cowman heard. He had not yet reached a seat. He walked back to his horse. He wasn't around when dinner was served on the ground, every family having brought fried chicken, lemon pies, and potato salad.

It was close to sundown when the ranch hack stopped at the front yard gate. The cowman was sitting on the front gallery twirling a spur rowel in silence.

"Well, brother," the preacher addressed him, "we had an outpouring of the spirit today. I'm sorry you weren't there to receive a share of it."

"Preacher," the cowman replied, "I know you saw me walk away, and I'm a-going to give you plain talk. When you got here Friday I asked you fair and square if you were a cowman's preacher or a sheepman's preacher, and you said you were a cowman's preacher. I did what I said I'd do, and you found a good crowd waiting to hear you preach. As I walked up to the arbor, the first words I heard you utter were about some damned sheepherder. The next time you want to preach in this country, you can go somewhere else."

"Aunt Mary," as people called Mrs. George Givens, looked up to preachers and ministered to them. She and her husband

ranched about seven miles east of us. He always seemed in
the background. A veteran of the Civil War, maybe of the
Mexican War, he was so inactive that Mrs. Givens had to do
most of the ranch work. She rode a sidesaddle, but that did
not hamper her in driving cattle to the pens and roping
wormy calves to be doctored. She had a few sheep, a curiosity
in the country at that time. I suppose that coyotes had too
many rabbits to eat to bother sheep. In season she grew garden produce and at all times had a bounty of chickens and
cats. Once in a while my mother would take the children
with her to eat dinner and spend a good part of the day with
Mrs. Givens. She was a staunch supporter of the Methodist
Church. The particular church house to which she went was a
little frame building near the Dinero store. An itinerant
preacher came here only on fifth Sundays.

He lived at Oakville, twenty miles or so away. He usually
rode his circuit in a buggy. His pay from the five churches in
his circuit may have amounted to three hundred dollars a
year, and as two horses eat more corn than one, he drove a
one-horse buggy. One year the Methodist Conference as-
signed to the Oakville circuit a newly married young
preacher who decided to save by not supporting even one
horse. Soon after his appointment he came down from Oakville for the Dinero services. He rode a bicycle, though he
probably had to push it a good part of the way, for sand was
heavy on stretches of the road.

According to custom, the Dinero preacher spent Saturday
night at the Givens ranch. There he could count on all the
fried chicken, cream gravy, hot biscuits, fresh vegetables,
pound cake, with the best of coffee, milk, and butter, that any
appetite could compass. Aunt Mary Givens had heard of the

BILL JENNINGS, about 1900. When somebody asked him if he'd ever been broke, he said, "Yes, except in 1893. I went broke three times that year." He did not approve of anything modern but whiskey. He was not hell-bent on having his way, but maintained a kind of you-be-damned attitude towards people whose ways he disliked.

new preacher and was expecting him late Saturday preceding the fifth Sunday. Her house stood in sandy loam amid great live oaks. She saw a man coming down the sandy road — wheeling his bicycle. It was the first she had ever seen in Live Oak County. She would never have expected a preacher to be bicycling. When he arrived at the front gate and called, she said, "Come in." When he introduced himself as the preacher, she told him to keep going. She thought a preacher should be a real man. Every real man she knew rode or drove horses.

One preacher coming fresh to a cow country church read books. He stood up behind a homemade pulpit to expound a doctrine new to his growing mind. He had the bits in his teeth.

Not everybody took what he had to say sitting down. Following the benediction, a cowman of set features stepped up to him. "Who are you," he demanded, "to be changing what the Bible says?"

"I am a student of religions and know what I am talking about," the young preacher answered. "Now, I'd like to know who you are to be questioning me."

"Who am I?" the cowman retorted. "I'll tell you who I am. I am a follerer of the meek and lowly Jesus. I say to hell with all this newfangled theology."

Like most cowmen, John Chisum of the Jinglebobs did not care for soup. One time soon after the Brown Palace hotel was erected in Denver he went there. The meals were served at regular hours and in courses. Dinner was at evening instead of at noon: soup first; then meats and vegetables in bowls and platters, all passed around by liveried waiters. The diners sat down to empty bowls on plates, and presently waiters brought tureens from which they ladled the soup. When a waiter got to John Chisum, he said, "No soup." Dressed in white uniforms, the waiters looked considerably alike. Presently another one came along to John Chisum saying, "Your soup, sir." "No," Chisum replied, "I told you I didn't want any soup." "Very well, sir." But these were energetic and watchful waiters, and in less than two minutes another was at Chisum's side trying to ladle soup into his bowl. "How many times do I have to tell you," Chisum asked in a rising voice, "that I don't want any soup?" He ate a full meal without it.

In those days consumptives, called "lungers," frequented Denver and other western towns and cities. Chisum's room in the hotel had for months been occupied by a lunger, and every night some time after twelve an attendant dressed in a white uniform resembling that of the table waiters had given him an injection in the arm. Chisum talked, played poker, and otherwise diverted himself after supper, and was tired and sleepy when he went to bed. He neglected to lock the door. He was dead asleep when he was aroused by a uniformed figure leaning over him with a hypodermic needle already piercing his arm. The light was on. Without remonstrance, Chisum, still more than half asleep, said, "Well, damn your soul, you are getting that soup into me after all!"

I know other stories connected with John Chisum, but I have never heard an intimation that he exercised his mind on any subject not connected with cattle.

The more room a man has, the more apart from population he operates, the more of his own way he can have. It is easy to be independent in solitude. To maintain independence amidst crowding people and opinions requires self-discipline, accommodation to others, intellectual perspective. "Independence is my happiness, and I view things as they are, without regard to place or person." In that sentence Thomas Paine struck a universal note. Nowhere were stands for personal independence more pronounced than on the old-time cattle ranges.

Those who so choose may talk about "cattle kings," "the cattle kingdom" and "feudal estates," but no real cattleman, however big, ever tried any feudal lord business over spur-wearing employees. I have never heard of a cowman's alluding to himself or another cowman as king.

When he comes to feel obligations to society, the independent understands that he himself is a small potato in a big hill. Assertions of independence by many cowboys grew out of prejudice and provincialism. The final form (1928 reprinting) of Charles A. Siringo's autobiography, entitled *Riata and Spurs,* affords an example — probably of folk creation, which makes it representative of the creators.

In the provincial-minded way of many cowboys, Siringo calls John G. Adair, moneyed owner of an estate in Ireland and backer of Charles Goodnight, a "lord." One time, he says, while "Lord" and "Lady" Adair were visiting the J A ranch, Goodnight absented himself to oversee cattle work and sent a top hand named Cape Willingham in from camp for the mail. Willingham arrived just at supper time, dirty, greasy, bloody from castrating bull calves. As he stepped into the door of the headquarters house, he saw Mrs. Goodnight sitting at the dining table with the Adairs. Hat in hand and leather chaps on legs, he stood still for a minute until Mrs. Goodnight invited him to sit and eat. She placed cup and saucer, plate, knife, fork and spoon on the table opposite "the Irish lord and his wife."

Both laid down their forks and drew somewhat back. "We are not in the habit of eating with the servants," Adair explained to Mrs. Goodnight. This, remember, is a cowboy story. The Adairs had too much sense to act as related.

As the story goes on, Mrs. Goodnight spoke out, "Mr. Goodnight and I don't consider cowboys servants. Cowboys are good enough to eat with anybody." Whereupon, the Adairs moved to a side table and there finished their meal.

A few days later Goodnight persuaded Adair to spend a night at the cow camp. He occupied a tepee-shaped tent some distance away from the chuck wagon. After dark a cold, wet norther blew up, and when Cape Willingham rode in from the herd to wake the next guard, the tepee tent aroused his resentment. He untied the rope from the horn of his saddle, made a loop, pitched it over the top of the pole holding up the tent, and socked the spurs into his horse's sides.

The outraged Adair was left "exposed in his silk night-gown." Goodnight and awakened cowboys got him into some sort of shelter. Next morning Goodnight fired Cape Willingham, but as soon as his partner left the country hired him back.

Having one's own way because the way is right in work is different from having it out of personal pique. Dillard R. Fant used to travel to Dodge City, Kansas, by rail, and there, trading around, await the herds of cattle he had started up the trail from southern Texas. By June they would be arriving, one at a time. One year John Rigby bossed a Fant herd. He knew that the big owner would be eager to see how much the steers had gained on their slow travel north and would give him orders to deliver the herd or drive it on to Wyoming or somewhere else.

Dodge City is just north of the Arkansas River. The evening before he was to cross, John Rigby camped two or three miles south of the river. He knew from scouting at what bend of the river and at what hour the sun would shine least in the eyes of the cattle.

Everything was going according to plan and the herd was being pointed into the water when, to quote John Rigby, "Mr. Fant showed up in a livery rig. He had crossed on the ferry below. He was driving a pair of fancy blacks and the top to his buggy was down. I just had time to tell him howdy and the next thing I noticed he was sliding that rig down towards the river. The bank wasn't steep. He seemed to think he would help us string the cattle across. Then the next thing I knew he had edged into the water.

"About a minute later horses, buggy, Fant and all went out of sight. He had struck a jump-off. The cattle went to milling and the big cowman was under water. It looked like there was hell to pay and no pitch hot. I was on a good swimming horse, and I·rode out downstream from where the outfit had gone under. I thought something would bob up d'reckly, and it did. I had my loop fixed and I pitched it over Fant's shoulders, tightened the rope and made for shore.

"When he hit the bank, he got up a-sputtering. 'Jesus Christ and General Jackson,' he says, 'what are you roping me for? Why don't you get that pair of livery stable horses out? Don't you know they're worth a carload of steers?'

"I told him the horses was already drownded and that if I

hadn't roped him he'd a-been drowned too. 'Mr. Fant,' I says, 'if you ever come around again interfering with my herd of cattle, you can get another boss.'

"He saw he'd been in the wrong. The boys had broken the mill and were stringing the herd across the river in good shape. Fant went back to Dodge and paid $800 for the outfit he had lost. 'Jesus Christ and General Jackson,' he used to say, 'move about and make things go.' That was the only swear word he used. He was kindhearted and easy with his men and we all liked him."

As Bob Beverly used to tell, Barnes Tillous, boss of the Quien Sabe outfit on the Plains, had trained a grullo-colored colt named Possum. He was very fond of Possum. One day when he rode Possum into Midland, a buyer of polo ponies tried to stop him and buy the pony. Barnes Tillous rode on without paying him any attention. The buyer kept an eye on him, though, and followed him eight miles back to camp, where he found Tillous feeding Possum oats. "My name is Savage," he said.

"I can't help what your name is," Tillous retorted. "I didn't give it to you."

The polo buyer went on to say that before he left San Antonio he had talked to M. Halff, owner of the Quien Sabe, and that Halff had told him he would sell — at a fancy price — any horses suitable for polo to be found in his remudas.

"It is about time for chuck," Barnes Tillous said. The polo buyer followed to the wagon, saying over and over how he liked the looks of Possum and how he would like to try him out after dinner. As soon as dinner was over, Barnes Tillous without a word put his saddle on Possum and rode away. Some of the hands told the buyer that he had just as well go back to town. He went and wired M. Halff. Halff wired Tillous to sell any horse the buyer would take.

Tillous did not answer the telegram. He was something more than a "hired man on horseback."

Literature and biography are studded with characters of one passion, one desire, one ambition. Silas Marner lived to hoard; Bismarck, to make Germany dominant; Chaucer's Pardoner, to hoax mankind under the cloak of piety. Yet, however one-sided a man may be, he has other sides.

George West had. He paid for sending off to a good school the two daughters of a boss, on condition that no word get out on what he was doing. If it did, he would fire the boss and quit schooling the daughters. I grew up on George West anecdotes. They are still passed around. He had notions.

Whatever bacon and lard his ranch hands got had to come from wild razorback hogs ranging along and out from the Nueces River winding through his Live Oak County ranch. Deer were plentiful. Even "poor doe" is meat. West was against any sweet in camp, whether he furnished it or not. Once he fired four men for buying a jug of molasses with their own money. He rode up to a herd of steers lying down in peace, full of grass and water, too lazy to move, and found three herders congregated in the shade of a tree. He ordered them to headquarters for "a little pink check." Shade and sociability might be good for fattening steers; fattening hired men was not business. Sometimes he seemed bent on cultivating irritation. After firing hands, he more than once sent a rider, a day or two later, to rehire them. This was at a time when job-hunters were more plentiful than jobs.

GEORGE W. WEST, rancher of southwest Texas. When he and his men lost their horses in Kansas on an early-day drive they moved the herd on afoot. All his life he was resolute in having his way.

Having His Own Way

Having his own way seemed to mean more to George West than making money. One time he came to corrals where broncs were being cut through a gate. He wanted to keep the best horses, said he would watch the gate. A fine looking bronc that he wanted to hold back nearly ran over him trying to pass through the gate. He told one of the men to watch the gate, walked to his buckboard, got his Winchester, leveled it on the headstrong bronc, and shot him dead there in the pen.

Dr. Simmons, of Simmons Liver Regulator fame, bought thousands of acres of land that Mr. West had once run and that joined his ranch. Simmons stocked it with steers and branded them with a brand shaped like a liver. He proposed to cut the land up, sell it out, and establish a town called Simmons City. He did not appeal to Mr. George West. About 1899 he sold his steers to J. M. Dobie, and Uncle Jim got my father to stay on the Simmons ranch for weeks cutting out fat steers for shipment while they were being gathered from the brush. A few George West cows were still running in it. After they and their maverick offspring were caught, Mr. West was notified. He sent his boss to receive the cattle — by shooting them and dragging the carcasses a short distance away from the pens.

When a railroad — the San Antonio, Uvalde and Gulf, "the Sausage" — built into Live Oak County it ran through the heart of George West's ranch. He subsidized it heavily. The county seat was moved to George West, on the railroad. He proposed to make this a town according to his own ideas. He refused to sell a lot to anybody who would not agree to certain restrictions or who was obnoxious to him. He built a bank building, engaged a San Antonio man to organize the bank and sell stock in it. Before the shares were issued he looked over the list of subscribers and cut out about half of them.

He erected a modern hotel across from the railroad station and prevailed upon the railroad company to stop trains there for meals, in Harvey House style on the Santa Fe railroad. The "Sausage" passengers were not numerous enough or hungry enough to make the hotel pay. Mr. West was not satisfied with the way it was run anyhow. He locked it up with all the furniture, bedding, dishes, kitchenware and everything else in place. It remained locked for six years until he died in 1926 in San Antonio.

The George West ranch still exists, under lease. In front of the courthouse, a glassed-in case holds a mounted Longhorn steer that was once George West's and that he gave, with the case, to the county. The Witte Memorial Museum in San Antonio exhibits mounted heads of Longhorn steers that came from him. He belonged more to Longhorns and ranch spaces than to population and developers.

It is something beyond demonstrating one's "rights" that indicates nobility of nature, regard for the human race, breadth of mind. Al Capone had his way — for a while. Captain Richard King, founder of the million-acre King Ranch, had his way — to wealth. In order to maintain it he rode with an armed guard. While most Southerners lost during the Civil War, Captain King gained gold on Confederate cotton. After General Robert E. Lee was dead, Captain King's descendants claimed a strong friendship between their ancestor and the great southern gentleman. Nothing in history indicates rapport between the two.

Major — a title attained in the Civil War — George W. Littlefield had the ponderous bronze doors to his bank in Austin, Texas, bas-reliefed with cattle, cowboys, chuck wagon and his L F D brand. He hired a mediocre sculptor to erect figures of Jeff Davis and other Southerners on the University of Texas campus. He gave the university a fund for purchasing Southern history books. As regent he used his power to oust from the university a civilized president with whose ideas he did not agree. He said, "The only practical knowledge I have gained in ranching is that a cow will have a calf." For all his patriotism — sectional in nature — he was hellbent, above all else, on having his own way.

18

Civilized

SOUTH AMERICANS used to say, to bind themselves to an oral agreement, *"por la palabra de un Ingles"* (on the word of an Englishman). Will Waddell, a cowman of cultivated deportment, married Ella Byler, eighteen years older than he. My mother was her niece and namesake. They had no children but ample ranch property. As the years added up, they talked of bequeathing it to relatives, but she made no will. Thus, when she died, her part of the estate became his, by law. This was before inheritance taxes became high. Later, he found in a table drawer a piece of paper on which she had penciled the first names of a few relatives, including my mother's, and opposite each name a number. The numbers added up to ten. A name with the figure three following it meant that the individual was to receive three-tenths of her half of the estate. An oil company leased the ranch for mineral rights and struck oil. Will Waddell had a lawyer draw up a will. In it be bequeathed his half of the estate to his own kin; the other half he willed to the individuals, some of them his own kin, named by his wife, portioning the amounts out according to her figures.

Men you could tie to, honest, generous, open-natured, decent in all ways, unfailingly self-reliant, dependable wherever they went, represented the entire cattle country. I could name a few big cowmen of open range days who with tough hirelings took cattle from other men, sometimes burning out the brands on them. The most active cow thieves were little operators preying from adjacent country on big ones. They included some nesters. Despite such activities, the word of a representative cowman has always been as good as his bond.

The best known name of an ex-cowboy is that of Will Rogers. As rope-twirler, actor, stage entertainer, writer of newspaper squibs frequently rich in sense, humanity and wit, he made the world more wholesome. Yet, sometimes he played up a corny sentimentality indicative of Bible Belt fundamentalism and ignorance of history. This sentimentality and this idea of heaven were supposed by the public to be cowboyish; to an extent they were. His friend Charles M. Russell, the western artist, died in 1926. The next year his rollicky collection of yarns, under title of *Trails Plowed Under,* was published with an introduction by Will Rogers in the form of a letter to Russell in heaven. Rogers asks for news on other angels gathered about him: Mark Twain and James Whitcomb Riley (imagine linking them together and imagine Twain among angels at all), Washington, Jefferson (who abjured personal immortality), Lincoln (profoundly spiritual but conceiving of God as impersonal and inscrutable), and his own mother cooking dinner at a ranch "up there."

Men of cultivated minds and civilized experience appeared more often in the western and northwestern states than in Texas. The majority were from Scotland, England, and New England. In reminiscences they reveal perspective, grace and reason, often break into the joyous. As a young man, I knew old-timers of the range who seemed to regard Indian troubles, killings, badmen, bad horses, stampedes and the like the only subjects worth relating. Autobiographies of the cattle world that look at life instead of being confined to action stand out as rarities among hundreds of bleak chronicles.

In the fall of 1883 young Theodore Roosevelt of New York, recently out of Harvard and already in politics, came to the Bad Lands of Dakota and contracted for four hundred head of cattle, to be managed by men he picked to trust. The following June he began what he called "a glorious career" as rider and cowman. While expanding his holdings and learning the life, his bedroom at the Maltese Cross ranch was also a study in which he read and wrote. He moved into a newly built house on another ranch, the Elkhorn. Unlike most cattlemen, he had outside resources to spend. Out of enormous energy he hunted, and he wrote of big game hunts as well as of ranching. He learned the birds of the region. He came to understand cowboys, cowmen, also six-shootered cow thieves, as human beings rather than as types for a Buffalo Bill exhibit. He wrote of them realistically. He owed to them a marked development in outlook and in what makes the whole man. After he became President, Dakota cowboys dined at the White House table with cabinet members and ambassadors.

About the time Roosevelt took to ranch life, without at all forsaking his political career, the fantastic Marquis de Mores, from France, was establishing a packing plant at Medora on the Little Missouri. He was far more successful in building up a legend, which has entered numerous books, than a business. Roosevelt could talk horses and literature with the Marquis but was more companionable with a university graduate publishing the sprightly *Bad Lands Cowboy,* a weekly, at Medora. Lincoln A. Lang, a Scot of cultivated mind and "a companion rancher," wrote a noble book, entitled *Ranching with Roosevelt* (1926). Then there were Howard Eaton and his brothers. Another educated gentleman-rancher was Wallis Huidekoper, from Pennsylvania. He later wrote various historical sketches, came to know Charles M. Russell well, and gave a fine collection of Russell paintings to the Montana Historical Society. I prize a beautifully bound copy of *Swiss Family Robinson* that he had kept from boyhood and gave me upon reading of my boyhood pleasure in the book.

Hermann Hagedorn's *Roosevelt in the Bad Lands,* in which all sorts of men of the cow country stand out, is a relief against imaginationless action. Yet it is not among many out-of-print titles of Western Americana that soar in price. Such is the taste for violence and such is the conception of the cowboy West that an obscure pamphlet on Billy the Kid will run bids up into the Abraham Lincoln signature category.

Billy the Kid: The Bibliography of a Legend, by J. C. Dykes (University of New Mexico Press, 1952) not only lists but digests 437 books, pamphlets, and magazine articles, along with phonograph records and motion pictures, bearing in part or wholly, whether fact or fabrication, on the Kid. Subsequent years have added scores of additional items. In all that range men have written on the heroized thief and murderer only one narrative, in so far as I have read, can be called charming. That is in R. B. Townshend's *The Tenderfoot in New Mexico,* published in London, 1923.

Fresh from Trinity College, Cambridge, Townshend began ranching in Colorado in 1869. He went back home to England in time to translate Tacitus under the spires of Oxford before World War I put him to training men how to shoot. His book *A Tenderfoot in Colorado* (1923) contains in a chapter entitled "A Texas Nursery" more natural history on Longhorn cows than anything contributed by hundreds of range men to the *Trail Drivers of Texas* volumes. It is told serenely without striving for effect, as W. H. Hudson of the pampas or Gilbert White of Selborne might have told. Townshend had a blend of grace and gay anticipation. He raised calves and he drove a herd of horses and mules from below "the deadline for sheriffs" (the Nueces River in Texas) to mines in Colorado. He was friends with Mexican vaqueros and Pueblo Indians.

In England, near the Scottish border, John H. (Jack) Culley was born, 1864, to the purple and to cattle breeding. After graduating from Oxford University he went west and in 1893 became manager of the Bell Ranch, comprising seven hundred and fifty thousand acres, in New Mexico — where he cultivated a flower garden. He came to operate a ranch of his own. His reminiscences, *Cattle, Horses and Men of the Western Range,* were published in 1940, after he had retired. While I was working in the Huntington Library, nineteen years later, he invited me by letter to visit him in his home in El Monte, an outpost of Los Angeles.

I perceived at first glance a very fine gentleman. A little later he picked up a book on the table beside him to show me. It was *An Essay on Style* by Walter Pater, presented to Culley by Pater himself as his tutor at Oxford. Mr. Culley said to me in a letter that his own book, full of particular horses and men both good and bad, was "written with the scrupulous pains and restraint I learned from Flaubert and my Oxford master and friend, Walter Pater — with something owing to our own Hemingway." To read it is to realize how far away a truthful writer with a civilized sense of values can get on the same subject from one always too-muching the wild and sensational: from Will James in *Lone Cowboy,* for example.

Of upper-class descent, Montague Stevens graduated in 1881, at the age of twenty-two, from Trinity College, Cambridge. The year before he had hunted in Wyoming with James H. Cook, whose *Fifty Years on the Old Frontier* remains a landmark among books written by keen-minded cowmen. In this book, mentioning Montague Stevens among other "distinguished" sportsmen, mostly English, whom he outfitted on hunts, Cook says he sometimes received as much as $750 a month from a hunter but was primarily benefited by association with men of knowledge and natural nobility.

Montague Stevens knew what he wanted and he had the means to follow his want. He wanted to ranch and hunt big game. In 1882, while Apaches were still on the warpath, he began ranching in western New Mexico and in time had ranches on both sides of the continental divide of the Rocky Mountains, "scattered over an area of some eighty by thirty miles." His autobiographic *Meet Mr. Grizzly: A Saga of the Passing of the Grizzly,* was not published until 1943, first by the University of New Mexico Press and then in London. He had a foreman to oversee cattle work. He rode with his cowboys, but his narratives are mainly concerned with bears, both black and grizzly, and hunters, including a hired helper, General Nelson Miles and Frederic Remington, who put an account, profusely illustrated, of the hunt in *Pony Tracks.*

Stevens gives his dogs and horses far more emphasis than he gives other hunters.

He was a factual man. Geographical particulars on chasing grizzlies up one canyon, above timber line, and down another canyon make me favor the style of the Bear Hunter of Arkansas. Called upon for a bear story, he said, "There ain't nothing to it. A bear is started and then he is finished." Old Susie, a cow-killer, was a notability among grizzlies of the Rockies. Montague Stevens has a full chapter on her. His account of repeated huntings and final killing of her is fully corroborated by Agnes Morley Cleaveland, who joined the hunt, in *No Life for a Lady.* In 1937, before either had published a book, I told in the *Saturday Evening Post* Nat Straw's story of his having killed Old Susie. In 1944 Montague Stevens sent me a letter of about fifteen hundred words annihilating Nat Straw's claim on the famous grizzly.

What he observed about bears and bear days makes *Meet Mr. Grizzly* the best book on the sense of smell in animals that has been published since *A Hind in Richmond Park* by the great naturalist W. H. Hudson came out in 1922.

He "suffered from a superiority complex," one New Mexican wrote me. Certainly he never ceased to use the broad *a* and to be an educated English gentleman. He realized that proving "popular beliefs" to be erroneous made him appear "queer." He rode the best of horses. "That kind of horse does not need a spur," he wrote. His not wearing spurs made him appear "queer." At the same time, to quote Agnes Morley Cleaveland, "No one respecting life or limb tried to keep up with Montague Stevens as Montague Stevens rode in those days of bear-hunting."

He did not like the professional bronco-buster's way of

breaking the only thing he should not break in a high-spirited horse — his spirit. He had an old-fashioned threshing machine to which four sweeps, pulled by horses, were attached. He began breaking broncs by hitching them to the sweeps and thus gentled thirty without abusing a single one. His method "became the talk of the country." Men riding horses broken by threshing machine sweeps complained that they were made fun of. His foreman did not like the ridicule. "As he was an excellent foreman," Montague Stevens told him to "hire a bronc-buster and carry on according to the custom of the country." He himself did not mind remaining "queer" in holding that "the most high-spirited wild horses become the most gentle by kind treatment."

The English have written the best travel books of the world since Herodotus. To consider all who write of ranching in the Americas is beyond my province. John Clay was Scotch. He came to America in 1874, having known cattle, farmers and literature from childhood. He became the outstanding representative of the great British-owned cattle companies of the 1880's. His *My Life on the Range* (privately printed, 1924) is packed with facts on cattle, cattlemen and ranches. I cite it here for its pictures of life and a sense of the beautiful.

A chapter of the book had been printed in 1901 under title of "The Silence of the Sibelle." The title expresses the tone. I would not know where to find in another cowman's writings a treatment of a sheepherder comparable to John Clay's description of old "English Joe" in Wyoming. He had come from Northumberland, lived alone in a sheep camp. "He seemed to love the mountains." He liked talking to this cowman from across the Tweed. Then, during a blizzard, he was found frozen to death. "We wrapped English Joe in blankets and in a niche between rocks, a ready-made grave, up Wild Horse Canyon, laid him in his narrow bed. Gus Lankin selected the flat stones and laid them across the little niche. . . . We piled the stones all over and around him, and today if you go there you will see a cairn heaped some three feet high. In my imagination I have stood by the bedside of little Nell, and have heard Colonel Newcome say *Adsum,* but this was a reality, for below those stones lay a British herder and all that was left of a life not crowned with success."

Edson C. Dayton (1860-1942), author of *Dakota Days,* privately printed 1937, was more sheepman than cowman. A much higher percentage of autobiographies by sheepmen have literary values than those by cowboys and cowmen. As Mrs. Dayton wrote me, four years after the death of her husband, "The questions cowboys and sheepmen asked him and the discussions that arose bringing out religious, historical, and philosophical views, would surprise people [who look for nothing but six-shooter culture in the West]."

On the second page of his book Dayton describes an "intellectual face." He had a spiritual content. Next to a sketch of a Dakota saloon-keeper, he remarks on the sustained exaltation of Milton and the growth of Gladstone in knowledge and intellect. He was from the East. He was not transmuted into a representative of the Raw West, but he understood harmony. Towards the end of his life he expressed awareness of being "an integral part of what Shakespeare called 'the whole race of mankind.' "

Granville Stuart (1834-1918) was born in Virginia of Scotch descent. He had a mind cultivated by parents, some months in country schools of Illinois and Iowa, and lifetime reading. After taking "considerable gold" out of California mines, he mined in Montana. He may not have become the richest cattleman of that state, but it has produced no other leader of such proportions. His ranch library of three thousand books, added to by magazines and newspapers, was open to whoever wanted to read. He led vigilantes in ridding the territory of outlaw thieves. The blizzards of 1886-87 wiped him out financially.

He had married a Shoshone woman and, not a squaw man, remained true to her until she died. His second wife was better fitted to go with him in 1894 as United States minister to the republics of Uruguay and Paraguay. In 1904 he became librarian of the Butte, Montana, library. His reminiscences, *Forty Years on the Old Frontier*, were published in 1925. A cowboy who worked for him and later married a daughter of his said: "He was the fairest of all big cowmen to cowpunchers and wanted to help them get a start in the cattle business." This was contrary to usual cowman practice. To him civilized life was not foreign to either mining or ranching.

19

Charles Goodnight of Amplitude

IN SEPTEMBER of 1926, during a period while I was writing numerous narratives and articles for the *Country Gentleman,* a magazine now extinct, issued by the Curtis Publishing Company, I suggested a story on Charles Goodnight. The editor said, "Go ahead." Not until years later did I know the experience that Lester H. Sheffy, professor of history at West Texas State College, Canyon, Texas, had just had in going ahead.

On a July day Sheffy and his wife ate a midday snack at a joint in the village of Goodnight and then drove to the Goodnight ranch house only half a mile away. For a short while, unseen, Sheffy watched Goodnight bent over repairing the bottom of a gate to a chicken yard. When he raised up, wet with sweat, the youthful stranger extended his hand, saying, "Colonel Goodnight, my name is Sheffy." "I don't give a damn what your name is," came the reply. "What do you want?" At this point the dinner bell rang, and he added, "Let's go in and eat." Sheffy's explanation that he had just eaten added to the old cowman's irritation, but after a meal that cooled him off he revealed "under that gruff exterior a

heart as gentle and kind as any man ever possessed." He led
Sheffy into the living room and for two or three hours talked
the history of which he had been a part. Then he got up and
began taking down pictures hanging on the walls to present
to the Panhandle Plains Historical Society, which Sheffy represented. At a remonstrance by Sheffy, he said, "I have already
given them to you. Take them and get out." He later gave
other things.

People called him Colonel Goodnight and still refer to
him by that title. He made a deeper imprint on the Great
Plains than any other man who has lived there. Born in 1836
in southern Illinois, he came to Texas in 1845 with his
mother, a stepfather and other children. At the age of twenty
he contracted, with a partner, to care for a herd of about four
hundred cows on shares. The grass was all free. During the
Civil War he served as scout and ranger against Indians on
the northwestern frontiers, becoming intimately acquainted
with Plains country beyond all settlements. He had a compass
inside his body, was never lost, day or night, alone or leading.
In 1866 he and Oliver Loving drove two thousand cattle of
their own across ninety miles of desert from the headwaters
of the Middle Concho to Horsehead Crossing on the Pecos
and on to Fort Sumner, New Mexico, where contractors to
supply government beef paid high prices. He trailed other
herds west over the Goodnight-Loving Trail, now traced out
on maps; he ranched for a while in Colorado; in 1876, driving thousands of buffaloes out of Palo Duro Canyon to make
room for his cattle, he established the first ranch in the Panhandle of Texas. The next year John Adair of Ireland backed
him with money.

He made the J A cattle on the Palo Duro perhaps the best-

CHARLES GOODNIGHT. He laid off the Goodnight-Loving Trail from north Texas to Fort Sumner, New Mexico, immediately after the Civil War, driving a herd ninety-six miles without water. In 1876 he established on the Palo Duro Canyon the first ranch in the Texas Panhandle. He always stood for law and order and education. He established the Goodnight Academy at Goodnight, Texas, when there were almost no schools in the region. Here he is pictured after years and life had sculptured his features (about 1920). He could wait as well as act.

bred herd in the West. He blazed a trail to Dodge City, Kansas, his market. He roped a few buffalo calves, raised them and established the first controlled buffalo herd in the West. He led in maintaining law and order over a vast territory. In 1885 Adair died. Two years later, in the depth of a financial panic, Goodnight dissolved the partnership, leaving the Adair estate in control of half a million acres stocked with J A cattle. He soon sold his own holdings, one hundred and forty thousand acres and twenty thousand cattle — at panic prices. After a disastrous plunge in Mexico mining, he settled down on the ranch where I met him.

In response to a letter, he had replied that he would be "pleased to entertain" me any time I came. He had been interviewed and written about various times. He had himself written brief articles on handling a trail herd and other experiences. He was plainly not elated at my arrival, though courteous enough. He told me right off that he did not care a damn for any "publicity" that I or any other writer could give him. He was now ninety years old. His wife, married in 1870, had died the preceding spring. A woman of mature years was cooking and keeping house for him.

At supper I noticed on the table the biggest bottle of pepper sauce I have ever seen — red Mexican peppers in maybe two quarts of vinegar. He regarded, I learned, a mixture of whiskey and extract of buffalo meat as the best of tonics. I saw nothing of this tonic. He ate, without talking, as if he meant business, finished, pushed his chair back, said, "I never was a hand to dally around the table, excuse me," and left.

I stayed with him for three or four days, taking down voluminous notes. On the second morning he told me that his men were going to bring in and pen his buffalo herd. I

wanted to ride with them. "You'd be in the way and probably scare the buffaloes beyond control," he said. He made a
good deal of the "cattalo," a cross between Polled Angus cows
and buffalo bulls. He became irritated when I asked if the
cross could reproduce itself. It could not, consistently. An ab-
solute master at breeding cattle, he had ideas on crossbreed-
ing two species of animals that knowledge of biology would
have dispelled. In Mexico he had heard of — not seen — a
cross between a sheep and a hog. When I visited him he was
keeping and feeding in a pen a sow and a ram, expecting a
cross. The Christmas following this visit he sent me by mail
a fine buffalo roast.

While he narrated experiences and observations to me, I
sometimes had to prod for facts. Yet our chemistries mixed.
I developed a positive admiration for him as a man of large
nature, wisdom, concern for other people, and a noble sense
of values. At mention of "my old pardner Oliver Loving," his
voice grew warm and tender.

He told me about Old Blue, his lead steer on the great
J A Ranch. Old Blue led beef herds from the Palo Duro Canyon to Dodge City and came back with the cowboys and the
remuda. He was a camp pet. Many an outlaw steer roped in
the breaks was necked to him to be led straight to the ranch
corrals. Buffalo calves that Goodnight saved to start a buffalo
herd with were necked to Old Blue for bringing in.

When I evidenced lively interest in Old Blue, Mr. Goodnight's spirits rose. While he would not give half of a damn
for anything that anybody might write about Charlie Goodnight, he would "like to have Old Blue given his dues." Out
of the rich stores of his memory he related instance after
instance of the old Longhorn's behavior; he gave me a bi-

ographical sketch of him that he had written in doggerel verse. Back in Austin, I wrote the story of Old Blue as best I could and sold it to a magazine published in New York. After I sent Mr. Goodnight the story as printed, he responded: "My eyes filled with tears when I read what you had written of my faithful old friend." Years later I put it in my book *The Longhorns*. He told me that if he felt dispirited and rode down into the buffalo pasture and looked at his buffaloes and the canyons, he always came back heartened and refreshed. The honesty of nature never failed him.

Another of his favorite characters was Old Bose Ikard, who had been born a slave in Mississippi and who for years rode with Goodnight on the long cattle trails and on ranges where Indians and white murderers and thieves made life dangerous. Later H. B. (Tex) Willis of Dallas gave me an account of a trip he made, in 1919, with Charlie Goodnight in a car to Weatherford, where Bose was living.

Tex said that as they approached Waco about four o'clock in the afternoon he asked Goodnight if he'd like to go by Sul Ross's place. He had been with Sul Ross in a fight with the Comanches when Cynthia Ann Parker was captured from them. She was the white mother of Quanah Parker, who became the most noted of Comanche chiefs. The dour Parker people to whom she was restored were utterly alien to her. She belonged to the Comanches, to her children, and to nomadic life on the plains. She died of grief. Goodnight understood her tragedy. Sul Ross's subsequent vote-seeking and then governorship of Texas lessened him in Goodnight's eyes.

"Why in the hell," Goodnight snorted, "would I want to see anything connected with that old lying four-flusher named Sul Ross?" He had known him in camp and had known him as politician. He had an instinctive dislike for people always eying the gallery and seeking "suffrages." He himself never had been afflicted with the itch for being noticed — that pimply outbreak on small natures who cannot abide with equanimity their own smallness. Tex Willis said he showed more pleasure at meeting Bose Ikard than at meeting anybody else on the whole trip. He gave him a hundred-dollar bill, sent him money after that. After Bose Ikard died Goodnight had a marker placed over his grave attesting to his "splendid behavior."

It was close to six o'clock before he and Tex Willis got breakfast in Weatherford — mighty late for Goodnight. Word had got around town that the noted frontiersman was back on his old stomping grounds. Before they left the restaurant some important-appearing individual walked up to him boldly and said, "Mr. Charles Goodnight, I believe." Goodnight never moved a muscle. The enthusiastic greeter kept coming, holding out his hand. "My father used to be an Indian fighter," he brightened. With that, Charlie Goodnight rared back like a buffalo bull and, glaring right into the gladhander's eyes, growled: "God-damn poor recommendation, considering one Comanche warrior could drive all the sorry white people out of five counties." Goodnight had fought the Comanches himself. Also, while feeding beef to Quanah Parker's warriors on the Palo Duro, he had made a treaty with them. He respected their rights and respected them as human beings. They had once claimed all the country south of Red River and west of the Cross Timbers to the Rio Grande. They had, in Goodnight's words, "held for ages the land I and other white men controlled. By all laws of justice, it was theirs. We wanted it, fought for it, took it." He was a great friend to some of the Pueblo Indians. He rated natural men and nature above anything else.

At one time Goodnight partly owned and wholly controlled about 1,300,000 acres of land, some of it leased from individual owners, some of it fenced-in state land. Often over a hundred cowhands worked under him. He forbade gambling and drinking on the ranches, demanded cleanness in person and camp. He encouraged his men to save money and invest it in cattle and horses, allowing their stock to graze on ranch property. He said he had not known of a genuine cowboy's having been tried for crime in the Panhandle. He did not rate outlaws as genuine cowboys. He recalled only two fights, merely fist fights, among his hired hands over a fifty-year period.

Mrs. Goodnight knew all the men, nursed them when they were sick, sewed buttons on their clothes, now and then gave them a party, once in a while got a preacher to preach to them. Goodnight did not care to hear what he called "soul-sharpeners," was never "converted," felt no need of having his soul saved. Mrs. Goodnight cultivated flowers, brought books to the ranch, loaned them to whoever wanted to read.

As leader of the decent element, Charles Goodnight naturally became the fear of the bad element. When no legal power was at hand, he assumed it. The earliest settlement near the ranch was "Christian Colony," some twenty miles from headquarters. It was made up of well-meaning visionaries utterly incapacitated for pioneer life. One time a man with a wagon load of whiskey and another wagon loaded with dancing girls appeared in the Colony. He proposed to set up a saloon and dance hall. The colonists protested. The man laughed. The colonists sent for Goodnight. He came.

"Do you see that line of cottonwood trees?" Goodnight asked the promoter.

He saw. He understood the uses to which cottonwood branches, plus ropes, were sometimes put.

"You have half a day to pack up and get out."

"I want only two hours," the man concluded.

Another time when district court was to be convened at Clarendon, Judge Willis was informed by a gang of outlaws who had ridden down from Mobeetie, bent on keeping the country lawless, that there would be no court. Judge Willis reported to Goodnight, who "happened" to be in town.

"My outfit is here with me," replied Goodnight. "The guns are in the wagon. The men know how to use them. You can open your court and conduct it without trouble."

Court was held — without trouble.

About this time Goodnight had his attention called to the fact that the nesters of Christian Colony (Clarendon) had children in need of schooling, that the parents were too poor to provide a school, and that there were no public school funds. He laid the matter before the Panhandle cowmen. Not a single one of them had a child to send, but they instructed Goodnight to prorate among them the expenses of employing a teacher, and for two years they thus financed the first school of the Panhandle.

The teacher was Tom Martingale, "a kind of roustabout and head of the cow thieves." But he was well educated and as smart as a steel trap. "We ought to hang the son-of-a-gun," said Goodnight, "but let's put him to teaching school and keep him busy." The next year the Panhandle Cattle

Raisers' Association made a brand inspector out of him, on the theory that a thief can catch a thief. He made a good inspector.

Goodnight said he could learn more about a man by camping out with him in Comanche country for ten days than by neighboring with him for ten years in a settlement. As he put it, "The purest metal comes out of the greatest heat." He found educated men more teachable, quicker learners, than ignorant men. He believed in educating young women, mothers of men to be. His wife was educated. They had no children. He built a combined church and schoolhouse at Goodnight when there were only six children within reach of it and hired a teacher for them. In 1898 he and his wife opened Goodnight Academy. Hundreds of young people were benefited by it, though it was hardly the equivalent of a modern high school.

His own schooling had ended when he was nine years old, but he read. He observed not only profit-making stock but all kinds of flora and fauna, and, above all, human beings. He reflected. He thought. As his own mind ripened, even while his energy ebbed away, he grew more interested in the development of intelligence and character than in the calving of his cows. Offshoots of wild plums he selected to plant along the Palo Duro bear fruit annually. At the end he was far from being wealthy.

Even while he was making big money, more for a partner than for himself, his reach was for something in life beyond money. I never forget his telling of coming back from Fort Sumner, New Mexico, across the desolate, waterless Pecos country, where not a single bird was sighted. He had a pack mule loaded with $6000 in coin. He and his men were traveling mostly at night, "laying up," out of Indian sight, by day. They were short on food. Then on the desert, not far from Horsehead Crossing on the Pecos, they met a man with a wagon load of watermelons.

"Where he came from, where he was going, what he was doing alone in that wild country, I have never imagined," Goodnight told, "but he was a godsend to us. As I rode along filled with watermelon we had bought, I thought, 'Here we have plenty of money. We can't eat money. We can't carry it with us when we leave this world. I believe I don't care much for money.' I have never since cared much for money." A generous nature is generous with money — if he has any; often he has not. For years the widows of men who had kept the frontiers against the Comanches sent letters to Goodnight asking for help. They received it.

One day while I was with him, we drove in my car a short distance from the house to the big pens. After we got out and looked around, he had difficulty sidling his thick body back into the car. While struggling he said, "Old age hath its honors but sometimes it is damned inconvenient."

Another day I drove alone to the caprock rim of the Palo Duro and for the first time gazed upon the pillars, hills, canyons, mesas and slopes leading down to a small stream, miles away, twelve hundred feet below. When I returned and said something about the impression the fantastic sight had given me as I came upon it suddenly after crossing level land, his face brightened with remembrances. The spring after placing his cattle in the wide depression, fenced by palisades, he had returned with Mrs. Goodnight and camped overlooking the canyon. All night the rumbling of ten or fifteen thousand rutting buffaloes so frightened her that he could hardly "pacify" her.

At the age of ninety-one, early in 1927, he married a young woman who had cared for him in sickness and who typed letters as he dictated them. His correspondence was heavy. As a wedding gift I sent a pair of bronze bookends depicting an Indian on horseback, hands stretched out toward the sky, a replica of "The Appeal to the Great Spirit." These were trivial things. I did not select them in a spirit of irony but because I thought the Indian subject would appeal to Mr. Goodnight. He wrote back: "If you had studied for a hundred years, you could not have found anything that would have pleased me more. If Providence permits, I hope to have some little Goodnights to hand them down to."

In October of 1928 he and his wife came to our house in Austin on their way south for a gathering of the Old-Time Trail Drivers of Texas at San Antonio. He had never been to the annual meeting. Sixty-two years had passed since he blazed the Goodnight-Loving Trail on his first long cattle drive. He was now well stricken in years. His strong young wife evidenced respectful dedication to him. He told me she had had a miscarriage.

The trail drivers always met in the Gunter Hotel. Mr. Goodnight did not make a talk to the gathering, but greeted many men and was the center of curiosity and attention. For hours through two days he sat, wide and thick, on a long lounge in the big hotel lobby. Two or three times while I sat with him talking, a stranger came up to say, "This is Colonel Goodnight, I take it," or something like that.

His invariable reply was, "This is Charlie Goodnight." He

had not been even a captain. He did not like complimentary titles implying a status contrary to fact. The present concern over personal "images" would have disgusted him. He preferred, I judge, *Mister* to *Colonel*.

He did not mind naming, to me at least, known cow thieves who had prospered — and even been coloneled. "No more night work for me," he said. "I've done my share of night work — and it wasn't after other people's cattle." In his adamantine code of honesty, thieves were among the primary enemies of society.

Some man said, "You have been a man of vision." "Yes," he retorted, "a hell of a vision." "My life," he said to me on this last visit I had with him, "has been mostly a failure." That self-depreciation did not keep him from feeling superior in a you-be-damned way to all hypocrites, liars, pretenders, leeches and bootlickers, even when it was his own boots they tried to lick. I have never, however, known an authentic earth-man who licked anybody's boots.

On December 12, 1929, he died in Phoenix, Arizona, where he had been eating buffalo meat sent from an animal of his own herd. He was buried in Goodnight, Texas, not far from the rim of the Palo Duro Canyon. I reserve severely use of the word great. Charles Goodnight approached greatness more nearly than any other cowman of history.

A Note on Sources

IN SEPTEMBER, 1939, I began writing an article or a narrative for the Sunday issue of a few Texas newspapers. I have not yet missed a Sunday. Preceding publication, pieces of several of my books, including *Cow People,* have appeared in these Sunday columns.

Chapter 1. In 1931 I took notes on Ike Pryor's narrative as he told it to me in his office in San Antonio. He checked what I wrote for facts. I knew many people who knew him. Parts of "Hunting Cousin Sally" were syndicated by the New York *Herald Tribune Magazine,* July 10, 1932. The final form as now published appeared in the *Southwest Review,* Dallas, Texas, Summer, 1963.

Chapters 2 and 3. To gather materials on Ab Blocker, Shanghai Pierce and other outstanding characters of the range, all one had to do was associate with old-time ranch people, in whose talk "characters" lived. The old-timers knew each other, either in person or in talk, from Montana to the Rio Grande. Chapter 2, "Ab Blocker, Trail Boss," appeared in *Arizona and the West,* the Quarterly Journal of History, published by the University of Arizona Press, Tucson, Arizona, Summer, 1964 (Vol. 6, No. 2).

Chapter 10. While I was writing *Up the Trail from Texas* (1955), I put into it a brief segment on "The Cook and His Chuck Wagon." I had materials for a full book on trail drivers and wrote out for my own satisfaction a full treatment on camp cooks. A good part of it, under the title "Cooks of Range and Trail," was published in a paperback entitled *Riders West* (1956). The book was as ephemeral as a pulp magazine and copyright was turned over to me. Other cooks came into my collection. The chapter in *Cow People* entitled "Cooks of the Chuck Wagon" has some parts out of the chapter in *Riders West* and some hitherto unpublished material.

Chapter 12. Jack Potter, a cowman and trail driver friend, author of *Lead Steer* and *Cattle Trails of the Old West,* told me the Billy the Kid story in the "Man and Horse" chapter. *Owen Wister Out West,* quoted in this chapter, was edited by Fanny Kemble West and published by the University of Chicago Press, 1958. In treating of cutting horses I have drawn from a narrative-essay I wrote for *Mustangs and Cowhorses,* edited by me for the Texas Folklore Society, 1940, and from Luther North's *Recollections,* edited by Donald F. Danker, University of Nebraska Press, 1961. My long regard for Asa Jones influenced my giving something about him beyond his cutting horse story, and I have taken an incident of his early cowboying from "Asa Jones, Early Day Cowman," by Florence Fenley, published in *The Cattleman,* Fort Worth, Texas, June, 1962, pp. 43 f.

Chapter 13. "The Drouthed" is largely autobiographical. Some folk traditions I have not credited to anybody. They belong to the atmosphere, though everything in talk, like every folk song, had to be started by somebody.

Chapter 14, "The Right Tempo," appeared in the *Texas*

Quarterly, University of Texas, Austin, Texas, Summer, 1964 (Vol. 7, No. 2).

Chapter 19. Full facts on the career and character of Charles Goodnight are in *Charles Goodnight, Cowman and Plainsman* by J. Evetts Haley (1936), to whom I turned over my Goodnight notes while he was writing the best biography yet published of a cowman. I have derived some facts from it and have referred to it to bolster what I took from Goodnight directly. William Timmons, author of *Twilight on the Plains* (1962), began working for Goodnight in 1892 and was befriended by him. *Prose and Poetry of the Live Stock Industry,* Vol. I, 1905, has a full and able account of Goodnight. He is in other books.

Index

Index

Index

Index